ENGLISH THROUGH TOPI

TRANSPORT
KEY STAGE 2

TEACHER'S BOOK

Sue Palmer

Acknowledgements

The authors would like to thank all those involved in the production of English Through Topics 'Transport' (Key Stage 2) especially Janet Weller, Liz Cartmell, Heather Richards, Geoff Gwatkin; the staff and pupils of St Columb Minor Primary School, Newquay, Matt Tudor and other children who contributed handwritten material; Bert Fortune, Sue Biscoe and others who gave dialect words and expressions; the Commonwealth Institute, Edinburgh; Robbie Butler for the use of her library; Ann Singleton of Cumbria Library Services, Stuart McLean of the Institute of Cornish Studies, and the Staff of Truro County Library, Moray House College Library, the Scottish Poetry Library, Cornwall Schools' Library Service and Truro Bookshop; Cardiff Bus Company; the teachers and children all over Britain who reported on the pilot material; and finally Maggie Ward, without whom the Teacher's Notes could not have been compiled.

We are grateful to the following for permission to reproduce copyright material:

The Controller of Her Majesty's Stationery Office for extracts from *English in the National Curriculum* (1989).

The 'Record-keeping checklists' on pages 15, 57 and 103 refer to the National Curriculum in English at the time of going to press (Spring 1993). Updated checklists for the revised curriculum, when known, are available free to purchasing schools, from Oliver & Boyd, Longman House, Burnt Mill, Harlow, Essex CM20 2JE.

Oliver & Boyd

Longman House
Burnt Mill, Harlow
Essex CM20 2JE

An imprint of Longman Group UK Ltd

First published 1993
ISBN 0050 05070 2

© Oliver & Boyd 1993

Set in Cheltenham 10/12pt

Printed in Great Britain by Bell and Bain Ltd., Glasgow

Designed and illustrated by Celia Hart

Page layouts by Jonathan Barnard

The publisher's policy is to use paper manufactured from sustainable forests.

CONTENTS

GENERAL INTRODUCTION

What is ETT?

English Through Topics provides:
English resource material based on the National Curriculum English documents linked to the theme of Transport.

At Key Stage 2, the material is graded for three levels of ability, based on **National Curriculum Attainment Target Levels:**

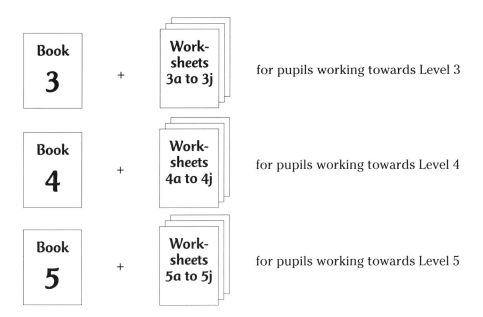

Book **3** + Work-sheets 3a to 3j   for pupils working towards Level 3

Book **4** + Work-sheets 4a to 4j   for pupils working towards Level 4

Book **5** + Work-sheets 5a to 5j   for pupils working towards Level 5

This Teacher's Book contains:
- detailed notes for each page of the pupils' books
- suggestions for teaching strategies
- additional resource material
- Notes for Book 3   pages 17 – 53
- Notes for Book 4   pages 59 – 98
- Notes for Book 5   pages 105 – 152

What ETT isn't

English Through Topics 'Transport' is not a topic pack. It does not provide detailed suggestions for activities in curricular areas other than English.

Fitting ETT into the school curriculum

English Through Topics 'Food' is flexible:

1

> At our school we like to keep the subject areas separate. But I do see the point of having a theme to provide a context for a term's work.

Use it as an integrated English course linked by a common theme.

2 Use it as an integrated English course providing starting points for cross-curricular work on transport.

> Our school policy is to start with English work, and to exploit cross-curricular links wherever possible. It's good to make links but English should never be subordinated to other curriculum areas.

3

> We believe in cross-curricular teaching — integrating the subject areas need not mean you neglect anything. You just have to take care to cover all aspects of the English curriculum.

Use it as a ready-structured English strand for a cross-curricular project on Transport or a related topic (e.g. Journeys, Exploration and Discovery, Communications).

English Through Topics is intended to supplement the ongoing literacy learning in the primary classroom. It assumes that children will, in addition to *English Through Topics*, have access to a wide range of fiction and non-fiction material within a structured reading and writing programme.

Using ETT in the junior classroom

English Through Topics provides resource material on the Transport theme for pupils at every developmental level in Key Stage 2, e.g.:

> I've got a mixed junior class. Most of them are Level 3, working towards Level 4, but a few have reached Level 4.

Use Book 4 with the majority of the class, but supplement it with work from Book 5 for the more able children.

> Our school sets children for English by developmental level. All the children in my class are working towards Level 5.

Use Book 4 as a basic class text.

> My class is a real mixture! Some aren't at Level 3 yet. Most are on the way to Level 4, and a few are already there and heading for Level 5.

Using the Teacher's Notes

A reduced facsimile of each pupil's book page is shown in the Teacher's Book. This is so that the teacher can see what the pupils are seeing, and at the same time check the relevant notes.

Organisation
In the margin are notes and suggestions for using the page, to cover particular areas of the English curriculum.

A brief explanation of the purposes of a resource or exercise.

Specific teaching targets

Suggested questions for you to ask pupils and specific instructions are in *italics*.

Notes are grouped, sometimes in boxes, to constitute one teaching session, one complete activity, or one unit of information.

Worksheets are linked to particular pages (these are listed on the first page of the introduction to each book).

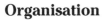

TRANSPORT BOOK 3 TRANSPORT BOOK 3 TRANSPORT BOOK 3 TRANSPORT B

26

Travelling Folk *(page 10)*

Poetry/Language
The poems provide starting points for using dictionaries/reference books/discussion to find out about unknown words/names.

'The Pedlar's Caravan'
For example: **pedlar-man**, **delf** (blue chinaware from Delf in Holland), **bathing machine** (movable cabin in which people changed for sea-bathing)
NB **Captain James Cook** (1728–79) – navigator and cartographer. On his first voyage in 'The Explorer' (1768–71) discovered the Southern continent, on second voyage (1722–75) circumnavigated the Antarctic.

'Me – Pirate'
For example: **man-of-war, cutlass, Crossbones, fire a salute, Caribbean Seas/ Spanish Main** NB Caribbean pirates flourished in 17th/18th centuries looting European ships returning from the New World. Famous pirates to investigate: William Kidd, Henry Avery, Mary Read, Ann Bonny.

Poem

One eyed Jack, the pirate chief
Was a terrible, fearsome ocean thief.
He wore a peg upon one leg;
He wore a hook, and a dirty look!
One eyed Jack, the pirate chief
Was a terrible, fearsome ocean thief.

(Anon)

'Soft Landings'
For example: **wake of flame, landscapes, unknown to human eyes**
NB Starting points for investigating Space Race: Sputnik (1957); first astronaut – Yuri Gagarin (1961); 'Apollo 11' landed on moon (1969); U.S. space shuttle programme (1981–86).

Discussion
For example: *Which of the three travellers would you most like to be, and why? Which poem gives the best description of the transport? Which gives the best description of the traveller?*

The Pedlar's Caravan

I wish I lived in a caravan,
With a horse to drive, like the pedlar-man
Where he comes from nobody knows,
Or where he goes to, but on he goes!

His caravan has windows too,
And a chimney of tin, that the smoke comes through;
He has a wife, with a baby brown,
And they go riding from town to town.

Chairs to mend, and delf to sell,
He clashes the basins like a bell;
Tea-trays, baskets ranged in order,
Plates, with alphabets round the border!

The roads are brown, and the sea is green,
But his house is like a bathing-machine;
The world is round, and he can ride,
Rumble and splash, to the other side!

With the pedlar-man I should like to roam,
And write a book when I came home!
All the people would read my book,
Just like the Travels of Captain Cook!

William Brighty Rands

10

Parts of speech: adjectives
(See Glossary, page 32 of Book 3.)
Worksheet 3e
Discuss and fill the 'adjective bank' in the top corner. Pupils then complete the worksheet individually or in pairs. | 3e |

Language work: adjectives
Look again at the poems and ask pupils to spot some of the adjectives in each. For each adjective, try to identify the noun it describes.

Game: add an adjective
Pupils are split into teams. Teacher chooses a type of transport, e.g. 'Mr Brown's car', 'Concorde', 'a scooter'. Teams take turns to give adjectives which describe that transport (shape, size, condition, type of movement, noise it makes, etc.). Team which can keep going longest is the winner.

On some pages (especially in Book 3) is a selection of fiction books which relate to the material on the page or the ideas explored in the Teacher's Notes.

Where space permits, further poems, songs, folktales, etc. are included.

ETT 'Transport' at Key Stage 2

The Pupil's Books and Copymasters include:

- poems about Transport

- short stories by recognised children's authors, extracts from children's fiction and English literature all related to the theme

- folktales, myths and legends from many cultures related to the theme

- other 'real' texts such as a timetable, letters, leaflets, etc. concerned with Transport

- starting points for drama, presentations, discussion, debates and a variety of group activities involving spoken language, all related to the Transport theme

- stimuli for a wide variety of writing activities, fiction and non-fiction, narrative and non-narrative, poetry and prose – for a variety of purposes and audiences, linked to the theme

- cartoon representations of the processes involved in information search and reading for information, for discussion and as models, linked to work on Transport

- information about language related to the theme of Transport.

The Teacher's Notes contain:

- suggestions for developing pupils' skills in speaking and listening, reading and writing, linked through the material to the theme of Transport

- suggestions for integrating teaching about language and the conventions of written English into pupil's work on the Transport theme

- additional resource material linked to the theme

- details of children's fiction and non-fiction for classroom use.

Using a Pupil's Book across one attainment band

The material in each pupil's book has been pitched about halfway between the Attainment Level pupils have already reached and that at which they are aiming.

Beginners

Pupils who have only recently reached the previous attainment level.
Beginners need plenty of support, e.g.:
– help with reading and writing
– plenty of clear explanations
– help with activities and worksheets.

Midway pupils

Pupils about halfway between levels.
Midway pupils need teaching support but are more independent than beginners. For example, they can:
– read the stories alone
– complete activities and worksheets with occasional help.
Teachers should watch for areas where concepts and vocabulary need more practice.

Independent pupils

Pupils who have almost reached the Level of Attainment by which the pupil's book is numbered.
Generally, they should be able to:
– read all texts with minimal help
– carry out activities independently.
Teaching help should now be
– 'fine tuning'
– encouraging independence and preparing for transition to the next level.

Assessment and record-keeping

Assessment

On the opposite page we outline the teaching input appropriate for children at various stages of development. Criterion-referenced assessment is the other side of this coin.

The resource material and teaching suggestions have been carefully matched to the National Curriculum Attainment Targets. Pupils' stage of development can be assessed informally through their performance on the suggested activities.

Included in the Introductory Notes for each stage in this Teacher's Book is a criterion-referenced assessment grid:

Level 3 Assessment Grid – page 15
Level 4 Assessment Grid – page 55
Level 5 Assessment Grid – page 103

These grids give a general indication of what can be expected of children as they progress along the continuum of achievement within each Level of Attainment, e.g. at Level 4:

- Pupils who can work independently from Book 3 but require considerable support on Book 4 (see grid on page 55) are **Level 4 Beginner** pupils.

- Pupils who achieve satisfactory results with an average amount of teaching input (see grid on page 55) are **Level 4 Midway** pupils.

- Pupils who work competently with minimum support, but are not yet quite ready for Book 5 (see grid on page 55) are **Level 4 Independent** pupils.

English Through Topics is appropriate for use in pupil assessment only insofar as all structured teaching materials are vehicles for informal assessment. It has not been designed primarily for this purpose, but as *teaching* material.

Recording assessment of individual pupil's development

Simplified versions of the three Assessment Grids are included in the Key Stage 2 Copymaster pack, for use as individual pupil assessment sheets. On these sheets, teachers may record the dates at which a pupil's performance on ETT material/activities indicates that s/he has reached particular stages of development (Beginner, Midway or Independent).

Record-keeping

Materials for recording details of individual pupils' progress are described above. You may also wish to keep a record of work undertaken in English with a class or group.

The Introductory Notes to each level of ETT include a checklist, correlating the activities for each page of the book with the National Curriculum Attainment Targets. These pages are reproduced in the Copymaster packs for record-keeping purposes. Copies may be included in a teacher's Record of Work for English, to record the English work undertaken through the medium of ETT by a particular class or group.

As the activities for each page of ETT are completed, the page number on the record sheet may be ticked off or highlighted. As a running record is built up, there will be clear indications of the areas where extra input is necessary.

The NC Attainment Targets are merely guides to pupils' overall performance. There are many elements of pupils' language development which are contributory factors to reaching each target, but which are not specifically mentioned (e.g. a vocabulary of language terms).

English Through Topics!

Sue Palmer, Avril Barton and Peter Brinton

Transport 3

A stone will sink, there is no doubt;

A little cork will float about;

A paper clip is bound to sink;

A paper cup will float, I think.

Book 3

For pupils working towards Level 3

PUPIL'S BOOK 3: resource material, linked to the theme of Transport, of the following types:
- poems and rhymes
- traditional stories from fable and folk literature
- fiction in a variety of formats (play, stories)
- picture stimuli for written work
- examples of a variety of written sources of information, different print styles and handwriting, including children's work
- picture stories showing the process of
    - drafting and editing a piece of writing
    - reading for information
- non-fiction material
- glossaries of specialist terminology related to English work.

THE TEACHER'S NOTES:
- suggestions (accompanying each page of Book 3) for using the resource material to cover Level 3 English requirements.
  (A guide to the layout of the Teachers' Notes – page 8.)
- more poems and rhymes
- fables and folk stories for teachers to read or retell
- titles of books for pupils (picture books, story books, anthologies of short stories) related to the theme
- titles of books which the teacher might read to pupils (we call these 'Read aloud' books).

WORKSHEETS: practice work on:

3a	Nouns	(link to Pupil's Book page 2)
3b	Verbs	(link to page 4)
3c	Statements and questions	(link to page 6)
3d	Singular and plural	(link to page 9)
3e	Adjectives	(link to page 10)
3f	Writing complete sentences/ reading comprehension	(link to page 14)
3g	Sentence punctuation	(link to page 14)
3h	Using an index	(link to page 21)
3i	Spelling (wordsearch)	(link to page 25)
3j	Sentence connectives	(link to page 30)

While detailed suggestions for the use of the resource material are provided, individual teachers have their own preferred methods of working and should use the materials as is most appropriate to their own teaching styles and their pupils' needs.

Covering the English Curriculum

The material is intended to **supplement** the ongoing language work of a class for children working towards Level 3 and link it to the theme of Transport.

Pupil's Book 3 has been designed to provide:
- stimuli for discussion, drama, and various group activities, including group presentations;
- opportunities to hear and respond to poetry, fiction, folktales and non-fiction writing;
- opportunities to use spoken language in a wide variety of ways, including relating narrative and giving and receiving complex instructions;
- opportunities to read aloud and silently from a variety of material;
- opportunities to read for a variety of purposes;
- understanding of the techniques applicable when reading for information;
- opportunities to use inference and deduction based on previous reading experience, and to employ developing knowledge of story structure in personal writing;
- stimuli for pupils' own writing, fiction and non-fiction, chronological and non-chronological;
- information about punctuation (and practice material);
- occasional links to the teaching of spelling;
- awareness of the rule-based nature of language, including the way words can be categorised by function, and the effects of tense and singularity/plurality on word endings;
- technical vocabulary in which to discuss the above;
- understanding of the process and purpose of drafting and editing written work, and opportunities to apply this;
- opportunities to practise joined-up handwriting and careful presentation of written work;
- opportunities to use word-processing facilities.

Keeping track

The Record-keeping checklist on page 15 correlates the National Curriculum English Attainment Targets for Level 3 with the activities suggested in these notes. The numbers used to record these correlations are the page numbers of the Pupil's Book against which activities are recommended in the Teacher's Notes.

Please see also the notes on page 11 about record-keeping.

Record-keeping checklist

Opportunities for covering Level 3 NC English Attainment Targets

See activities suggested to accompany the pages given below in Pupil's Book 3

	2	3/4/5	6	7	8/9	10/11	12–17	18	19–21	22/23	24/25	26	27	28–30	31
Speaking and Listening															
Relate a connected narrative					8/9		12–17							28–30	
Convey a simple message							12–17	18			24/25				31
Listen/question/respond to others			6		8/9						24/25		27		
Give instructions					8/9										
Follow instructions					8/9				19–21	22/23					
Reading															
Read aloud from familiar stories		3/4/5					12–17							28–30	
Read aloud from familiar poems	2		6			10/11						26			31
Sustained silent reading		3/4/5					12–17								
Listen to stories		3/4/5					12–17							28–30	
Talk about setting		3/4/5					12–17							28–30	
Talk about storyline		3/4/5					12–17							28–30	
Talk about characters		3/4/5					12–17							28–30	
Recall significant detail		3/4/5					12–17							28–30	
Appreciate meanings beyond literal using inference, deduction etc.	2						12–17								31
Recognise story structure		3/4/5					12–17					26		28–30	
Devise questions to guide information search and reading			6						19–21						
Writing															
Produce pieces of writing using sentences				7		10/11									
Use full stops, capital letters, question marks				7		10/11	12–17							28–30	
Shape chronological writing				7											
Use variety of sentence connectives				7		10/11								28–30	
Write more detailed stories/defined ending				7	8/9		12–17								
Non-chronological writing	2						12–17		19–21	22/23			27		
Begin to revise and redraft									19–21		24/25				
Check for consistent tenses	2				8/9						24/25				
Check for consistent pronouns					8/9										
Spelling															
Simple polysyllabic words observing common letter patterns						10/11									
Regular patterns for vowel sounds/common letter strings			6												
Word families and relationships		3/4/5				10/11								28–30	
Check accuracy when redrafting											24/25				
Handwriting															
Opportunities to practise handwriting				7		10/11					24/25			28–30	

This checklist refers to the National Curriculum in English at the time of going to press (Spring 1993). An updated sheet for the revised curriculum, when known, is available free to purchasing schools, from Oliver & Boyd, Longman House, Burnt Mill, Harlow, Essex CM20 2JE.

Assessing and teaching children using ETT Book 3

(See notes on assessment in General Introduction, page 11 and *Copymasters* page ix.)

The resource material is pitched for teaching purposes roughly halfway between a Level 2 and a Level 3 standard. Teacher input will, of course, vary to accommodate children's needs as they progress along the developmental continuum between Levels 2 and 3.

Progress can be informally assessed by observation of a child's performance when using the resource material and carrying out activities, e.g.:

Level of pupil:	Just above Level 2 (beginner)	Between Levels 2 and 3 (midway)	Nearing Level 3 (independent)
Spoken English	Requires supervision to carry out group work: requires repeated explanations of activities; unsure of vocabulary related to language and topic work; unsure how to express understanding of linguistic and topic related concepts.	Some teacher support required for group activities; requires few or no repetitions of instructions; developing control of vocabulary related to language and topic work; developing confidence in expressing linguistic and topic related concepts.	Little supervision required for group work; explanation usually grasped at first attempt; confident of vocabulary and able to talk clearly about concepts in language and topic work.
Reading	Requires considerable teacher support to read texts labelled as Level 2 +; reads with little expression or attention to punctuation; requires more than one reading to recall detail accurately.	Reads text labelled Level 2+ with reasonable fluency, requiring little support; developing expression in reading and beginning to attend to punctuation; generally recalls detail after one reading of a text.	Reads texts labelled Level 2+ easily, and can manage texts labelled Level 3 with some fluency; good expression and attention to punctuation; good recall of detail; predicts outcomes on basis of previous reading.
Writing	Requires considerable teacher support to complete writing tasks suggested in Teacher's Notes; simple pieces of writing with rudimentary punctuation.	Developing confidence to tackle writing tasks in Teacher's Notes with less support; stories and non-chronological writing showing evidence of structure; basic sentence punctuation developing.	Able to complete writing tasks in Teacher's Notes reasonably independently; stories and non-chronological writing demonstrate understanding of basic elements of structure; on the whole, correct punctuation of sentences.
Spelling	Requires help with polysyllabic spellings; generally of unknown words; considerable teacher support to identify and correct errors in own writing.	Needs less help with common polysyllabic words; beginning to use knowledge of common letter-strings and word-families to spell unknown words; developing confidence in checking for errors in own writing.	Good vocabulary of common polysyllabic words; developing confidence in using knowledge of common letter-strings and word-families to spell unknown words; able to check and correct own errors using established classroom strategies.
Handwriting	Requires considerable teacher support in order to produce joined-up writing.	Able to produce clear, legible joined-up writing, with some support, for final drafts.	Always able to produce clear, legible joined-up writing in final drafts.

Contents

'Up in the Air'... 'Down on the Road' *(page 2)*

Poems

Readability: 'Up in the Air' Level 2+
'Down on the Road' Level 3+
Read the poems, discuss as appropriate, relating to pupils' own experience.

Discussion/ Comprehension

For example: *What does the plane look like to the writer? What do the cars look like? Why are cars sometimes close together and not moving? Why does the writer think it is? What look like 'feelers' on the cars at night?* etc.

Discussion/ Preference

Which poem do you like best? Why?

Reading poems

When pupils are familiar with the poems, a few pairs or individuals can choose and practise one to read to the class.

Up in the Air

Zooming across the sky
Like a great bird you fly,
  Airplane,
  Silvery white
  In the light.

Turning and twisting in air,
When shall I ever be there,
  Airplane,
  Piloting you
  Far in the blue?

James S. Tippett

Down on the Road

From city window, 'way up high,
I like to watch the cars go by.
They look like burnished beetles, black,
That leave a little muddy track
Behind them as they slowly crawl.
Sometimes they do not move at all
But huddle close with hum and drone
As though they feared to be alone.
They grope their way through fog and night
With the golden feelers of their light.

Rowena Bastin Bennett

Parts of speech: introduction

An important part of pupils' language awareness is their recognition that words can be categorised by **function**. Words do 'different jobs' in a sentence.

Language/Parts of speech: nouns

(See Glossary, page 32 of Book 3.)

3a

Worksheet 3a

This introduces the concept of nouns as 'naming words' through association with labels, and familiarises pupils with the term 'noun'.
After discussion, pupils should complete worksheets individually or in pairs.

Group work/Nouns

Transport nouns

Under the heading of TRANSPORT NOUNS, pupils list on board the names of (a) forms of transport; (b) the names of people who travel in each of them (these can be general, e.g. pilot, sailor, or specific, e.g. Captain Kirk); (c) the names of places they travel in/to (e.g. air, sea, America, etc.)

Noun hunt and posters

Pupils in groups make (draw/paint/collage from magazine cut-outs) posters related to transport. In discussion with teacher, pupils make and stick on labels (as in the worksheet) for some of the nouns in the pictures, especially those with transport associations. Again, clear title TRANSPORT NOUNS helps link the terminology with the concept of 'naming words'.

The Tortoise Who Showed Off *(page 3)*

THE TORTOISE WHO SHOWED OFF

It was a hot summer. Every day the water in the lake got lower and lower. "What are we going to do?" the animals said. "If the lake dries up we will have nothing to drink."

The cleverest animal was a little tortoise. "I know what to do," she said. "We must travel to another lake which is so big that the sun cannot dry it up."
"That's a good idea," said the other animals. The little tortoise smiled. "Yes," she boasted. "Aren't I clever?"

The animals didn't like the tortoise when she showed off. "Just a minute," said one of the elephants. "How will we find this lake?"

The little tortoise thought again.
"I know," she said. "We must ask the birds. They fly everywhere and see everything . They will know where the biggest lake is and they can tell us how to get there. That's a good idea, isn't it?"

3

Reading a story

Readability: Level 2+
Pupils who have just reached Level 2 may need to hear the story read aloud before attempting to read it themselves. Others, who are approaching a Level 3 standard, should be able to read it unaided.

Recall of detail

For example:
- *What season of the year was it in the story?*
- *What was happening to the lake where the animals lived?*
- *What did the tortoise suggest they should do?*
- *Who did the tortoise suggest they should ask to find the new lake?*
- *What transport did the tortoise arrange for herself?*
- *Who saw the tortoise flying and thought it was a good idea?*
- *Why did the tortoise fall down?*
- *Where did the tortoise land?*
- *What did she decide?*

Discussion: story structure

- *This story has a beginning, at middle and an end. Which bit would you say was the beginning?*
- *Which bit would you say was the end?*
- *Which section is biggest - beginning, middle or end.*

Discussion: fables

This story is an adaptation of a fable from South East Asia.
- *A fable is a story which makes a point, usually about how people should/should not behave. What is the point in this fable?*
- *The British saying 'Pride goes before a fall' fits the story well. Can you think of examples of pride going before a fall in everyday life?*
- *What other fables do you know?*

(page 4)

The animals had to agree that it was a good idea, so the tortoise showed off again. "It was my idea," she boasted. "Aren't I clever?" The animals hated it when she showed off.

"Just a minute," said one of the elephants. "You are a very little animal, and tortoises are always slow. How are *you* going to travel to the big lake?" The tortoise thought again.

"I know," she said at last. "I shall get transport to the big lake. I shall fly!" "How can a tortoise fly?" asked the other animals. "I shall ask two birds to help me," said the tortoise. "They will hold a stick between them, and I shall hold on to it with my mouth. I shall reach the lake before any of you." The animals had to agree that it was a very good idea, so the tortoise showed off more than ever. "It was *my* idea," she boasted. "Aren't I clever? Aren't I clever? Aren't I clever?"

Books
Picture books
Aesop's Fables
(Picturemac)
Fables, Arnold Lobel
(Picturemac)
Wordless picture book about flying:
Up and Up, Shirley Hughes (Bodley Head)

Language/Parts of speech: nouns and verbs
Revise nouns by looking for the names of some places/animals/things in the story.

Parts of speech: verbs
(See Glossary, page 32 of Book 3.)

3b *Worksheet 3b*
This may be used after pupils have read 'The Tortoise Who Showed Off'. It uses an illustration from the story to familiarise pupils with the term 'verb' and introduce the concept of a 'doing word'. After discussion, pupils should complete worksheets individually or in pairs.

Group work: verbs
The best way to instil the concept of 'doing words' is through **doing** some of them, e.g.:
What's my verb?

DISCUSS and list on board 'animal verbs' (i.e. things which animals do, e.g. creep, crawl, screech, gobble, sleep, etc.). Pupils take it in turn to choose a verb and mime/act it. Rest of group guesses which verb it is.

Mime and movement
Use 'transport verbs' (e.g. roll, zoom, fly, slide) as the focus of a movement lesson; use the term 'verb' frequently so pupils come to associate it with activity.

Verbs in reading
• *Look back at poems on page 2.*
  Can you find the verbs associated with (a) the plane, (b) the cars? - interesting contrast.
• *Look back at the story.*
  Which verbs did the tortoise 'do'?
  What's the most common verb in this story?
  (said)

(page 5)

The tortoise set off, flying between the birds. They soon reached the big lake. Just as they got there two eagles flew past.
"Gosh, that's clever," said one eagle. "Those birds are giving that tortoise a lift." The tortoise smiled to herself.
"What a good idea," said the second eagle. The tortoise smiled even more.
"I wonder who thought of it," said the first eagle. The tortoise could keep quiet no longer. She opened her mouth to boast.
"It was m. . . . . ." she said, and she started to fall.

Splash! The tortoise swam to the edge of the lake.
"I wish I hadn't done that," she said to herself. "Maybe it isn't a good idea to boast. Maybe I should think before I speak." And as she was a *very* clever little tortoise, she never showed off or boasted again.

5

Story for telling

Another story of an ingenious flight which went wrong, also linking to the 'pride goes before a fall' moral, is the Greek myth of Daedalus and Icarus.

Daedalus was a brilliant designer and craftsman, who had been imprisoned on an island by a wicked king (Minos of Crete, for whom Daedalus had built the labyrinth, and who feared Daedalus might give away its secret). Daedalus' son, Icarus, was imprisoned with him.

They decided to escape using wings, and fly home to Greece. They secretly collected birds' feathers and drips of candlewax, and bound the feathers into wings, setting them in place with the wax.

When they set off, Daedalus warned Icarus not to fly too near the sun. But Icarus began to enjoy flying so much that he started showing off and forgot the warning. When he went near the sun, the heat melted the wax, the wings fell apart and Icarus plummeted into the sea and drowned.

Which parts of this story are like the story of the tortoise? Which parts are different?

Spelling links

- Some commonly used/commonly misspelled words which occur in the story are given in **bold** print. Other words which may be linked to them for teaching purposes are given in brackets:
  every/everywhere/everything (everybody/everyone: some+where/thing/body/one; no+where/thing/body/one)
  know   minute   maybe
  thought (fought, bought, brought, ought; -ight words)
  again (-ain words, e.g. rain, Britain)
  always (al+most/ready/though/so/together but not **all right**)
  could/should (would)
- Spelling rules exemplified by words in the story include:
1) ke words (e.g. lake) as opp. -ck words (e.g. lack)
   (Other examples: snake/snack; bake/back; rake/rack. Also duke/duck, smoke/smock, like/lick, etc.)
2) or- and -oi- words, as in tortoise
   (e.g. -or- words: for, short, story, boring,/more, before, store, etc.;
   -oi- words: oil, spoil, coin, point, as opp. boy, joy, destroy.

Questions of Transport *(page 6)*

Readability: Level 2+

Poetry/Discussion

Read the poems aloud with the group and discuss as appropriate, relating to pupils' own experience.

'Can I Come Along?'

The speaker in this poem watches the train approach ('rattling along'), watches it pass ('thundering along'), and watches it recede into the distance ('whistling along') until it disappears.

'The Ferryman'

What is a ferry? What words in the poem suggest that this poem is from Africa? etc.

Original of 'The Ferryman':
'Ferry me across the water,
Do, boatman, do.'
'If you've a penny in your
    purse
I'll ferry you.'

'I have a penny in my purse,
And my eyes are blue;
So ferry me across the water,
Do, boatman do".

'Step into my ferry-boat.
Be they black or blue.
And for the penny in your
    purse
I'll ferry you.'

(Christina Rossetti)

Reading poetry

When pupils are familiar with the poems, pairs or individuals can practise them for reading aloud. 'The ferryman' may be presented as a dialogue. 'Can I Come Along' is effective if other pupils provide accompanying 'tiddly-tum, tiddly-tum' sound effects of the train passing by. This should start softly, rise to a crescendo in the middle stanza so that the reader has to shout, then die away again.

Questions of Transport

Can I Come Along?

Train, train,
rattling along,
where are you going to?
Can I come along?

From station to station,
From coast to coast,
where do you like going
the most?

Train, train,
thundering along,
where are you going to?
Can I come along?

From sunrise to sunset,
from east to west,
where do you like going
the best?

Train, train,
whistling along –
where are you going to?
Where have you gone?

Tony Bradman

The ferryman

"Ferry me across the water,
Do, boatman, do."
"If you've some money in your purse,
I'll ferry you."

"I have no money in my purse,
But will a pawpaw do?
Please ferry me across the water,
Do, boatman, do."

"Step into my ferry boat,
A pawpaw will do,
And though you have no money
I'll ferry you."

Christina Rossetti
(African adaptation)

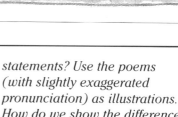

6

Language: statements and questions

(See Glossary)
*Which sentences are questions/statements in 'Can I Come Along?' 'The ferryman'?
What is different in the way we use our voices to ask questions a opposed to making statements? Use the poems (with slightly exaggerated pronunciation) as illustrations. How do we show the difference between a statement and a question in writing?*

Worksheet 3c
This gives practice in recognising and writing questions and sentences.

3c

Language/Spelling

Note the 'wh' spelling of many question words, e.g. where, why, when, what, who. Linking these together under the conceptual umbrella or 'question words' can help when children confuse the spellings of where/were and which/witch.

Picture books featuring ferries

The Harbour, Philippe Dupasquier (Walker)
Katie Morag books by Mairi Hedderwick (Picture Lions)

22

Missing the Bus *(page 7)*

This page is intended as a focus for the development of children's writing skills and appreciation of story structure. It should be tackled in two parts, on different occasions.

Session 1: Discussion/Planning

The picture and caption on page 7 represent the middle of a story:

- Discuss what is happening in the picture, e.g.: *Where has Harry been and where is he going? Why has he missed the bus? What's likely to happen to him now?* etc.
- Discuss – *what should the beginning tell us, so that we will understand what is going on?* (See questions on top left of picture)
- Elicit a variety of possible beginnings.
- Each pupil now **draws** the beginning s/he chooses.

Discussion/Writing: a good beginning

Discuss what makes a successful beginning in terms of writing, e.g.: *How long should the beginning be compared to the rest of the story?* (NB Avoid the unnecessary detail with which many children get bogged down when starting stories - encourage pupils to 'jump straight in'.)
What questions should the beginning answer? (see note on illustration)
Each pupil to write a **beginning** for the Harry story, using own drawing as a focus. When the beginning is complete, s/he can write more **middle**, extending the picture's caption.

These pieces of writing may be retained for later use with pages 22-23 (Drafting and Editing)

Session 2: Discussion/Writing

The ending of a story should provide a clear resolution. Using examples of pupils' beginnings + middles, discuss, e.g.:
What would be a happy ending? What would be a sad ending? What points need to be made clear/tied up?
Each pupil draws an illustration of the ending s/he wishes for his/her own story. Pupils then write their endings, focusing on their pictures.

Again writing may be retained for use with pages 22-23.

The Way to School *(page 8)*

Spoken language: Relating a connected narrative

Children to work in pairs: A and B.

Pictures 1 –11.

A can see the picture story, B cannot. A to relate the story exactly to B, giving all necessary detail so that B can envisage the pictures. B to ask for more information where necessary.

Science link: observation and reporting

Pictures 12-24:

B to relate narrative, A to listen and question if necessary.

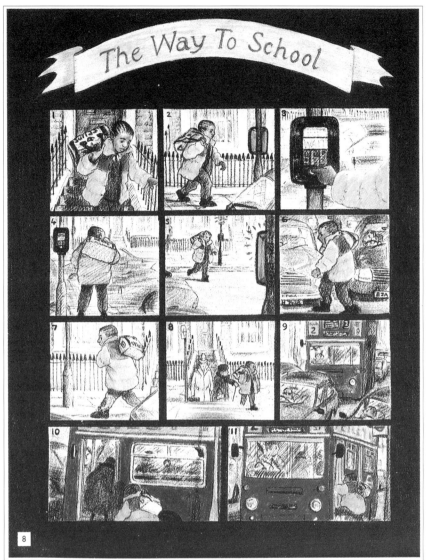

Language work: verbs and tenses

(Definition in Glossary, page 32 of Book 3)

When children attempted the above exercise, did they speak in the past or present tense (probably the present)? Help the children identify that tense is a feature of **verbs.**

In a group, invent narrative for several frames in past/present/future tenses. Once pupils seem confident try the following game.

Tense swapping game

Pupils each have copy of 'The Way to School'. Going round the group, they take turns to tell the story of one frame in the strip. Before each pupil's turn, the teacher calls 'past tense' or 'present tense', and pupil must adjust verbs as necessary. This can be converted into a team game (members of opposing teams taking alternative turns, and scoring a point for the team if tense is correct).

Spoken language

Another activity which can be carried out using a picture story (e.g. this one/pages from a book such as Raymond Brigg's *The Snowman*/a comic):

Giving/following instructions: cooperative group work

Children work in groups: some are actors and should not be able to see the pictures. One is the director, and should be looking at the pictures. The director must give the actors detailed instructions so that they can mimic the actions of the characters in the pictures exactly. They may ask for further information if they require it.

One is the judge, also with access to the pictures, who decides whether the acting is accurate enough.

(page 9)

Writing within a clearly defined framework

Pupils write an account of the boy's activities in the picture story (or another cartoon strip).
Before beginning:
- Each pupil decides whether to write as the protagonist (I) or about the protagonist (he). Those choosing the latter should invent a name for the character.
- Each pupil decides whether to write in the past or present tense.
- Lists of useful vocabulary/spelling words can be compiled on the blackboard.

Assess accounts for clarity and detail – do pupils explain the stages in the process clearly? Have they maintained their chosen tenses?

Language work: pronouns

(See Glossary)
- Revise nouns: look back to 'The Tortoise Who Showed Off' and spot some of the nouns in the story.
  In the story, the pronoun 'she' often stands in place of 'the tortoise'.
- Demonstrate by reading the story and substituting 'the tortoise' for each use of 'she'. *Why doesn't it sound as good as when the pronoun is used?*
- Pronouns used by the tortoise when talking about herself include 'I', 'me', 'my'. Try reading the tortoise's speeches, substituting 'the tortoise' for these words.
- Use the same technique on a pupil's story written about 'I' or 'he/she'.
- Draw attention to the 'I pronouns' and the 'he/she pronouns'. Two pieces of children's writing (one in the first person and one in the third) would provide illustrations. Can children list some 'I pronouns'? Some 'he/she/it pronouns'?
- Discuss the problems of slipping from 'I' to 's/he' or vice versa, which often happens in children's writing.
- Pupils can attempt to convert (orally) their own pieces of writing from the person in which they have written into the alternative person.

Language work: singular and plural

(See Glossary)

Worksheet 3d   **3d**
This worksheet revises nouns and pronouns, and introduces the terms singular and plural. It should be completed some time after pages 6–7. After discussion, pupils should complete the worksheet individually or in pairs. When the terms 'singular' and 'plural' are established, look for singular/plural nouns in real texts (e.g. stories or plays in this book/children's own writing).

Travelling Folk *(page 10)*

Poetry/Language

The poems provide starting points for using dictionaries/reference books/discussion to find out about unknown words/names.

'The Pedlar's Caravan'

For example: **pedlar-man, delf** (blue chinaware from Delf in Holland), **bathing machine** (movable cabin in which people changed for sea-bathing)

NB **Captain James Cook** (1728–79) – navigator and cartographer. On his first voyage in 'The Explorer' (1768–71) discovered the Southern continent, on second voyage (1722–75) circumnavigated the Antarctic.

'Me – Pirate'

For example: **man-of-war, cutlass, Crossbones, fire a salute, Caribbean Seas/ Spanish Main** NB Caribbean pirates flourished in 17th/18th centuries looting European ships returning from the New World. Famous pirates to investigate: William Kidd, Henry Avery, Mary Read, Ann Bonny.

Poem

> One eyed Jack, the pirate chief
> Was a terrible, fearsome ocean thief.
> He wore a peg upon one leg;
> He wore a hook, and a dirty look!
> One eyed Jack, the pirate chief
> Was a terrible, fearsome ocean thief.

(Anon)

'Soft Landings'

For example: **wake of flame, landscapes, unknown to human eyes**
NB Starting points for investigating Space Race: Sputnik (1957); first astronaut – Yuri Gagarin (1961); 'Apollo 11' landed on moon (1969); U.S. space shuttle programme (1981–86).

Discussion

For example: *Which of the three travellers would you most like to be, and why? Which poem gives the best description of the transport? Which gives the best description of the traveller?*

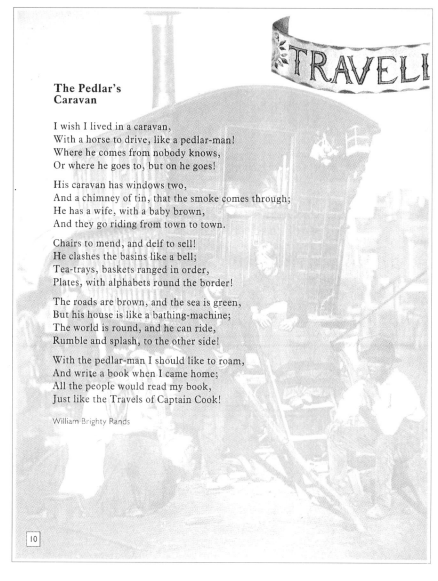

The Pedlar's Caravan

I wish I lived in a caravan,
With a horse to drive, like a pedlar-man!
Where he comes from nobody knows,
Or where he goes to, but on he goes!

His caravan has windows two,
And a chimney of tin, that the smoke comes through;
He has a wife, with a baby brown,
And they go riding from town to town.

Chairs to mend, and delf to sell!
He clashes the basins like a bell;
Tea-trays, baskets ranged in order,
Plates, with alphabets round the border!

The roads are brown, and the sea is green,
But his house is like a bathing-machine;
The world is round, and he can ride,
Rumble and splash, to the other side!

With the pedlar-man I should like to roam,
And write a book when I came home;
All the people would read my book,
Just like the Travels of Captain Cook!

William Brighty Rands

10

Parts of speech: adjectives

(See Glossary, page 32 of Book 3.)

Worksheet 3e
Discuss and fill the 'adjective bank' in the top corner. Pupils then complete the worksheet individually or in pairs. **3e**

Language work: adjectives

Look again at the poems and ask pupils to spot some of the adjectives in each. For each adjective, try to identify the noun it describes.

Game: add an adjective

Pupils are split into teams. Teacher chooses a type of transport, e.g. 'Mr Brown's car', 'Concorde', 'a scooter'. Teams take turns to give adjectives which describe that transport (shape, size, condition, type of movement, noise it makes, etc.). Team which can keep going longest is the winner.

(page 11)

ING·FOLK

Me – Pirate

If ever I go to sea,
I think I'll be a pirate:
I'll have a treasure-ship in tow
And a man-of-war to fire at.

With a cutlass at my belt,
And a pistol in my hand,
I'll nail my Crossbones to the mast
And sail for a foreign land.

And when we reach that shore,
We'll beat our battle-drum
And fire a salute of fifteen guns
To tell them we have come.

We'll fight them all day long;
We'll seize their chests of gold,
Their diamonds, coins and necklaces,
And stuff them in our hold.

A year and a day at home,
Then off on the waves again –
Lord of the Caribbean Seas
King of the Spanish Main!

Clive Sansom

Soft Landings

Space-man, space-man,
Blasting off the ground
With a wake of flame behind you,
Swifter than passing sound.

Space-man, ace-man,
Shooting through the air,
Twice around the moon and back
Simply because it's there.

Space-man, place-man,
Cruising through the skies
To plant your flags on landscapes
Unknown to human eyes.

Space-man – Race, man,
Scorching back to earth –
To home and friends and everything
That gives your mission worth.

Howard Sergeant

11

Discussion/ Imaginative writing

What other types of transport would you like to be a traveller in? What sort of traveller would you be? Where would you go? etc.
Each pupil decides on a form of transport and a traveller's identity for self (e.g. pilots, submariners, time-travellers, etc.).
Pupils describe:
• appearance of transport
• how it moves, sounds, smells etc.
• appearance of self as traveller
• details of travels, destinations, activities.
Stress the use of adjectives in description.

Poem

'The Island' in *When We Were Very Young*, A A Milne (Methuen)

Spelling links

For example:
• **-ar** ending of pedlar – like sugar, cellar, beggar, pillar, vicar, collar, etc.
• **-ace** of space/ace/race/place (also face/palace, etc.) – like ice/nice/rice/notice/office/police, etc.
• homonyms of words in 'Me – Pirate', e.g. main/mane; tow/toe; sail/sale; their/there; sea/see (see song 'A Sailor went to Sea Sea Sea' with notes to Book 2, back page).
• **-or** ending, of sailor – like doctor, actor, tractor, visitor, inspector, major, author, operator, etc.

Language/Parts of speech

Long-term follow-up to adjectives on previous page. Create an adjective bank in the classroom, with adjectives filed in alphabetical order. Start with adjectives pupils have written on their worksheets and those which have come out of discussion. Whenever a pupil comes up with a good adjective, s/he can add it to the bank. The cards can be used for games (e.g. teacher draws out 3/4 adjectives at random and pupils must draw a 'monster' to fit them; pupils in teams draw out an adjective each, give an example of something it describes, etc.).

Picture books

Around the World in Eighty Days, John Burningham (Cape)
The Man Whose Mother Was a Pirate, Margaret Mahy (Dent)
Patch the Pirate Cat, Andrew Martyr (Hamish Hamilton)
Professor Noah's Spaceship (Cape)

Alexander and the Leaky Junk *(page 12)*

This play provides material for group reading. There are parts for 12 readers, but the smaller ones could if wished be doubled: e.g. wise men/old man and woman; solider/Emperor of China.

Readability levels:

Narrator 1	Level 3
Narrator 2	Level 3
Alexander	Level 2+
Roxana	Level 2+
Timothy	Level 2+
Emperor	Level 2+
Messenger	Level 2+
Wise man 1	Level 2+
Wise man 2	Level 2+
Soldier	Level 2
Old man	Level 2+
Old woman	Level 2+

Alexander and the Leaky Junk

from an old legend

People in the Play

King Alexander the Great
Queen Roxana
Timothy, Alexander's friend
A soldier
Narrator 1
Narrator 2
The Emperor of China
A messenger boy
Wise Man 1
Wise Man 2
An old man
An old woman

Narrator 1   Long ago, there was a king called Alexander who was a great soldier. He and his army travelled all over the world. Every time they came to a new land they took it over.

Narrator 2   At last they reached a land of mountains and deserts. People said it was the end of the world. Alexander went walking there with his wife, Roxana, and his friend, Timothy.

Alexander   (*sighing*) Oh dear. I'm bored!

Roxana   Bored! But you are king of the whole world!

Timothy   Why are you bored, my lord?

Alexander   I am bored because there is nothing left for me to do. Now I have reached the end of the world, there are no lands left to take over. What I am going to do for the rest of my life?

Roxana   Oh, Alexander – there is plenty for you to do. We can go back home.

Alexander   I suppose we can.

Timothy   You can rule wisely over all your lands.

Alexander   I suppose I can.

Roxana   You can read books or write poems or paint pictures.

Alexander   Yes, Roxana. I suppose I can do all that. But I like being a soldier best. I wish there was just one last land to conquer.

12

Recall of the story After first reading:
- Why was Alexander the Great bored at the beginning of the play?
- Who was Roxana?
- Who first told Roxana about a land beyond the mountains?
- What was the land called?
- How did Roxana travel on the journey to China?
- What animals did Alexander take for transport?
- When Alexander camped, how far was he from China?
- Why did the Emperor of China fear Alexander?
- What did the messenger ask the Emperor to give him?
- How long did the old people say they had been travelling?
- What did they say the nails had been when they set out?
- What did they say the fruit tree had been when they set out?
- Who did they say the boy was?
- Why did Alexander turn back?

(page 13)

Roxana	Well my lord, when I was a little girl, I lived not far from here. My nurse used to tell me stories at bedtime. She told me stories of another land . . .
Alexander	Did she? Where was it?
Roxana	She said there was a land beyond the deserts and mountains – a beautiful, rich land. She said its name was "China".
Alexander	China! I shall go there. I shall conquer it!
Roxana	Oh, but it might be dangerous. No one knows how far away it is.
Alexander	I don't care how far it is! I am Alexander the Great and I can do anything. No matter how far it is, I am going to conquer China!
Timothy	But how will we get there? How will we carry our weapons and stores across the mountains?
Alexander	We'll take elephants and horses.
Roxana	What about me and the other ladies?
Alexander	You can travel in sedan chairs.
Timothy	What about our war machines and catapults?
Alexander	Get oxen to drag them! Get all the transport we need.
Roxana	But what if China is a million miles away?
Alexander	I've told you – I don't care how far it is. We are going to China!
Narrator 1	So Alexander set off to find China. He took more animals and men than he had ever taken anywhere before. After they had been travelling for weeks, they camped for a while by a river. Alexander did not know that China was only a few days' journey away.
Narrator 2	But the Emperor of China knew how far away Alexander was. A messenger boy brought news every day to the Emperor's palace.
Emperor	(sounding worried) How many soldiers do you say he has?
Messenger	Thousands, your majesty. Tens of thousands. Hundreds of thousands!
Emperor	(more worried) And does he have lots of weapons?

13

Inference from the text/Expression in reading

- *What sort of character is Alexander?* (Children's responses to such a question are usually far from concise. However, the teacher can attempt to summarise them with suitable adjectives, which could be added to the adjective bank, e.g.: proud, important, vain, bossy, impatient, bored, warlike, etc.)
- *What sort of character is the Emperor?*
- *What sort of character is the Messenger?*
- *What sort of voices should they have?*
- *Do you think Roxana wants to go to China? Why? (Can you find evidence in what she says?)*
- *How do you think Alexander's voice should sound at the beginning of the play? Can you speak the lines in the right tone of voice?*
- *How do you think the Wise Men should sound when the Messenger says he has an idea? Can you say their lines in the right sort of voice? Why do they sound like that?*

Punctuation: statements and questions
(See Glossary, work for page 6 and Worksheet 3c.)
Ask pupils to find some questions in the play and read them in appropriately 'questioning' voices.

Discussion: Language

- *What do the following words and phrases mean?* 'conquer'; 'a sedan chair'; 'oxen'; 'starve someone out'; 'bargain with someone'; 'a junk'.
- Titles of respect. *What special names do the Messenger and the Wise Men use to address the Emperor to show their respect?* (Your Majesty, Sire) *How does Timothy address Alexander?* (My lord) *What other titles do you know which people use to show respect when they speak* (Sir, Miss, Mr...., Mrs...., your Highness, etc.) *and to whom would they use them?*

29

Language: complete sentences

(See Glossary: **phrases** and **sentences**.)

When writing, pupils should generally use complete sentences. However, when people are speaking they often use phrases rather than sentences.

In this play, there are both sentences and phrases. Help children to spot the obvious phrases (i.e. those which do not contain a verb, such as 'Oh dear'/'Yes, Roxana'/'China!'/'Tens of thousands!' etc.).

Worksheet 3f: How to answer in sentences

3f

Responding to comprehension questions gives pupils an opportunity to look at how sentences are formed. Section A of the worksheet provides three questions about 'Alexander and the Leaky Junk'.

For the first question the answer is provided as a phrase (in the speech bubble) and as a sentence (hand-written on the line). The latter provides a model for completing the remaining sentence – answers in Section A. Pupils who have only recently reached Level 2 will need much teacher support to grasp the point of this.

Once pupils seem secure, Section B gives questions about 'Alexander and the Leaky Junk' which pupils should answer in complete sentences.

(page 14)

Messenger	Spears and swords and knives, your majesty.
Emperor	*(even more worried)* What about transport?
Messenger	Elephants, horses, sedan chairs. Camels, carts and oxen.
Emperor	And how far away is he?
Messenger	Just a few days' journey, your majesty.
Emperor	This is terrible news. Our army has no chance against him. Call my wise men! I need advice.
Messenger	Wise men! Come to the Emperor!
Narrator 2	The wise men came hurrying in.
Emperor	What are we to do? What are we to do? Alexander the Great is only a few days' journey away, and his army is much stronger than ours.
Wise Man 1	Well, we could lock ourselves in the palace, your majesty, and wait for him to go away.
Emperor	That's no use. He'd starve us out.
Wise Man 2	Perhaps we could all run away before he gets here, sire.
Emperor	That's no use. There's nowhere to run. Alexander has taken over the rest of the world.
Wise Man 1	Then maybe we could bargain with him, your majesty.
Emperor	How could we bargain with him? He has nothing to lose. Oh dear, you aren't helping at all. What am I to do?
Messenger	Please, your majesty, I have an idea.
Wise Man 1	What?
Wise Man 2	You're only a boy!
Emperor	NO – let the boy speak. I will hear what he has to say.
Messenger	Well, your majesty, Alexander is a very great soldier, and very powerful, but there is something we know that he doesn't know.
Emperor	What is that?

14

3g

Worksheet 3g: sentence punctuation

This worksheet consists of two short passages for punctuation – one fiction and one non-fiction – which can be cut up for use on separate occasions. Pupils could either 'correct' the worksheet, or copy out each passage adding punctuation. Alternatively, the passages could be transferred to a file on Pendown or other word-processing package.

(page 15)

Messenger	We know how far away China is!
Wise Man 1	What do you mean?
Messenger	Alexander has been travelling for a long time. He doesn't know how far he still has to go. For all he knows, China could be a million miles away! If you give me a few things, I think I can make him turn round and go home.
Emperor	What sort of things do you want?
Messenger	I want an old old boat – a leaky, rotten junk – filled with rusty nails. I want two fruit trees in tubs to put in it. And I want three old old men and three old old women to help me sail it down the river.
Wise Man 1	What nonsense! What can you do with a leaky junk full of old people? Alexander has elephants, horses, sedan chairs and thousands and thousands of soldiers.
Wise Man 2	Don't listen to him, your majesty. He's mad.
Emperor	No, I don't think he is mad. He has an idea, and at the moment any idea is worth trying. You shall have your junk, your old people and all the other things, my boy. You shall have my blessing too. Good luck go with you!
Messenger	Thank you, your majesty. I shall do my best.
Narrator 2	So the messenger boy got what he had asked for. He spent a long time telling the old people what they had to do. Then they set off in their junk to sail down the river.
Narrator 1	Meanwhile, Alexander, Roxana, Timothy and the army were still camped on the river bank.
Roxana	Oh dear, I wonder how much farther it is to China.
Timothy	We seem to have been travelling for ever.
Roxana	My sedan chair is very bumpy.
Timothy	My horse keeps losing his shoes on the mountain roads.
Alexander	I'm sure it can't be all that much farther. We'll be there soon!
Timothy	I hope so, my lord, because the soldiers are getting very fed up.

15

Group work: group presentation

Once pupils are familiar with the play, groups could attempt presentations of it.

Taped reading
A taped presentation could involve the production of a musical introduction/accompaniment and sound effects.

Puppet play
The characters could be made from sock puppets or stick puppets. The puppet theatre could be tables simply covered or a more elaborate arrangement. Pupils could work in pairs to make puppets, then one could operate the puppets as the other reads the lines.

Staged play
A staged presentation, perhaps for another class, could also involve the design and production of appropriate masks/costumes for the characters.

Information technology
Any production of the play provides an opportunity for the design of a programme, using Pendown or other desk-top publishing package.

(page 16)

Roxana	They keep saying they want to go home.
Alexander	They'll cheer up when we see China.
Narrator 1	Suddenly one of the soldiers spotted a junk coming down the river.
Soldier	My lord, my lord! There is a boat!
Alexander	A boat! It must be from China. We must be nearly there at last. Stop the boat! Ask who they are!
Soldier	Halt! Who goes there?
Narrator 2	An old leaky junk sailed up to Alexander's camp and stopped. In it there were three very old men, three very old women and a young boy. There were two fruit trees growing in pots and a lot of rusty old nails. One old man and one old woman came forward.
Old Man	Good day to you, my lord.
Old Woman	Have we arrived at last? Is this the west?
Soldier	Who are you? Tell us your name!
Old Man	My name is Lee Hwang, my lord.
Old Woman	I am his wife, May Ku.
Old Man	The other people in the junk are our friends and that young boy is our grandson.
Soldier	Where have you come from?
Old Man	We have come from China!
Alexander	China! At last! How far away is it? Are we nearly there?
Old Man	What, sir? Did you hear that, wife? He asked if he is nearly at China. (*All the old people laugh.*)
Soldier	Silence! Do you know who you are speaking to? This is Alexander the Great, King of the World!
Old Man	I am sorry, my lord. But let me explain. My wife and our friends here left China to seek a new life in the west.

16

Poem

Edward Lear's poem about another leaky sea-going vessel makes an excellent mime presentation:

The Jumblies

Far and few, far and few,
    Are the lands where the Jumblies live;
Their heads are green, and their hands are blue,
    And they went to sea in a Sieve.
They went to sea in a Sieve, they did,
    In a Sieve they went to sea:
In spite of all their friends could say,
    On a winter's morn on a stormy day,
In a Sieve they went to sea!
    And when the Sieve turned round and round,
And everyone cried, 'You'll all be drowned!'
    They called aloud, 'Our Sieve ain't big,
But we don't care a button! We don't care a fig!
    In a Sieve we'll go to sea!'
Far and few, far and few,
    Are the lands where the Jumblies live;
Their heads are green, and their hands are blue,
    And they went to sea in a Sieve.

They sailed away in a Sieve, they did,
    In a Sieve they sailed so fast,
With only a beautiful pea-green veil
    Tied with a ribbon by way of a sail,
To a small tobacco-pipe mast;
    And everyone said, who saw them go,
'Oh won't they be soon upset you know!

    For the sky is dark, and the voyage is long,
And happen what may, it's extremely wrong
    In a Sieve to sail so fast!'
Far and few, far and few,
    Are the lands where the Jumblies live;
Their heads are green, and their hands are blue,
    And they went to sea in a Sieve.

The water it soon came in, it did,
    The water it soon came in;
So to keep them dry, they wrapped their feet
    In a pinky paper all folded neat,
And they fastened it down with a pin.
    And they passed the night in a crockery-jar,
And each of them said, 'How wise we are!
    Though the sky be dark, and the voyage be long,
Yet we never can think we were rash or wrong,
    While round in our Sieve we spin!'
Far and few, far and few,
    Are the lands where the jumblies live;
Their heads are green, and their hands are blue,
    And they went to sea in a Sieve.

Old Woman	We bought a brand new junk and set off along the river.
Old Man	That was fifty years ago.
Alexander	Fifty years!
Old Man	We have been travelling down this river for fifty years.
Old Woman	When we set off we were all young people.
Old Man	These rusty nails were bars of iron, which we were going to sell.
Old Woman	The fruit trees in these pots were just seeds.
Old Man	Our children had not even been born. Now they are all dead.
Old Woman	If it weren't for our grandson here, we would be dead too. He sails the boat for us.
Old Man	Please tell us, sir – have we reached the west now?
Alexander	I cannot believe it. Fifty years! China is fifty years away.
Timothy	By the time we get there the army will be too old to fight.
Roxana	The horses and elephants will be dead.
Soldier	Our weapons will have rusted away.
Roxana	Oh husband, please change your mind now. Let's go home.
Alexander	You are right. We shall have to turn back. China is too far away.
Narrator 1	So Alexander and his army turned around and went home.
Narrator 2	After they had gone, the messenger boy and his friends sneaked back up the river to tell the Emperor what had happened.
Emperor	Wonderful! China is saved! You shall have gold and jewels as a reward. And I shall put the junk, the nails and the fruit trees into a museum for all our people to see.
Wise Man 1	They show that a good idea can turn back an army.
Wise Man 2	And that a boy can sometimes be wiser than a wise man.
Messenger	And that sometimes a leaky boat is better transport than all the elephants, horses and sedan chairs in the world!

17

Books

Picture books:
Little Tim and the Brave Sea Captain, Edward Ardizzone (OUP)
Tim and Lucy Go To Sea, Edward Ardizzone (Kestrel)
and many other Little Tim titles.
Story book for reading alone by Level 3:
Red Fox and His Canoe, Nathaniel Benchley (Puffin)

And all night long they sailed away;
And when the sun went down,
They whistled and warbled a moony song
To the echoing sound of a coppery gong,
In the shade of the mountains brown.
'O Timballo! How happy we are,
When we live in a Sieve and a crockery-jar,
And all night long in the moonlight pale,
We sail away with a pea-green sail,
In the shade of the mountains brown!'
Far and few, far and few,
Are the lands where the Jumblies live;
Their heads are green, and their hands are blue,
And they went to sea in a Sieve.

They sailed to the Western Sea, they did,
To a land all covered with trees,
And they bought an Owl, and a useful Cart,
And a pound of Rice and a Cranberry Tart,
And a hive of silvery Bees.
And they bought a Pig, and some green jackdaws,
And a lovely Monkey with lollipop paws,

And forty bottles of Ring-Bo-Ree,
And no end of Stilton cheese.
Far and few, far and few,
Are the lands where the Jumblies live;
Their heads are green, and their hands are blue,
And they went to sea in a Sieve.

And in twenty years they all came back,
In twenty years or more,
And everyone said, 'How tall they've grown!
For they've been to the Lakes, and the Terrible Zone,
And the hills of the Chankly Bore;'
And they drank their health, and gave them a feast
Of dumplings made of beautiful yeast;
And everyone said, 'If we only live,
We too will go to sea in a Sieve –
To the hills of the Chankly Bore!'
Far and few, far and few,
Are the lands where the Jumblies live;
Their heads are green, and their hands are blue,
And they went to sea in a Sieve.

Transport in the Playground *(page 18)*

Discussion

For example:

Do you know any of these playground rhymes? What sort of game do you think is played to 'Kitsy Katsy'? What other playground rhymes do you know? (Are there any about transport? e.g. many examples in Book 1 and notes; 'The Good Ship Sails Through the Alley-Alley O' with notes to Book 2, page 10, etc.)

Discussion/Language awareness

The Hindi rhyme is pronounced thus:

Haati ghora palki
Jai Kanaiya lalki

Does anyone in the class speak Hindi? Which country does Hindi come from originally? What is different about the way Hindi and English are written? What do they have in common? etc. Does anyone in the class speak any other languages? Does anyone know any children's rhymes from other cultures/in other languages?

Spoken language/Group work/Language

Pupils could ask parents and grandparents for further examples of children's rhymes.

If they can collect enough material (especially rhymes from a variety of cultures) they could compile an illustrated booklet/newsheet of playground rhymes from their own playground, for circulation to parents/grandparents.

Another Hindi rhyme

Chuk Chuk Chuk Chuk

Chuk Chuk Chuk Chuk
Rail chale
Rail ka injan shor karey
Aachhey bacchey khel karey.

Chooh, Chooh, Chooh, Chooh!

Chooh, chooh, chooh, chooh!
The train is going
The engine is making a noise
Good children play.

The Voyage *(page 19)*

The Voyage

This box is a boat,
The carpet's the sea,
Those patterns are fishes,
That armchair's the quay.

I've undone the rope
And pulled up the sail,
I'm now on the ocean
And it's blowing a gale.

The wind's loud and fierce,
The waves leap up high,
But I'm sailing her well
In the dark thundery sky.

The sun has appeared,
I've sailed through the storm.
The sky has turned blue
And the air has grown warm.

Look, there are some stars!
I'll stay here the night
And sleep on the waves
Beneath the moon's light.

Michelle Magorian

19

Discussion: imaginative play

Do you ever play at travelling in a pretend boat/plane/space ship, etc.? What do you use for your imaginary transport/environment? What/who do you take with you? etc.

Drama/Role-play

Pupils in small group or pairs choose forms of transport, 'create' them using classroom furniture, etc., and role-play their journeys. Groups can then explain their constructions and imaginary environment to the rest of the class and volunteers can act out their journeys to an audience.
See also notes to Book 2, page 5.

Poetry/Expressing preferences

Compare poem to Robert Louis Stevenson's 'A Good Play', written in the 1880s:

We built a ship upon the stairs
All made of the back-bedroom chairs,
And filled it full of sofa pillows
To go a-sailing on the billows.

We took a saw and several nails,
And water in the nursery pails;
And Tom said, 'Let us also take
An apple and a slice of cake;' –
Which was enough for Tom and me
To go a-sailing on, till tea.

We sailed along for days and days,
And had the very best of plays;
But Tom fell out and hurt his knee,
So there was no one left but me.

Which of the poems do you like best and why?
Pupils can then look back through all the poems in the book and pick the ones they like best and least. Organise a voting session, and discuss reasons for their preferences/dislikes. Perhaps compile a Top Ten list of transport poems.

Books

Story book:
Ursula Sailing, Sheila Lavelle (Young Corgi)

Picture books about boats: see also Book 1, page 3; Book 2 page 3.

Reading for information

Reading for information

This picture story provides a stimulus for discussion of the processes involved in reading for information and introduces the vocabulary required to talk about it.

IT IS NOT AN ALTERNATIVE TO REAL INFORMATION SEARCH AND READING.

Once discussion is over, pupils must engage in the process themselves. It is therefore important that enough suitable information books are available for the group's use (we recommend a minimum of 2 books available per pupil). On the whole, the reading level of information books should be a little lower than that with which pupils cope in narrative material.

Overview

Pupils should read the whole picture story through with the teacher before discussing individual frames.

Reading/Discussion

More detailed reading and discussion would best be done in two parts:
- frames 1–6 (followed by an opportunity for pupils to browse themselves)
- frames 6–14 (followed by an opportunity for pupils to find answers to their own questions).

Frame 1

Children working towards Level 3 should be aware of the difference between 'story books' and 'fact books' (use Worksheet 2d, if required). We use the terms 'fiction' and non-fiction' to describe them. (Definitions in Glossary)

Frames 2–5

There is a great deal of new vocabulary here. Definitions of **captions**, **headings**, **sub-headings**, and **keywords** are given in the Glossary (page 32 of Book 3). The illustrations in these frames should help pupils learn these new words. However, discussion and opportunities to find examples in real non-fiction books in the classroom are essential to understanding.
- Treasure Hunt in classroom project books: Can you find a book with a Contents Page? a picture with a caption? a chapter heading (and the reference to it in the Contents)? a sub-heading?
- Keywords: What are some keywords about *transport/different sorts of transport?*

Frame 6
This frame shows children becoming involved in browsing, and thus acquiring some of the background knowledge they require to think about the subject for themselves. At this point, pupils should have the opportunity to browse in the class project collection.

Frame 7: formulating questions
Questions have already been covered from other angles in work for 'Alexander and the Leaky Boat' (pages 10–15 of Book 3) and Worksheet 3. See also **statements** and **questions** in the Glossary (page 32 of Book 3).
Formulating good questions for information-finding purposes is not easy. To some extent, you need to know the answers before you can formulate the questions.
One way round this is to ask each pupil to write down a good question about transport to which, as a result of browsing, s/he already knows the answer. Questions can then be vetted and doled out to other pupils, so that they can try to track the answers down.

Frames 8 and 9
Vocabulary: **title**, **contents page** (these are not included in the Glossary). Most good children's information books these days include a contents page. Its use is fairly straightforward and can be practised, if necessary, using the contents page of this book.

Frames 10, 11 and 12
Vocabulary: **index**, **key-words** (both in Glossary), **alphabetical order**.
Practice of alphabetical order is given in Worksheet 2c.
After discussion, practice in locating keywords in an index, and in using these to find the appropriate pages in a book is given in **Worksheet 3h**.

3h

Frame 13
Vocabulary: **skim**, **scan** (both in Glossary)
Pupils should have already begun to skim and scan. They were probably skimming rapidly through books during their browsing period, and using an index involves scanning for keywords.
The application of these reading modes to text can really only be developed through practice. Thus, the more questions pupils attempt to answer, the more skilled they are likely to become.

Frame 14
When the relevant section of text is identified, careful attentive reading is required, and pupils must reflect on what they read to ensure their full understanding of the words and concepts concerned. Again, this is a very different sort of 'reading' from that involved in enjoying a story. The test of pupils' success in reading for information is their subsequent ability to answer questions on the topic without reference to the book. At Level 3, such retailing of information learned is probably best done orally.

Once children have learned the elements involved in reading for information, the teacher should take every opportunity to encourage its use. When questions arise within the project, pupils should seek answers in the books available. Whenever a new topic is introduced, relevant non-fiction books should be provided, and the skills demonstrated here applied.

Submarines *(page 23)*

Submarine

A baby sardine
Saw her first submarine:
she was scared and watched through a peephole.

'Oh, come, come, come,'
Said the sardine's mum.
'It's only a tin full of people.'

Spike Milligan

How do submarines go up and down?

Submarines are ships that can dive down under water. They can also float on top of the sea, like other ships.

Submarines have big tanks on their sides called "ballast tanks". The tanks have holes in them which can be open or shut. These holes are called vents.

When the submarine is floating on top of the sea, the ballast tanks are full of air. The vents are shut so no water can get in.

If the submarine's crew opens the vents, water rushes into the ballast tanks. When the tanks are full of water the submarine is much heavier, so it sinks down.

To make the submarine come back up, the crew has to force the water out of the ballast tanks. The sailors pump air into the tanks very hard indeed. This forces the water out of the vents. When the tanks are full of air again, the submarine is much lighter, so it rises up to the surface.

 23

Poetry/Reading 'Submarine'

This poem can be read as an introduction to 'How Submarines Go Up and Down' below.

Discussion

Later session: Reread the poem. What is a sardine? Have you ever seen a tin of sardines?
Points of view: *What might a plane look like to a bird? A space module to a Martian? A car to a hedgehog?* If children are interested in this idea, and make some good suggestions, it may provide a starting point for writing.
NB see poem 'Southbound on the Freeway' In Book 4, page 30.)

Science links:
floating and sinking;
formulating questions.

Reading non-fiction material

How submarines go up and down.
In 'Reading for Information' we presented a model for the process of children's information-search. The final frames describe the intensive reading required once relevant material is located. In this section we provide a short piece of non-fiction material on which intensive reading methods can be practised.

Questions, explicitness, factual information

Pupils should read the passage and, in their own words, provide a brief oral answer to the question 'How does a submarine go up and down?' They can then make up more questions inspired by the passage (e.g. What are the tanks on the sides of submarines for? How does water get in and out of the tanks? How do sailors force water out of the tanks when they want to go up to the surface?) and frame clear explicit answers.

When the passage has been read in depth, proceed to page 20.

Reading a diagram

What is a diagram? What information in the writing on the previous page is not shown in the diagram? How does the diagram show the order in which things happen? This is a cycle-diagram. Can you think why it's called that? What other cycles can you think of which could be represented in this way?

> Science links: diagrammatic flotation

Spoken explanation, factual explicitness

In pairs, pupils explain to each other exactly what is happening in the pictures (taking alternate ones). They should not look back at the passage.

Written factual information

Pupils next write a simple explanation of the cycle of the submarine's descent and ascent, using the diagrams as a stimulus and not looking back at the previous page. This exercise develops a pupil's confidence to write using his/her own words, rather than copying verbatim from a non-fiction text. (This might be a suitable piece for drafting and editing.)

Diagrams and writing

Teachers may find it helpful in other information finding/ recording activities to ask pupils to represent what they have learned pictorially in the first instance. Their pictures can later become the stimulus for each pupil's written account.

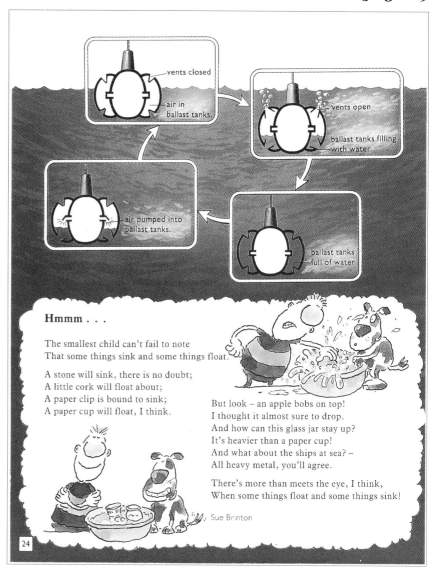

Hmmm . . .

The smallest child can't fail to note
That some things sink and some things float.

A stone will sink, there is no doubt;
A little cork will float about;
A paper clip is bound to sink;
A paper cup will float, I think.

But look – an apple bobs on top!
I thought it almost sure to drop.
And how can this glass jar stay up?
It's heavier than a paper cup!
And what about the ships at sea? –
All heavy metal, you'll agree.

There's more than meets the eye, I think,
When some things float and some things sink!

Sue Brinton

> Science links: flotation; characteristics of materials.

Poem: 'Hmmmm'

Discussion, e.g.: *Why do you think the stone and the paper clip sink? Why do the cork and the paper cup float? Would you expect an apple to float or sink? Why? Why do you think it floats? What about the glass jar?* etc.

The poem is divided into two **stanzas**. *How is the child feeling in the first stanza? What about the second? What is different about the child's opinion in the first two lines of the poem, and in the last two?*

The poem has a strong **rhyme scheme**, known as AA, BB, CC. *Can the pupils work out what this means? Using the same notation can they work out the rhyme schemes of other poems in the book?* (e.g. 'Submarine on page 22 is AA, B, CC, B.)

A letter from Java *(page 25)*

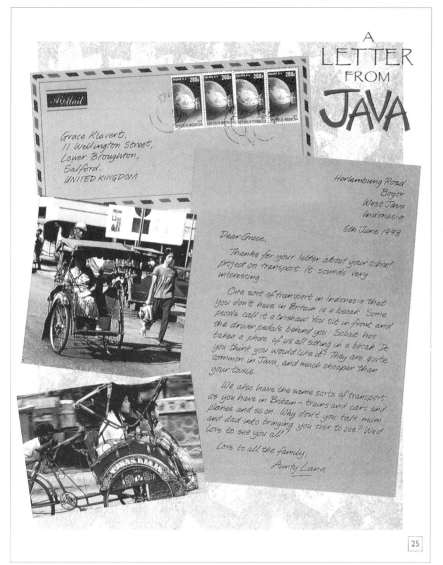

Reading Level: Level 2+
The letter is from a woman in Java to her niece in Britain.

Reading/Discussion

Read letter and discuss, e.g.:
This letter is obviously a reply – who wrote first, what do you think she asked, and why? Where is Java? (atlas? any books in the library with pictures?)
Does anyone have any relations in the Far East? Is it hotter or colder there than Britain? Do you like the idea of riding in a becak?
What do you think is the most typically British sort of transport? How would you describe it to someone who had seen it? Have you ever been abroad and seen other sorts of transport?
etc.

Language: proper nouns

(See Glossary)
Names and addresses are obvious examples of proper nouns. After looking at the example on the envelope, each pupil should write:
• own name and address,
• best friend's name and address,
with particular attention to layout and capital letters for proper nouns.

Letter writing

If pupils do not have any relatives abroad whom they can contact, as Grace obviously has, to find out first hand about transport in other countries, you can establish links with schools in other countries through the Commonwealth Linking Trust, 7 Lion Yard, Tremadoc Road, London, SW4 7NF; 071 498 1101. Genuine writing opportunities of this kind are ideal for teaching letter-writing skills. The letter from Aunty Lana provides a model for layout, etc., which should be discussed at length before pupils are expected to produce their own letters:

> own address in top right-hand corner,
> date beneath it
> Dear......., and indentation of first line of letter
> layout of letter, 'signing off line' and signature.

Discuss suitable 'signing off lines' for particular circumstances ('Best wishes', 'Love', 'All the best', etc. in a personal letter of this kind). Lana's envelope similarly provides a model for addressing an envelope.

Drafting and editing *(page 26)*

This picture story in intended as a focus for discussion of the process of drafting and editing and the introduction of vocabulary. Before beginning work on this section, it will be helpful if the pupils are familiar with these metalinguistic terms:

punctuation
pronoun
tense

Other metalinguistic terms which have been covered (**noun, verb, adjective, singular** and **plural**) may also be useful.

Overview

Pupils should read the whole comic strip through with their teacher before discussing it.

Frames 1 and 2

Drafting and editing gives the opportunity to improve:
- correctness
- composition.

Frame 3

Discussion should elicit that Ava's work is difficult to read because of errors, e.g.:
- Missing punctuation causes difficulties with phrasing.
- Incorrect spelling disrupts fluency.
- Use of 'he' to refer to both Harry and his friend leads to ambiguity.
- Inconsistent tenses disrupt the sense.

It could also be more explicit – 'a nice time' does not convey much to the reader. Ava could use more adjectives and explanation to improve the atmosphere of her story.

Frame 4

When children read their own work they often read what they think they wrote rather that what is on the page. To avoid this happening, Ava has left her work for a day or two (which 'distances' her from it). She is now reading it aloud (which slows her down and makes her pay more attention to the text) and a friend is following her reading and helping her to spot errors.

Frame 5

Discuss the terms 'draft' and 'edit' to ensure children understand them. As well as editing a complete draft, children will find themselves editing work as they go along. (As Ava did when she added 'winter's' to her opening phrase in the first draft.) Ava has now identified words which she thinks are incorrectly spelled and requested correct spellings from her teacher.

(page 27)

Frames 6 and 7

Many children feel that tidiness is the most important feature of written work, and are reluctant to edit because it looks scruffy. Frames 6 and 7 provide discussion material on this problem. Children can identify the changes Ava has made, and why she has made them. Can they spot any she's missed?

Frames 8, 9, and 10

Making a fair copy of a story is often seen as a punishment, but it is an essential part of drafting and editing. As often as possible, children should be relieved of the burden of making the final copy by hand. There are suggestions in the picture story as to how this can be done. However, fair copying is sometimes necessary and then it can be seen as an opportunity to create a beautiful piece of work, using the presentation skills children have been refining over recent months.

Final frame

A comparison between Ava's original composition and this final draft shows how drafting and editing can improve a piece of writing. Pupils could discuss how this one could be made even more interesting by the addition of further detail. Comparison between the scruffy second draft and the final copy shows how attention to presentation in the final stages is worthwhile.

Drafting and editing own work

When pupils fully understand the process and purpose of drafting and editing, they can try applying their knowledge to some of their own writing. Their own short pieces on 'Missing the Bus' (page 7 of Book 3) or 'Submarines' (page 20) may be appropriate. It is strongly recommended that, at this stage, children should not be expected to produce edited versions of many pieces of work.

3i

Worksheet 3i

This worksheet provides two wordsearches. The first consists of commonly used words on the Transport theme, the second of words which are commonly misspelled by pupils approaching Level 3. Pupils might also be provided with empty wordsearch frames and asked to compile their own wordsearches, using words they have recently learned to spell, to be completed by their friends.

The Bike   *(page 28)*

Poem

First reading: for pleasure and discussion as appropriate.

Descriptive writing/ story structure

The poem is provided as a stimulus for a structured piece of descriptive personal writing.

Session 1

Lead discussion on to the subject of 'Bikes', relating to pupils own experience, e.g.: *Do you have a bike/ have you ridden on a bike? Where do/did you go on it? Where did you get it?* etc.

For those children who do not have bikes (or access to a bike), allow other sorts of transport, e.g. 'Our car', 'A horse-ride', etc. and adjust notes below appropriately.

Each pupil chooses a significant moment in relationship to bikes (e.g. buying the bike/learning to ride/falling off). Pupil should then:

• Draw/paint a picture of self and bike at this moment
• Collect (either round the picture or on scrap paper) as many words as possible to summon up:
  – what you could see, e.g. colours/shapes/environment
  – what you could hear
  – what you could smell
  – what you could feel/touch
  – your feelings inside.
• Using these notes, each pupil to produce a detailed piece of writing describing **what is happening** in his/her picture (NOT the events leading up to it, or afterwards). This passage could be redrafted and improved if necessary.

This bike was bought
For my cousin, Mark;
He once fell off it
In the park.

But now it's mine.

Then it belonged
To his little sister;
She said the saddle
Gave her a blister.

And now it's mine.

Their little brother
Had it then;
And he fell off it
Again and again.

But now it's mine.

My big sister
Was next in line
And she stayed on it
All the time.

And now it's mine.

Then my brother
(Whose name is Mike)
Was the next to get
That bike.

But now it's mine.

This bike is old,
And covered in grime,
It's battered and rusty,
But to me it's fine . . .

For now it's mine, all mine.

Tony Bradman

28

Story

Friends and Brothers in *Friends and Brothers*, Dick King-Smith (Puffin).

Session 2 (optional)

The passage produced could provide the middle section of a story. Look back to 'Missing the Bus' (page 7 of Book 3). If appropriate, each child could write:

• A beginning, answering the who, when, where, why questions.
• An end, explaining what happened next.

Provide wall posters to jog memories:

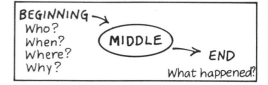

What could you FEEL?   HEAR?
          SMELL?   SEE?
          TASTE?   TOUCH?
What were your FEELINGS INSIDE?

BEGINNING →
Who?
When?   MIDDLE
Where?   → END
Why?   What happened?

The Sledge at Hilltop Rise *(page 29)*

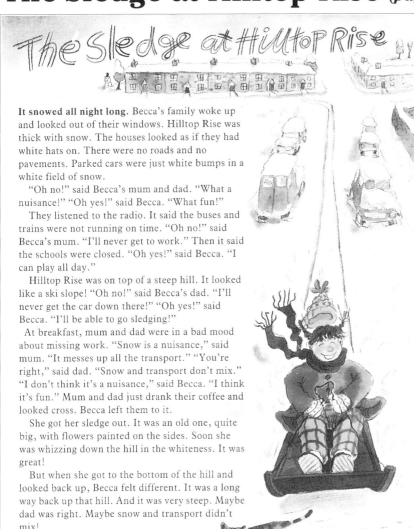

The Sledge at Hilltop Rise

It snowed all night long. Becca's family woke up and looked out of their windows. Hilltop Rise was thick with snow. The houses looked as if they had white hats on. There were no roads and no pavements. Parked cars were just white bumps in a white field of snow.

"Oh no!" said Becca's mum and dad. "What a nuisance!" "Oh yes!" said Becca. "What fun!"

They listened to the radio. It said the buses and trains were not running on time. "Oh no!" said Becca's mum. "I'll never get to work." Then it said the schools were closed. "Oh yes!" said Becca. "I can play all day."

Hilltop Rise was on top of a steep hill. It looked like a ski slope! "Oh no!" said Becca's dad. "I'll never get the car down there!" "Oh yes!" said Becca. "I'll be able to go sledging!"

At breakfast, mum and dad were in a bad mood about missing work. "Snow is a nuisance," said mum. "It messes up all the transport." "You're right," said dad. "Snow and transport don't mix." "I don't think it's a nuisance," said Becca. "I think it's fun." Mum and dad just drank their coffee and looked cross. Becca left them to it.

She got her sledge out. It was an old one, quite big, with flowers painted on the sides. Soon she was whizzing down the hill in the whiteness. It was great!

But when she got to the bottom of the hill and looked back up, Becca felt different. It was a long way back up that hill. And it was very steep. Maybe dad was right. Maybe snow and transport didn't mix!

29

Readability: Level 3

Recall of detail

For example:
- *Where did Becca's family live?*
- *Why was her mother fed up about the snow?*
- *Why was her father fed up about the snow?*
- *What did it say on the radio that made Becca very happy?*
- *What was Becca's sledge like?*
- *When Becca had sledged to the bottom of the hill, why did she think for a while that maybe snow and transport didn't mix?*
- *Who was the first/second/third person Becca met?*
- *Why did each of these people need help up the hill?*
- *Why was Becca pleased when she went in for lunch?*

Discussion

For example: *Have you ever had a go on a sledge? What was it like? Do you like snow? Why/why not?*
Why do many grown-ups dislike the snow? What other things do children usually like and grown-ups usually dislike? In each case, can you think why?

How does a sledge move? Why is it a suitable vehicle in snow? What other forms of transport are useful in snow? Why can cars and vans be dangerous in snowy/icy conditions? (See punctuation passage on 'How brakes work' in Worksheet 3g)

Science links: forces and movement; friction.

Group work/reading with expression

Once the pupils are familiar with the story, it can be split up among various readers to be read almost like a play. We suggest that pupils are allowed lightly to underline the words they are to read in pencil on the text.

Narrator 1 – all the narration on pages 28 and 30

Narrator 2 – all the narration on page 29

'Actors', to read all the words of direct speech:

    Becca
    Mother/Milkman
    Father/Postman

This activity directs pupils' attention to the organisation of a piece of writing, and the punctuation of direct speech.

Attention should be drawn in reading to punctuation and expression.

Spelling links

Some commonly used/commonly misspelled words which occur in the story are given in bold print. Other words which may be linked to them for teaching purposes are given in brackets:

field (shield, chief, thief, etc.; friend)

bre**akfast/gr**e**at** (break)

different (interest)

because

another (other, mother, brother)

heavy (head/ready, instead, etc.)

Spelling rules Those exemplified by words in the story include:

- **-dge** ending of sledge – as in edge/wedge/ledge; and badge/badger; bridge/fridge; dodge/lodge; judge/nudge/fudge/grudge etc.

- **-ui–** in nuisance – as in fruit, suit, juice, bruise, cruise (and, with a different sound, in the commonly misspelled words: build/building/built; biscuit).

As she stood there, someone called her name. A man came through the snow, all wrapped up in coats and scarves and wellies. "Hello, Becca," he said. It was the milkman!

"You're a bit late today," said Becca. "I'm lucky to get out at all," said the milkman. "But I have to deliver the milk if I can. I've managed to drive the van this far because it's a flat run. Still, there's no way it'll go up Hilltop Rise. I might as well go home."

Then Becca had an idea. "Why not borrow my sledge?" she said. The milkman looked at the sledge and then at Becca. "That *is* a good idea," he said.

They put a crate of bottles on the sledge and tied them down with some rope from the milk van. "That's great," said the milkman. He started to drag the sledge up the hill, and Becca walked along with him, chatting. At the top she helped him deliver the milk to the houses.

"That was a great idea, Becca," the milkman said. "Thanks very much." "Thank *you*," said Becca. "It helped me as well!" Then she had another lovely sledge-ride down the hill.

30

Use of English: the apostrophe in shortened forms

Because the story involves direct speech, the apostrophe to show shortened forms is used quite frequently:

page 28 'I'll never get to work/never get the car down there/be able to go sledging' 'You're right...' 'I don't think it's a nuisance.'

Page 29 'You're a bit late.' 'I'm lucky…' 'I've managed…' 'There's no way it'll go…' 'That's great,' 'It's helped me…' 'Don't do that...'

page 30 'I've had some lovely....' 'And I haven't....'

NB in the second sentence, an apostrophe is used to show possession in 'Becca's family'. This occurs again later in 'Becca's mum' and 'Becca's dad' IGNORE THIS FUNCTION FOR THE TIME BEING.)

Pupils can provide the full forms of all examples of the apostrophe in shortened forms that they can find in the story (e.g. 'I will never get to work.'). Write up on the blackboard beside the shortened versions, so pupils can work out exactly where the apostrophe should be placed (i.e. where the letters are missed out).

This time at the bottom she bumped into the postman. He had managed to drive his van to the bottom of Hilltop Rise too, but that was as far as it would go. "It's such a nuisance," he said sadly. "I have five big parcels to deliver up the hill, but I'll never get the van up there. I might as well go home."

"No," said Becca. "Don't do that."

The postman was very pleased when Becca let him borrow her sledge to pull his parcels. She walked with him and chatted. When they got to the top she helped him deliver the parcels.

"That was a great idea, Becca," said the postman. "Thanks very much." "Thank *you*," said Becca.

She whizzed down the hill again. This time she met Mrs Alexander, her next-door neighbour. Mrs Alexander had walked to the shops in the snow to do some important shopping. Now she was wondering how to get her heavy bag up the hill. Becca showed her. At the top she helped Mrs Alexander unpack her shopping and clear some of the snow away from her path.

When she came in for lunch, Becca was smiling. "You look pleased with yourself," said her dad. "Yes," said Becca. "I've had some lovely sledge-rides. I've helped lots of people. And I haven't had to drag my sledge up that hill. Not even once!" She told her mum and dad about her morning, and they smiled too. "Well, we were wrong then," said dad. "Snow and transport *do* sometimes mix," said mum. "As long as the transport is a sledge!" said Becca. They all laughed. "Can I have a go this afternoon?" said dad.

31

Books

Stories which pupils should be able to read for themselves:
'The Snow Time Express', Lillian Moore from *Never Meddle With Magic*, ed. Barbara Ireson (Puffin)
'Down the Hill' in *Frog and Toad All Year*, Arnold Lobel (Puffin)
Postman Pat Goes Sledging, John Cunliffe (Deutsch)

Language: Pupils' use of a range of sentence connectives

Sentences can be connected in many ways. Sometimes through vocabulary (e.g. 'Hilltop Rise was thick with snow. The houses looked as if....'), sometimes through layout (e.g. several sentences grouped as a paragraph), sometimes by grammatical features (e.g. linking pronouns, adverbial phrases of space and time, conjunctions, etc.). Pupils' skill in using and varying sentence connectives is usually a reflection of the extent of their reading rather than the result of teaching. However, the more aware children are of how language works and can be manipulated, the more likely they are to develop a wide range of strategies.

Worksheet 3j: Joining sentences

3j

This worksheet provides discussion material on some of the different ways sentences can be joined using 'joining words'. The 'joining words' should be cut out, and the pairs of sentences also cut out (as they are required). Sentences and joining words can then be moved about and tried in various combinations. Teachers should supervise work on possible ways of joining the first pair of sentences (A). Pupils should then work in pairs to find as many variations as possible for joining the other pairs (jotting them down as they find them). The exercise can be turned into a team competition, and extra marks allotted for correct punctuation of jottings.

Glossaries (page 32)

The glossaries are provided to ensure that vocabulary needed for Level 3 work is available to pupils. Definitions are, as far as possible, in language appropriate to the age-group, and are therefore somewhat simplistic. (A more complex definition sometimes appears in later books.) Some terms, such as 'capital letter' and 'full stop' are not included, as we have assumed that pupils approaching Level 3 are already familiar with them.

All definitions require plenty of discussion with the teacher. Pupils must then experience the concept concerned within the context of real language before they can be expected to grasp the meaning. Wherever possible vocabulary has been introduced in the teachers notes to individual pages, often with follow-up in an exercise or worksheet.

By the time pupils have finished the book, therefore, they should be familiar with most of the terms.

Suggestions for introducing words pupils have not met through exercise/worksheets:

abbreviation: note the use of e.g. in many Glossary notes. Collect other common abbreviations and their meanings.

consonant: see vowel

glossary: do any books in the project collection have glossaries?

word-family: collect families related to transport on the basis of the examples given.

GLOSSARY of words about reading and writing

♦ **abbreviation**
A short way of writing something, often using initials, e.g. the letters *e.g.* mean *for example*.

♦ **browsing**
Looking through books to get an idea of what they are about.

♦ **caption**
Words written underneath a picture, to tell you about it.

♦ **diagram**
A simple picture which helps to explain something clearly.

♦ **draft**
A writer's try at expressing what he/she wants to say. The draft can then be **edited** and improved.

♦ **edit**
To change or correct a piece of writing to make it better.

♦ **fable**
A short story which teaches you a lesson or moral.

♦ **fiction**
A story which is invented.

♦ **glossary**
A list of difficult words, with their meanings, usually arranged in alphabetical order. You sometimes find a glossary at the back of a **non-fiction** book.

♦ **heading**
The title at the top of a piece of writing, or at the beginning of a chapter in a book.

♦ **index**
An alphabetical list at the back of a **non-fiction** book. It lists **key words** for all the topics in the book, and tells which pages contain information about each topic.

♦ **key words**
The important words about a particular topic, e.g. the words in this **glossary** are key words about reading and writing.

♦ **non-fiction**
Facts.

♦ **notes**
You write notes to help you remember something. They are short, quick reminders and they do not have to be in **sentences**.

♦ **reference books**
Books which you use to look up particular bits of information. You do not read them from beginning to end.

♦ **scanning**
Looking quickly over pages to find particular key words.

♦ **skimming**
Looking quickly over pages of a book to get an idea of what they are about.

♦ **sub-heading**
The title given to one section of a longer piece of writing. There may be several sub-headings under one main **heading** or chapter-heading.

♦ **summary**
A short description of the main points of something.

♦ **word processor**
A computer used for writing.

GLOSSARY *of words about language*

♦ **adjective**
A describing word, e.g. *quick, slow, rusty*.

♦ **apostrophe**
A **punctuation mark** like a flying comma. It shows where letters have been missed out of a word or words, e.g. *didn't* (short for did not), *I've* (short for I have).

♦ **consonant**
Any letter of the alphabet which is not a **vowel**, i.e. B, C, D, F, G, H, J, K, L, M, N, P, Q, R, S, T, V, W, X, Y, Z.

♦ **joining word**
A word which joins groups of words together, e.g. *and, but, when, so, as, while, because, after*. It can be used to join two sentences together to make one sentence, e.g.
The battery was flat. The car did not start.
1. The battery was flat *so* the car did not start.
2. *When* the battery was flat, the car did not start.
3. The car did not start *because* the battery was flat.

♦ **noun**
A naming word – the name of a person, place, animal or thing, e.g. *man, country, horse, train*.

♦ **part of speech**
The job a word is doing in a **phrase** or **sentence**, e.g. **noun, verb, adjective, pronoun, joining word.**

♦ **phrase**
A group of words which go together, but do not make a complete **sentence**.

♦ **plural**
See **singular** and **plural**.

♦ **proper noun**
First see **noun**. The special name of a particular person, place, animal or thing, e.g. *Alexander, China, Black Beauty, Flying Scotsman*. Proper nouns always begin with a capital letter.

♦ **punctuation marks**
These marks help a reader make sense of a piece of writing. Some show how words are grouped together to make sense (e.g. comma and full stop). Some also show the tone of voice you should use (e.g. question mark).

♦ **questions and statements.**
Sentences can be questions or statements. A question-sentence asks something and it ends with a question mark, e.g. *What is your favourite sort of transport?*
A statement-sentence is an ordinary sentence and it ends with a full stop, e.g.
My favourite sort of transport is the train.

♦ **sentence**
A group of words that go together to make complete sense. A sentence always contains at least one **verb**. It begins with a capital letter and ends with a full stop.

♦ **singular and plural**
Nouns can be either singular or plural.
Singular = just one,
plural = more than one,
e.g. *plane* (sing.), *planes* (pl.)
    ferry (sing.), *ferries* (pl.)

♦ **tense**
Verbs can be in the past, present or future tenses, e.g. past – the plane *flew*; present – the plane *flies*; future – the plane *will fly*.

♦ **verb**
A word of doing or being, e.g. *fly, travel, be, become*.

♦ **vowel**
One of these five letters of the alphabet: A, E, I, O, U. (The letter y is a 'part-time vowel', sometimes standing in for the sound of 'i').

♦ **word family**
A group of words that come from the same root e.g.
1. *fly* (noun), *flies* (verb)
   flying (adjective), *flight* (noun).
2. *parts of the* verb '*to drive*':
   drive, drove, driving, driven.

At Book 3 level the development of pupils' awareness of language as a system becomes very important. This necessitates the introduction of many metalinguistic terms, which we have presented in a separate glossary. We hope that the separation will help children grasp that some words are related to **how we use language**, while others are the specialised vocabulary required to **talk about language** (Just as we need specialised vocabulary to talk about maths).

Language: metalinguistic terms

A way of checking that pupils are familiar with this vocabulary is to copy the words and their definitions on to separate pieces of card and ask pupils to match them up correctly.

Punctuation marks

NB The definition given here does not cover the use of the apostrophe in contractions – the apostrophe is always a rogue punctuation mark.
Punctuation at this stage is related mainly to sentence punctuation of which practice is given in Worksheet 3h. Another useful activity for sensitising pupils to punctuation is the 'Talking punctuation game'.

Talking punctuation game

Assign a sound to each punctuation mark in a particular passage. (e.g. for the letter on page 27:

full stop = 'splat'
question mark = 'boing'
exclamation mark = 'thwack'
comma = clicking noise with tongue
capital letter = 'Hrrumph', immediately before the capital)

Ask one child to read the letter aloud slowly, while the rest of the group, guided by the teacher, make the punctuation noises.

Punctuation marks are dealt with again in Books 4 and 5, and the subject is given more comprehensive treatment there.

The Song of the train *(back cover)*

Poetry reading

Ask the pupils in pairs to read the poem aloud to each other, working out how it should be read, and perfecting their rendition. Ask a few pairs (who seem to have got the idea of the train's rhythm) to demonstrate to the class (or read it yourself). *What was the poet trying to do in the second and fourth stanza? Can you tap the rhythms with your fingers?* etc. Pupils could then read the poem together:
First stanza – voice 1
Third stanza – voice 2
Second and fourth stanzas – whole class in chorus

Discussion

What sort of train is this, and which word in the poem tells you so? (steam train: puffs)
The poet refers to the train as 'she' – this is a female pronoun. Do you think of trains as male or female? Why? What about other sorts of vehicles? etc.

English Through Topics

For pupils working towards Level 3

Transport 3

Oliver & Boyd

THE SONG OF THE TRAIN

(Slowly)
With snort and pant the engine dragged
Its heavy train uphill,
And puffed these words the while she puffed
and laboured with a will:

(Very slowly)
"I think - I can - I think - I can,
I've got - to reach - the top,
I'm sure - I can - I will - get there,
I sim - ply must - not stop!"

(More quickly)
At last the top was reached and passed,
And then - how changed the song!
The wheels all joined in the engine's joy,
As quickly she tore along!

(Very fast)
"I knew I could do it, I knew I could win
Oh, rickety rackety rack!
And now for a roaring rushing race
On my smooth and shining track!"

H. Worsley-Benison

ISBN 0-05-005054-0

9 780050 050545

Song

This train is bound for glory, this train,
This train is bound for glory, this train,
This train is bound for glory,
If you ride in it, you must be holy, this train.

This train don' pull no extra, this train,
Don' pull nothin' but de Midnight Special.

This train don' pull no sleepers, this train,
Don' pull nothin but the righteous people, this train.

This train don' pull no jokers, this train.
Neither don' pull no cigar smokers, this train.

Books

Picture books:
The Little Shunting Engine, Ib Spang Olsen (World's Work)
Stories:
'Train story' in *Time for A Story*, ed Eileen Colwell (Puffin)
'Melanie Brown Goes for A Ride' in *Melanie Brown and the Jar of Sweets*, Pamela Oldfield (Faber)

Extra material for prediction

The Fool and the Flying Ship

A story from Russia

There were once three brothers called Ivan, Yuri and Boris. Ivan and Yuri were clever, hard-working and smart. Their mother was proud of them and loved them very much. Boris, however, was rather lazy. He liked to sit around dreaming all day, and never got any work done. People called Boris 'The Fool', and his mother was ashamed of him.

One day, the three brothers heard that the king of their country wanted to own a ship that could fly. He had offered a rich reward to anyone who could find such a ship – half of his kingdom and the hand of his daughter in marriage. The three brothers all fancied winning this prize, and they decided to leave home and search for a flying ship.

Ivan left first: their mother was heartbroken to see her eldest son go away. She baked him a special loaf of bread, and put it in a bag with wine and meat for him to eat on the journey. As Ivan walked down the road, an old beggar asked him where he was going, and then pleaded with the young man to give him some food and drink. Ivan ignored him and strode off to seek his fortune.

Next, Yuri set off; again their mother was very sad, and gave him bread, wine and meat to eat on his journey. As Yuri walked along, the same old beggar accosted him with the same request, but Yuri ignored the old man as his brother had done, and strode off into the world.

Last of all, the youngest brother left home: this time their mother was glad to be rid of the 'The Fool'. She gave him a bag containing nothing but a burnt loaf of bread and a bottle of water and sent him on his way.

The Fool had not gone far when he met the old beggar, who asked him where he was going. The Fool explained, and then the beggar asked him for some food and something to drink. The Fool replied that he had nothing but burnt bread and water, but that the old man was welcome to share it with him. Imagine his surprise when he opened the bag and found good bread, meat and a bottle of the best wine! The old man was really a magician, and had rewarded the brother who had been kind to him.

The magician had another reward for The Fool. He told him to go into a nearby wood and cut down a certain tree. The tree would turn immediately into a flying ship, which the young man could pilot to the King's palace. If the Fool was kind and understanding to all he met, the magician said, he would gain his heart's desire. The Fool thanked him, did as he had been told,

and soon found himself in possession of a magnificent flying ship. He climbed in and set off in the direction of the palace.

The Fool had not been flying for long when he saw a man kneeling on the ground with his ear pressed to the earth. 'Excuse me for asking,' he said, 'but what are you doing?' The man explained that he was listening to all the news going on in the country. His hearing was so powerful that, with his ear to the ground, he could hear everything everyone was saying. 'Gosh,' said the Fool. 'That must be both a blessing and a nuisance. But is there any way I could help you? Would you like a lift in my Flying Ship?' The man accepted gratefully as he had been travelling for a long time, and he quickly climbed in.

They flew on and soon saw another man, who was hopping along on one leg, with the other one tied to his ear. Again, the Fool asked what he was doing and whether he would like a lift. The man told them that he was such a fast runner that he had to tie one leg up or he would travel much too fast. He too happily accepted a lift on the flying ship.

They travelled on, picking up other travellers they saw along the way – and a strange crowd they were. The Fool's third passenger was a man whom they spotted apparently shooting his gun into an empty sky. This man turned out to have such amazing eyes that he could see birds and beasts a hundred miles away. The fourth passenger was a man carrying an enormous sackful of loaves on his back. He explained that he had such a huge appetite that he had to carry the sack with him, for a snack between meals. The fifth was a man kneeling beside a lake. He told The Fool that he had such a terrible thirst that drinking the whole lake would not quench it for him.

The sixth person they picked up was a man carrying a bundle of sticks on his back. He explained that the sticks were magic and that if he scattered them on the ground a huge army would spring up in their place. The seventh was a man carrying a bale of hay. He told them that if he spread the hay on the ground it would immediately freeze it up, and snow and ice would appear everywhere.

By this time, the flying ship had travelled through the night and was almost at the palace. They eventually landed in the king's garden just as dawn was breaking, and sent a message in to where the king was having his breakfast. The king was pleased that someone had brought him a flying ship, but very displeased when he found out what sort of person The Fool appeared to be.

'I don't want some low-born, foolish peasant marrying my daughter and taking over half my kingdom, he said. 'I'd better get rid of him. We'll set an impossible task for him to do.' The king told his servant to tell The Fool to bring him a flask full of the Water of Life, for which he would have to search across half the world. He commanded that The Fool must return with the flask before the people of the court had finished their breakfast. 'That should sort him out,' he muttered to himself.

However, the king had reckoned without The Fool's passengers, who were grateful for the lift in the Flying Ship and wanted to help their friend. The man with the powerful ears had heard everything the king said, and told the others. The man who could run with giant steps immediately untied his leg from his ear and set off. Within minutes he had crossed the world and found the Waters of Life. He was so confident of his speed that he decided to have a short rest beneath a shady windmill before setting off on the return journey.

Unfortunately, the runner fell asleep. He might not have wakened up in time to return with his flask full of the Water of Life, but the man with the amazing eyesight was keeping an eye on him. He raised his gun and aimed at the windmill, knocking off one of the arms, which fell on the sleeping runner and woke him up. The runner quickly returned, and handed over the flask to The Fool, who gave it to the king's servant. The king was amazed to receive the Water of Life before he had even buttered his toast!

However, the king was also very angry. He was determined not be outwitted by this 'foolish peasant', so he set another impossible task. He ordered that The Fool should be given an enormous meal to eat at a single sitting: a dozen roast oxen, a hundred loaves of bread, and forty pails of wine. The food and drink was carried on to the Flying Ship, and of course the man with the huge appetite and the man with the terrible thirst polished it off in no time.

What do you think happened next? How do you think the story finishes?

Now the king was furious. He ordered that an iron bath-house in the grounds of the palace should be heated up until it was white hot, and The Fool should be forced to spend the night inside it. The Fool, of course, took his friend with the magic hay into this furnace with him, and when they had spread the hay on the ground it cooled down so much that The Fool was even able to take a cold shower. He came out the next morning shivering, and the king was more furious than ever.

The king went back into the castle and sent out orders for an enormous army to be gathered, to kill The Fool and his companions. But the man with the powerful hearing heard this plan too, and The Fool asked his friend with the bundle of sticks to come to his aid. They threw the sticks on the ground before the palace, and an army sprang up ready to defend the occupants of the Flying Ship.

At last, the king realised he was beaten. He sent out a messenger to apologise, taking The Fool some rich embroidered clothes to wear, and inviting him into the palace. And when Boris The Fool put on the clothes, he suddenly didn't look like a fool any more, but like a handsome prince. He went into the palace and met the princess, who immediately fell in love with him. And from then on he ruled wisely over his half of the kingdom

---

Discussion

Were your predictions accurate? How did people decide on their predictions? What is the 'moral' or lesson of the story?
What is there about this story that makes it like a fairy tale? (e.g. Once upon a time/magician in disguise/fantastical happenings/repetition of events/happy ending)
What other fairy stories build up in this repetitive way, so you can almost guess the ending? (e.g. Three Little Pigs, Three Billy Goats Gruff) etc.

Sue Palmer and Peter Brinton

English Through Topics!

Transport

UNIQUE TALKING MODEL!
TEST DRIVE NOW

4

SOLD

Funny the way

Different cars run.

Some rattle and bang,

Some whirrr,

Some knock and knock.

Book 4

For pupils working towards Level 4

PUPIL'S BOOK 4: resource material, linked to the theme of Transport:
- *reading for pleasure:* poems; extracts from fiction; a short story; myth and folktale; a play based on a children's classic
- *reading for information:* using a library to find information; researching a topic
- *stimuli for writing in various genres:* stories and sketches; poetry; factual writing; letters; anthologies; records and reports
- *stimuli for spoken language activities:* class and group discussion; reporting; formal and informal presentations.

THE TEACHER'S NOTES:
- suggestions (accompanying each page of Book 4) for using the resource materials to cover most Level 4 English requirements.
  (A guide to the layout of the Teacher's Notes – page 8.)
- further poems and rhymes about Transport
- details of books for pupils related to the theme or to material provided in the pupil's book.

WORKSHEETS: practice work on:
4a	Parts of speech	(see notes to page 2)
4b	Comprehension questions – Section A: pages 3–5	(see page 3)
	Section B: pages 12–14	(see page 14)
	Section C: pages 22–28	(see page 22)
	Section D: pages 32–35	(see page 32)
4c	The apostrophe in shortened forms	(see notes to page 5)
4d	Using a library index	(see notes to page 8)
4e	Sentence punctuation	(see notes to page 11)
4f	Making parts of speech agree	(see notes to page 14)
4g	Capital letters	(see notes to page 21)
4h	Narrative and direct speech	(see notes to page 25)
4i	Prefixes	(see notes to page 31)
4j	Paragraphing	(see notes to page 34)

While detailed suggestions for the use of the resource material are provided, individual teachers have their own preferred methods of working and should use the materials as is most appropriate to their own teaching styles and their pupils' needs.

Covering the English Curriculum

The material is intended to **supplement** the ongoing language work of pupils working towards Level 4, and link it to the theme of Transport.

Pupil's Book 4 has been designed to provide:
- stimuli for large and small group discussion; drama and role-play; formal and informal presentations by individuals and groups;
- opportunities for group work involving planning and design;
- opportunities to read and respond to a wide range of literature, and especially to read aloud;
- opportunities to explore preferences, and to develop the ability to use inference, deduction and previous reading experience when reading;
- information about the use of a library and material to develop research skills;
- stimuli for writing of various kinds and for a variety of audiences;
- discussion material and models of various ways of drafting and organising written work;
- information about punctuation, sentence structure and paragraphing of texts;
- information about literary style and techniques;
- discussion material about regional and ethnic dialects of English and Standard English;
- technical vocabulary in which to discuss language use and the mechanics of reading and writing;
- opportunities to use word-processing facilities;
- occasional links to the teaching of spelling (although it is recommended that systematic teaching of spelling continues alongside use of ETT).

Keeping track

The Record-keeping checklist on page 57 correlates the National Curriculum English Attainment Targets for Level 4 with the activities suggested in these notes. The numbers used to record the correlations are the page numbers of the Pupil's Book against which activities are recommended in the Teacher's Notes.

Please see also the notes on page 11 about record-keeping.

Record-keeping checklist

Opportunities for covering Level 4 NC English Attainment Targets

See activities suggested to accompany the pages given below in Pupil's Book 4:

	2	3-5	6	7-9	10	11	12-14	15-17	18/19	20/21	22-28	29	30/31	32-35	36-37	38	39
Speaking and Listening																	
Deliver detailed oral account						11	12-14	15-17			22-28						
Explain with reasons		3-5				11	12-14	15-17			22-28	29	30/31	32-35			39
Ask/respond to questions		3-5	6			11	12-14	15-17			22-28	29	30/31	32-35			39
Participate in a presentation	2	3-5	6			11	12-14	15-17	18/19		22-28		30/31				39
Reading																	
Read from a range of familiar literature	2						12-14	15-17			22-28						39
Talk about and discuss preferences: stories							12-14	15-17			22-28			32-35			
poems	2												30/31				39
Develop inference, deduction			6				12-14	15-17			22-28			32-35			
Use classification system/catalogue				7-9	10												39
Use search reading		3-5			10									32-35			
Use contents/index				7-9	10											38	
Writing																	
Structured writing:					10		12-14									38	
sentence punctuation		3-5			10		12-14		18/19	20/21	22-28						
direct speech punctuation		3-5					12-14				22-28				36-37		
Write structured/crafted stories		3-5					12-14							32-35			
other chronological writing									18/19			29	30/31				
Organise non-chronological writing		3-5	6		10				18/19	20/21			30/31			38	
Standard English		3-5			10		12-14			20/21					36-37		
Revise/redraft work, talk about changes		3-5					12-14		18/19	20/21						38	
Develop metalanguage		3-5			10		12-14	15-17			22-28	29		32-35	36-37		39
Spelling																	
Main spelling patterns		3-5			10		12-14		18/19	20/21	22-28			32-35			
Handwriting																	
Fluent joined-up writing		3-5			10		12-14		18/19	20/21	22-28			32-35			

This checklist refers to the National Curriculum in English at the time of going to press (Spring 1993). An updated sheet for the revised curriculum, when known, is available free to purchasing schools, from Oliver & Boyd, Longman House, Burnt Mill, Harlow, Essex CM20 2JE.

Assessing and teaching children using ETT Book 4

(See notes on assessment in General introduction, page 11 and *Copymasters* pack page ix)

The resource material is pitched for teaching purposes roughly halfway between a Level 3 and a Level 4 standard. Teacher input will, of course, vary to accommodate children's needs as they progress along the developmental continuum between Levels 3 and 4. Progress can be assessed informally by observation of a child's performance when using the resource material and carrying out activities. For example:

	Just above Level 3 (beginner)	Between Levels 3 and 4 (midway)	Nearing Level 4 (independent)
Spoken English	Oral accounts not organised or detailed, reasoning not clearly expressed; tentative questioning and answering in group work; needs support in formal presentations.	Organisation of oral accounts improving, more detail, sometimes clear reasoning; skills in questioning and answering in group activities improving; developing confidence in presentations.	Oral accounts well organised, detailed; confidently questioning and answering in group activities; participating confidently in presentations.
Reading	Stumbles, lacks expression when reading aloud from prepared Level 4 texts; difficulty in defining personal response to poems and stories; not using much inference, deduction, previous experience when reading; unable to use a library classification system, catalogue or database.	Reads prepared Level 4 texts with some expression and developing confidence; beginning to explore preferences and define personal response to stories/poems; beginning to use inference, deduction and previous experience when reading; becoming familiar with library classification system, catalogue or database.	Reads aloud expressively and with confidence from Level 4 texts; able to explore personal preferences and indicate personal response to stories and poems; using inference, deduction and previous experience when reading; able to use library classification system or database.
Writing	Writing lacks clear organisational features, paragraphs and adequate punctuation; unable to punctuate direct speech; stories and chronological writing lacking clear structure; unsure of forms for formal letters and poems; using spoken language forms for written work; still needing support in drafting and editing own work; needs much support to complete worksheets.	Able to use appropriate organisational features, paragraphs and punctuation with teacher support; occasional correct use of direct speech punctuation; beginning to structure stories and chronological writing; using appropriate forms for formal letters and poems with help from teacher; developing awareness of difference between spoken and written language; beginning to draft/edit work independently and discuss with the teacher; complete worksheets with some support.	Making use of organisational features, paragraphs and punctuation to clarify writing; beginning to use direct speech punctuation as a matter of course; able to structure stories and chronological writing; able to use appropriate forms for formal letters and poems; sometimes using Standard English written forms; aware of major differences between Standard English and local dialect forms; drafting and editing work and explaining changes; completes worksheets with little/no support.
Spelling	Aware of the most common spelling patterns of English.	Developing awareness of spelling patterns.	Few errors on common words or regular spellings.
Handwriting	Legible joined handwriting in most final drafts.	Legible joined handwriting throughout work.	Fluent joined handwriting throughout work.

Contents

Off to a Good Start?

Reading poetry
Give pairs or groups of pupils one poem each to discuss and prepare for presentation to the class. Divide it between different voices to achieve the best effect.

Discussion: poetry
Two common aims of poetry featured here:
- surprising the reader into looking at familiar things in a new way;
- playing with, and enjoying, language.

'Funny the way different cars start'
What sort of car would start with a chunk and a jerk/a cough and smoke/a little click? What sort of cars would run in the four ways described? Can you make all the different sounds (using voices or items available in the classroom)? Think of a vehicle you know with a distinctive starting/running sound – how would you describe this sound in words? etc.

'Superstink'
Which of the 'words in the cloud' would you say were real words? What does each of them mean? Are they all spelled correctly? (dictionary?) In the case of catarrh, why do you think the poet spelled it wrong? What do you think the non-words mean? Do you know these engine noises and smells – if so, where from? etc.

Exploring preferences
Pupils might rate each poem on a scale of 1 – 10 and give reasons for their decisions.

Book about a bus
King Fernando, John Bartholomew (Puffin)

Funny the way different cars start

Funny the way
Different cars start.
Some with a chunk and a jerk,
Some with a cough and a puff of smoke
Out of the back,
Some with only a little click –
                with hardly any noise.

Funny the way
Different cars run.
Some rattle and bang,
Some whirrr,
Some knock and knock.
Some purr
And hummmmm
Smoothly on
                with hardly any noise.

Dorothy Baruch

Superstink

Big bus at the bus stop.

Ready to go again.

Big noise.

Big cloud of

shudder gasp cough gulp
stench retch stifle
sniffle snuffle wheeze strangle choke
poison choke *#@?&%£*
cataarrhh sneeze katchooo
ghughughughu

Robert Froman

Language: onomatopoeia
(See Glossary at back of Book 4.)
Which of the words in these poems would you say were onomatopoeic? Think of a few onomatopoeia for: a bicycle bell; a train; rocket taking off; windscreen wipers in the rain; a sledge going down a hill, etc.

Onomatopoeic art
Pupils choose an onomatopoeic 'transport word' and write/paint it using appropriate lettering/shapes/colours/background.

Language: parts of speech
(Revise **nouns**, **verbs**, **adjectives** – all in Glossary to Book 3.)

Worksheet 4a
Pupils complete the sheet individually or in pairs. After categorising words from a list as nouns, verbs or adjectives, they are asked to make sentences which might, with some reorganisation and editing, be converted into poems.

In 'Funny the way', what part of speech are chunk/jerk/cough/puff/click? Could you use each of these words as a verb? What parts of speech are rattle/bang/whirr/knock/purr/hum in the poem? Could you use the same words as nouns? In the cloud in 'Superstink', which words would you say were nouns/verbs?

4a

The Talking Car *(page 3)*

THE TALKING CAR

'It's a great car, Dad,' Rob said. 'But the voice is the best bit. It really is. Fancy us owning a new car that actually *talks*!'

After a week, the new car was still the new car, but now it was not quite so new. Rob's father had already found a few things to complain about at the dealer's. Rob's mother had broken a fingernail on the boot lid and called the new car some rude names. And the silvery, metallic finish of the new car was already a little dulled by road dirt.

Inside, however, the car seemed as new and exciting as ever to Rob. He sat in it for hours, sniffing the new smell, exploring all the new controls. As he was a sensible boy, his father and mother let him. '*Don't* turn on the lights because you'll drain the battery. Right?' said his father.

'Right,' replied Rob.

'And *don't* blow the horn or the neighbours will go mad and murder you. Right?' said his mother.

'Right,' said Rob.

'And *don't –*'

'All I want to do,' Rob interrupted, 'is *sit* in the car and *look* at everything. And make the voice work.'

'Yes, well, all right, then. But don't –'

'The voice is *magic*,' Rob said. 'I like the voice, I really do.'

So his parents gave him the keys and Rob went and sat in the new car, making the voice say all the different things it knew.

3

Comprehension/Reading for details/Writing in sentences

Questions on the story for pupils to answer in writing can be found on **Worksheet 4b** (Section A).

This exercise gives pupils practice in scanning a text for information and writing in complete sentences.

(This worksheet also contains similar questions on other passages from Book 4, for use at a later date.)

4b

Group work/Reading/Presentation

Groups of 4 each devise their own way of splitting up the extract for reading, e.g. perhaps like a play, with two narrators and two actors. Groups which are pleased with their renditions might present them (or parts of them) to the class.

Reading aloud

Reading level: Level 4

Divide the passage between a group of pupils to prepare beforehand (beginners will need help).

Pupils should read the whole passage aloud as the class/group follow in their books.

Discussion/Comprehension

(Pupils may note similarity to Walt Disney's 'Herbie' films.)
What sort of personality does the new car have? What makes you think this? Why do you think her first speeches are given in **italic print**? (see Glossary at back of Book 4) *Why have the words been split up with dashes?*
What do you imagine the car's voice would sound like in her later speeches, and why?
On the first page of the story, what do we learn about Rob's personality – from what is said about him? from what he says himself?
For what is the 'choke' used in a car? What happened when Rob's father accidentally left it out? Why did the car leave trickles of water on the road? How did she feel about this, and why?
The car says 'No one could call me a snob' – do you agree? Why/why not?
What do the following words and phrases mean: 'State of the art'; 'computerised, electronic, ergonomic'?
What do you think might happen next in the story?
etc.

Poem

The Army Horse and the Army Jeep

'Where do you go when you go to
   sleep?'
Said the Army Horse to the Army
   Jeep.
Do you dream of pastures beside a
   creek
With meadow grass to make you
   sleek?
Do you dream of oats and straw in a
   stall
And never a load in the world to
   haul?
Do you dream of jumping over the
   wall
To get at the apples that fall in the
   Fall?
Do you dream of haystacks steeple-
   tall?
Or what do you dream if you dream
   at all?'

   'Rrrrrrrrrr,' said the Jeep
   And 'Chug!'

'I dream of being greased for a
   week
On the Happy Rack by Gasoline
   Creek
In the Happy Garage where there's
   never a squeak,
But lakes of oil so black and sleek,
And Spark Plug bushes, and no
   valves leak.
That's where I go when I go to
   sleep,'
To the Army Horse said the Army
   Jeep.

   And 'Rrrrrrrrrr,' said the Jeep
   And 'Aaaaaaaaaaa!'

     (John Ciardi)

Book
Another book by Nicholas
Fisk for Level 4 readers:
The Backyard War (Piper)

On the car's eleventh birthday (it had been in the family for eleven days) Rob settled himself in the driver's seat, switched the key to the right position so that the electrical services worked but not the motor; and said, 'Hello, car, I'll clean you this weekend.'

The car said, *'The front pass-en-ger's door is not shut, per-lease make sure all doors are sec-urely locked.'*

Rob said, 'I know all that, I wish you'd say something different for a change.'

The car said, *'Kind-ly fast-en your seat belt.'*

Rob said, 'Boring, boring!' and waggled the gear-lever about.

'Boring yourself!' said the voice of the car.

'WHAT?' said Rob, amazed.

'Boring, boring, boring!' said the Voice. Rob could not believe his ears. But he had to believe them when the car said, 'You're Rob. You're the Mini, aren't you? There's a biggish one, a two-litre job, I'd say, that you call Dad. Then there's a family saloon of about one and a half litres. Then you, the Mini.'

'You've got it all wrong!' Rob said. 'I'm not a Mini and my mum's not a family saloon and my dad's not a two-litre job. He's a *man*, he's my *father*, we're all *humans*.'

'That accounts for it,' said the Voice, sounding a bit spiteful but still ladylike.

'Accounts for what?'

'The rotten way you treat me. Boring, boring. You know what that two-litre one, the dad, did the other day?'

'What?'

'He left my choke out! You'd never believe . . . He started me up with the choke right out and the petrol fumes getting in my lungs and everything. I was coughing and spluttering, but *he* didn't notice – oh, no, not him! Then off we went, mile after mile, with my choke still out!'

Rob couldn't think of anything to say, so he muttered, 'Oh, dear.'

'Well may you say, "Oh, dear!"' said the Voice. 'I mean, to begin with it was just cough, cough, splutter, splutter. But all the time I was getting warmed up, you see. Well, you know what *that* leads to, when your choke's out.'

'I don't,' Rob said. 'Was it horrible?'

'I thought my motor would *die*!' said the car's voice, hollowly and solemnly. 'I was just *gasping*! And then – and then . . .'

'And then, what?' said Rob. He was so interested that he leaned right forward and accidentally blew the horn.

'And then my water boiled!' said the Voice, in a horrified whisper. 'Need I say more?'

'Please do,' said Rob.

'Oh, but I can't,' said the Voice. 'I can't speak the words, it's no good asking me.'

'Tell me,' whispered Rob. 'I won't tell anyone else.'

'*Trickles*!' said the Voice, in a whisper even lower than Rob's. 'Trickles all along the carriageway!'

'Was it a main road?' said Rob, sympathetically.

Role-play/Characterisation/Writing
Pupils choose a vehicle (known to them or imaginary) and imagine its personality:
- draw/paint the vehicle in question;
- make notes about its personality, e.g. brainstorm:
  verbs (that tell how it moves, 'eats', speaks, etc.);
  adjectives, e.g. appearance – size, shape, colour, texture;
  phrases about character – pleasant/unpleasant traits, etc.
- make notes about the vehicle's past experiences, which have influenced its personality; its hopes for the future; 'where it goes when it goes to sleep', etc.

Pupils then attempt to take on the role of their vehicle to answer questions from the teacher (e.g. *Where do you live? What do you enjoy most/dislike most? Tell me a little about your past?* etc.)

Pupils could use their notes/experiences to write a character sketch of their vehicle to accompany their pictures. Some pupils may wish to put their vehicle into a story.

'No, thank heavens. Just a thirty m.p.h. restricted. And very crowded, so no one could tell it was me. But all the same . . .!'

'How terrible!' said Rob.

'I nearly passed out,' said the Voice. 'From shame. Me, a newly registered vehicle, hardly anything on the clock but my delivery mileage. I could have died! In fact, come to think of it, I *did* die.'

'Completely?' said Rob.

'Completely. He – that dad of yours – he had to push me to the nearest garage. I don't know if you've ever suffered the shame of being pushed?'

'Oh, yes, often!' Rob said. He was thinking of his baby pram-and-pushchair days. 'Pushed all over the place, I was. Up and down the road, in the park – everywhere.'

'Hmm,' said the Voice, distantly. 'Hmm. Hmm. I see. Yes, well.' Then it sniffed in a nasty way.

When it spoke again, its voice was more ladylike and refined than ever. 'No one could call me a snob,' it said. 'There's not a snobbish nut or bolt in my entire chassis, def-in-ite-ly not, oh, no. But one does have to be rather careful about the company one keeps, doesn't one? I mean, if one happens to have this year's registration, all the latest refinements,

two-tone velour upholstery, black rubbing-strips and digital clock –'

'I see what you mean,' Rob said humbly.

The Voice did not hear him. 'You see, where *I* come from – robots gliding about everywhere, just *everywhere*, none of your nasty, dirty, human hands, certainly not! –'

'You're modern, really modern,' Rob said. 'I could tell that from the start.'

'We don't say "modern". We say, "State of the Art". Computerised, electronic, ergonomic.'

'I can tell you're ergonomic,' Rob said, wondering what the word meant. He wanted to please the Voice so that it would go on talking.

But then the front door of the house opened and his mother was there calling, 'Rob! Lunchtime, wash your hands, hurry now!' And he had to open the door of the car.

'You'll talk to me some more, later on?' Rob whispered as he got out.

But the voice only said, '*The front pass-en-ger's door is not shut, per-lease make sure all doors are sec-urely locked.*'

Rob ate his lunch thinking about the car and its voice, longing to get back to it.

From *The Talking Car* by Nicholas Fisk

5

Language work: pronouns/sentence connectives

With pupils' help, list the main personal pronouns on the board:

I, you, he/she/it, we, you, they

me, you, him/her/it, us, you, them

my, your, his/her/its, our, your, their

mine, yours, his/hers/its, ours, yours, theirs.

myself, yourself, etc.

Divide pupils into teams. Team members take it in turns to read part of the passage aloud, stopping whenever they reach a personal pronoun to hand over to the next team. Team earns a point if reader stops correctly, but a point is deducted if reader reads too far. Bonus point if team can say which noun or noun phrase the personal pronoun stands for, e.g.: *'It's* (i.e. **the car**: hand over to next team) *a great car, Dad,' Rob said. 'But the voice is the best bit. It* (i.e. **the voice**: hand over) *really is. Fancy us* (i.e. **Rob's family**: hand over) *owning a new car that actually talks.' After a week the new car was still the new car but now it* (i.e. **the car**: hand over) *was not quite so new …*

Language work: apostrophe in shortened forms

(See Glossary on page 39 of Book 4.) The dialogue in the passage includes several examples of the apostrophe in shortened forms. (As these frequently involve pronouns, this is a suitable follow-up to the exercise above.) Pupils can identify examples of shortened forms in the characters' speeches and provide an extended version each time. Revise the rule: when words are run together, an apostrophe is placed **where the letters have been missed out**.

Worksheet 4c

4c

This worksheet provides further practice for individuals or pairs.

The story also includes examples of the apostrophe to show possession, but we recommend that explicit teaching of the rules concerned be left until pupils are approaching Level 5.

Language: spelling links

- **-ic** ending as in "electronic", "ergonomic" (e.g. music, magic, topic, picnic, tragic, basic, public, metric, plastic, arithmetic, automatic, domestic, fantastic, etc.)
- "voice" involves a **soft c** (in contrast with **-ic** words).
  The letter **c** is usually softened when followed by an **e**, **i** or **y**, e.g. century, city, fancy. Some of the most commonly misspelled words featuring this rule are: **decide**, **bicycle**, **centre**, **certain**, **recent**, **sincere**, **necessary**, **medicine**. Pupils could look for more **soft c** words in the extract.

Travel Tags

Discussing the meanings of proverbs gives pupils an opportunity to investigate the symbolic use of language: the literal message of the proverb stands for a much wider message.

Further transport proverbs
Britain:
The rats are always the first to leave a sinking ship.
Any port will do in a storm.
He travels fastest who travels alone.
Don't put the cart before the horse.
It's a long road that has no turning.
You can lead a horse to water, but you can't make it drink.
Germany:
The heaviest baggage is an empty purse.
Estonia:
If you go once round the room, you are wiser than he who sits still.
China:
The man on horseback knows nothing of the toil of the traveller on foot.
In a calm sea, every man is a pilot.
Caribbean:
Sickness does come on horseback, but leaves on foot.

Discussion
Choose one of the proverbs illustrated, e.g. 'Don't spoil the ship ...': *What does this really mean? Can you give examples of the truth of the proverb which do not involve transport?* (e.g. Don't waste all the good work you've done writing a story by forgetting the punctuation.)

Group discussion/Reporting back
Each group takes a number of proverbs. For each proverb, the group must decide what it means and invent an example which is non-transport-based if possible.
Groups then report back.

OR

Paired discussion/Non-chronological writing
In pairs, pupils discuss the wider meaning of the proverbs in the illustration, and produce written explanations and examples.

Language awareness/Reporting back
Pupils collect proverbs from parents, grandparents, etc. for a class collection/display.

Poetry book
Say It Again, Granny – 20 poems from Caribbean proverbs, John Agard (Magnet)

Transport in the Library *(page 7)*

Focus of discussion
The comic strip is provided as a focus of discussion on the process of using a library. It explains the organisation of libraries and introduces the Dewey Decimal System of classification and the use of a library index. It is intended as a preparatory exercise for pupils who are about to use their own school or local library as part of their studies. It is NOT intended as a substitute for library use.

Reading aloud
The comic strip should be read through in its entirety before it is used for discussion, to give pupils an overview. The parts of the protagonists could be read by individual pupils as in a play.

Discussion
Variations in individual schools and libraries can be pointed out during discussion.

2nd frame: Fiction and non-fiction
What is the difference between fiction and non-fiction? Do you know how fiction is arranged on the shelves? etc.

4th frame
Vocabulary: **classification** (see Glossary)

(Dewey Decimal System devised, 1873, by US librarian Melvil Dewey.)

This frame introduces categorisation of knowledge, which is of great importance in information search – it can be related to sets and subsets in Maths.

Categorisation
Discuss main categories listed on the poster and their meanings. *What do you think 'Social Sciences' are? From looking at the examples, what is the difference between 'Natural Science' and 'Science and Technology'? What are 'Geography'/'History'?* etc.
Pupils who cannot identify categories and sub-categories of knowledge will find difficulty in information search. Children tend to go into a library with a specific topic in mind, and no idea of how that topic fits into the classification system. Unless they have some idea of categorisation, they will be unable to use an index effectively (e.g. the child who looks up 'pyramids' and doesn't find it listed must be able to work out that 'pyramids' is a sub-category of 'Egypt').
If you couldn't find the following, what would you try looking up next?
parrots   helicopters   sharks   dandelions   Mars   the spine   clouds   Paris   leopards   Elizabeth 1
Which Dewey number (hundreds only) do you think you'd find each under?

1st and 2nd frames

If pupils' understanding of decimals is adequate, explain that Dewey used a decimal system so that his subject categories could go on being sub-divided indefinitely (to cater for increasing knowledge and the books that go with it), e.g.:

385 Railways
385.3 Railway facilities
385.36 Locomotives
385.361 Steam locomotives

4th and 5th frames

The use of an index in books was introduced in Book 3, page 21. **Worksheet 3h** gives practice in the skill.

An index of some kind is essential in any school library. The 'Simplified Dewey Classification System' shown here was provided by:

Cumbria School Library
Service (North),
Botchergate,
Carlisle
CA1 1RZ
Tel: 0228 812158

Other local Schools Library Services also provide short indexes of this kind. Indexes can also be obtained on computer **data-banks** (see Glossary). *Look up 'data' – why is a 'data-bank' so named? What other ways could a data-bank be organised apart from by the Dewey System?*

Children may also hear indexes referred to as **catalogues** (see Glossary).
What other sorts of catalogues do you know about? Why do you think people call library indexes 'catalogues'? etc.

4d

Worksheet 4d
This gives practice in using a section of a subject index. Pupils should also have opportunities to practise using a real index.

(page 9)

2nd frame
Discussion of contents, index, etc. for individual books is provided in Book 3, pages 19–21, and practice of using an index in Worksheet 3h.

3rd frame
Vocabulary: **encyclopaedia**, **reference books** (see Glossary)
What other sorts of reference books are there? What other ways of storing reference materials are there?
What other books/information might you find in a reference library? etc. (e.g. directories of addresses for making enquiries by letter – see notes to page 20.)
Pupils should have the opportunity to browse among encyclopaedias to familiarise themselves with their content and organisation.

Final frame
Vocabulary: **browse**, **read to find information**. These terms were introduced in Book 3 (pages 19–21) to describe two sorts of reading strategies for information books.

Library visits
A visit to the local library for a guided tour by the librarian helps familiarise pupils with the building and facilities. Alternatively, the local Schools Library Service may provide a librarian to visit the school and talk to pupils and answer their questions.

Information finding/Spoken presentations/Written work
Pupils' visits to the library should culminate in their using it to find information for themselves. We suggest that they work in groups to produce talks and posters (see next page) on various types transport.

Writing instructions
Another type of writing follow-up is the compilation of booklets on 'How to use a library', explaining the processes they have learned for the benefit of other children.

Plane Poster

This poster was produced by pupils working towards Level 4 to accompany a talk they had prepared from their own research on the subject of transport. It is intended for use as a focus of discussion about the presentation of information and, if required, as a model for pupils' own posters.

Discussion

Vocabulary: **heading**, **subheading**, **illustration**, **caption**, **label**.

Most of the above vocabulary was introduced in Book 3 (page 19) and appears in the Book 3 Glossary. Ensure that all terms are familiar to pupils, so they can be used in discussion. *In what ways do you think this poster is well set out? Are there any ways you would change the layout? How do you think Chris and Inderjit went about making the poster? What would they need? What do you think they did first? next? etc. What sort of diagrams have they included? What is a timeline for? How would you make one? etc.*

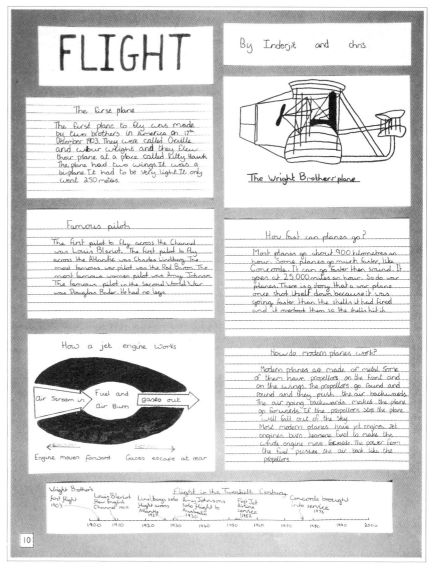

Information search/Non-chronological writing

Using the poster as a model, pupils should work in pairs to:
• choose a type of transport
• browse in the library and work out headings under which to write about it
• make a similar poster.

Spoken presentations

Pupils can use their posters as visual aids to give brief talks to the class on the type of transport they have chosen.

Fiction

Murder on the Midnight Plane (adventure game book), Usborne

Airborne *(page 11)*

Airborne

Taking off

The airplane taxis down the field
And heads into the breeze,
It lifts its wheels above the ground,
It skims above the trees,
It rises high and higher
Away up toward the sun,
It's just a speck against the sky
– And now it's gone!

Anon

Prayer for a Pilot

Lord of Sea and Earth and Air,
Listen to the Pilot's prayer –
Send him wind that's steady and strong,
Grant that his engine sings the song
Of flawless tone, by which he knows
It shall not fail him where he goes;
Landing, gliding, in curve, half-roll –
Grant him, O Lord, a full control,
That he may learn in heights of Heaven
The rapture altitude has given,
That he shall know the joy they feel
Who ride Thy realms on Birds of Steel.

Cecil Roberts

Reading aloud

Pairs/groups of children prepare and present poems to the class. Several presentations of each poem would provide interesting talking points.

Discussion: preferences

Which poem do pupils prefer, and why?

'Taking off'

What does 'taxis' mean here? Does the poem rhyme? How do the rhymes work? (teach notation for rhyme scheme, here: ABAB, CDCD) etc.

'Prayer for a Pilot'

What do the following words/phrases mean: 'flawless tone'; 'rapture'; 'altitude'? Do you think 'Bird of Steel' is a good description of a plane – why/why not? What is the rhyme scheme here? (AA, BB, CC, etc.) *What makes this poem like a prayer?*

Rhyme/Riddle

I fly – like a bird,
And buzz – like a bee,
Got a tail – like a fish,
Got a hop – like a flea.

(A helicopter)

Other poems about planes – see Book 3, page 2 and Book 5, page 7.

4e

Worksheet 4e: Punctuation

The worksheet provides a passage about the air pioneer Amy Johnson, for punctuation. (Further information on Amy Johnson, and a popular song about her, can be found in Book 5, pages 7–9.)
The passage requires:
  – capital letters for title/sentences/proper nouns;
  – full stops/question marks for sentences;
  – commas in lists.
It is suggested that pupils check with the teacher at the 'halfway line' to ensure that they are dividing sentences correctly before proceeding.

How to Keep Your Kitten on a Broomstick

(page 12)

Silent reading/ Comprehension

The extract may be used initially as a piece for individual comprehension. Questions are provided on **Worksheet 4b** (Section B).

Reading aloud

Alternatively, it may be split up among a number of pupils for preparation and reading aloud to the class. The worksheet questions could then be used after discussion.

Discussion: characters, setting and plot

Characters

For example: *Who are the main characters in this story? Without looking back, how much can you remember about Mildred – her appearance, habits, etc.?*
What about Maud?
(confirm and expand by consulting the text.)
How do you think the writer wants us to feel about Mildred? Which bits of the descriptions do you think most effective, and why? etc.

Setting

How much can you remember about the setting? (confirm and expand by consulting the text.)
How does the setting add to the effect of the story? Which details do you think are most effective in setting the scene, and why? etc.

Plot

What is the basic plot of the extract about the kitten? How briefly and succinctly can pupils summarise this? *A good plot often involves a problem, and a solution – what is the problem here? the solution?* etc.

MISS CACKLE's Academy for Witches stood at the top of a high mountain surrounded by a pine forest. It looked more like a prison than a school, with its gloomy grey walls and turrets. Sometimes you could see the pupils on their broomsticks flitting like bats above the play-ground wall, but usually the place was half hidden in mist, so that if you glanced up at the mountain you would probably not notice the building was there at all.

Everything about the school was dark and shadowy: long, narrow corridors and winding staircases – and of course the girls themselves, dressed in black gymslips, black stockings, black hob-nailed boots, grey shirts and black-and-grey ties.

Books

Worst Witch books:
The Worst Witch and *The Worst Witch Strikes Again*, Jill Murphy (Puffin)
Stories for Level 4 readers about other unconventional forms of travel:
'The Patchwork Quilt' from *A Necklace of Raindrops*, Joan Aiken (Puffin)
'The Fool and the Flying Ship' – prediction story for Book 3 (pages 51–53 of Teacher's Notes).

(page 13)

Miss Cackle's academy is the invention of the writer, Jill Murphy. Into this forbidding setting she puts her character Mildred Hubble, *The Worst Witch . . .*

Mildred Hubble was in her first year at the school. She was one of those people who always seem to be in trouble. She didn't exactly mean to break rules and annoy the teachers, but things just seemed to *happen* whenever she was around. You could rely on Mildred to have her hat on back-to-front or her bootlaces trailing along the floor. She couldn't walk from one end of a corridor to the other without someone yelling at her, and nearly every night she was writing lines or being kept in (not that there was anywhere to go if you were allowed out). Anyway, she had lots of friends, even if they did keep their distance in the potion laboratory, and her best friend Maud stayed loyally by her through everything, however hair-raising. They made a funny pair, for Mildred was tall and thin with long plaits which she often chewed absent-mindedly (another thing she was told off about), while Maud was short and tubby, had round glasses and wore her hair in bunches.

Mildred's problems with transport are the subject of the second chapter of *The Worst Witch*.

When the girls were first issued with kittens Mildred's rather dim-looking tabby kitten had trouble learning to ride pillion on a broomstick.

Riding a broomstick was no easy matter. First, you ordered the stick to hover, and it hovered lengthways above the ground. Then you sat on it, gave it a sharp tap, and away you flew. Once in the air you could make the stick do almost anything by saying, 'Right! Left! Stop! Down a bit!' and so on. The difficult part was balancing, for if you leaned a little too far to one side you could easily overbalance, in which case you would either fall off or find yourself hanging upside-down and then you would just have to hold on with your skirt over your head until a friend came to your rescue.

It had taken Mildred several weeks of falling off and crashing before she could ride the brookstick reasonably well, and it looked as

13

Personal reading/Discussion
Pupils consider the books they are reading at present/have just read. A few report on: *Who are the main characters? What are they like? How does the writer put their characters over to the reader? What is the main setting? What is it like? What is a brief summary of the plot?*

Book report/Non-chronological writing
All pupils write a report on the book they are currently reading, basing it on the above discussion.

Creative writing: characters, setting and plot

Characters
Pupils (individually or in pairs) create two/three characters of their own. Draw/paint pictures of them first, name them, and write a short description of each to accompany the pictures. For example: *What do they look like? What do they wear? What sort of things do they say/do? What are their personalities like?* etc. (See also notes to page 4 of Book 4 on characterisation.)

Setting
Pupils invent a setting in which to put their characters. Draw/paint it first, name it if necessary, then write a description to accompany it. *Where is it? What does it look, sound, smell like? What do the characters think about it?* etc.

Plot
Pupils plan a short episode involving the characters interacting within the setting, preferably involving transport of some sort. If possible plan this in note form first – beginning/middle(problem?)/end (solution?). Or write draft and discuss with teacher.

Writing a story
Pupils write and illustrate their short story.

Presentation
The finished writing (in three illustrated sections: characters, setting, plot) could be displayed on posters or as home-made books for other pupils to read.

Language/Spelling links

- **witch** – revise **-tch** ending.
- **comparative and superlative adjectives**, e.g.:
  good, better, best
  bad, worse, worst.
  Both of the above examples are irregular forms. There are two regular forms, e.g.:
  young→younger→youngest
  or
  stupid→more stupid→most stupid

  Discussion of these forms provides opportunities for revision of the **y→i** spelling rule, e.g.:
  silly→sillier→silliest
  and that for doubling medial consonants, e.g.:
  fat→fatter→fattest.

Pupils could provide comparative and superlative forms of:

regular

tall	dark
black	short

regular (more/most)

awful	clever
miserable	frightened

y→i

gloomy	ugly
easy	funny

doubling consonants

sad	grim
mad	wet

Language: agreement of word endings (singular and plural/tense)

When drafting and editing work, pupils must pay attention to agreement of word endings, especially when changing from singular to plural or changing tense.

Worksheet 4f
This provides discussion material and/or practice of this language point.

4f

though her kitten was going to have the same trouble. When she put it on the end of the stick, it just fell off without even trying to hold on. After many attempts, Mildred picked up her kitten and gave it a shake.

'Listen!' she said severely. 'I think I shall have to call you Stupid. You don't even *try* to hold on. Everyone else is all right – look at all your friends.'

The kitten gazed at her sadly and licked her nose with its rough tongue.

'Oh, come on,' said Mildred, softening her voice. 'I'm not really angry with you. Let's try again.'

And she put the kitten back on the broomstick, from which it fell with a thud.

Maud was having better luck. Her kitten was hanging on grimly upside down.

'Oh, well,' laughed Maud. 'It's a start.'

'Mine's useless,' said Mildred, sitting on the broomstick for a rest.

'Never mind,' Maud said. 'Think how hard it must be for them to hang on by their claws.'

An idea flashed into Mildred's head, and she dived into the school, leaving her kitten chasing a leaf along the ground and the broomstick still patiently hovering. She came out carrying her satchel which she hooked over the end of the broom and then bundled the kitten into it. The kitten's astounded face peeped out of the bag as Mildred flew delightedly round the yard.

Adapted from *The Worst Witch* by Jill Murphy

14

Poem about riding a broomstick

The Hag is astride,
This night for to ride;
The Devil and she together:
Through thick, and through thin,
Now out, and then in,
Though ne'er so foul be the weather.

A Thorn or a Burr
She takes for a Spur:
With a lash of a Bramble she rides now,
Through Brakes and through Briars,
O'er Ditches, and Mires,
She follows the Spirit that guides now.

No Beast, for his food,
Dares now range the wood;
But hush't in his lair he lies lurking;
While mischiefs, by these,
On Land and on Seas,
At noon of Night are a-working.

The storm will arise,
And trouble the skies;
This night, and more for the wonder,
The ghost from the Tomb
Affrighted shall come,
Called out by the clap of the Thunder.

(Robert Herrick, 1591–1674)

Unfinished Journeys ... *(page 15)*

Unfinished Journeys...

Baron Munchhausen and the Basket from the Sky

More than two hundred years ago, Rudolphe Raspe, a German living in England, wrote a collection of tall stories about a character called Baron Munchhausen. This Baron travelled the world, and everywhere he went impossible things happened to him. In the following story, he was living in Constantinople (now known as Istanbul), the capital city of Turkey.

When Baron Munchhausen was working for the Sultan of Turkey, he lazily spent his leisure time riding about on a barge on the Marmora River. He was in his barge one morning when he saw a strange shape in the sky. It looked like a silver globe with something hanging from it.

The Baron immediately took up his pistol and fired at the shape. After he had hit it several times the globe seemed to shrink and Baron Munchhausen was surprised to see an elegant golden basket come falling gently out of the sky into the river.

15

Group reading, discussion and prediction

Pupils' performance in these activities will be improved if they are informed in advance of what will be expected of them.

Group reading

Split class into roughly equal sections, A and B.

Divide each section into subgroups with 3/4 pupils in each. Subgroups in section A read the story about Baron Munchhausen; subgroups in section B read the story 'Arion the Singer'.

Group discussion/Prediction

Each story is incomplete. After reading it, each subgroup should discuss how they think it should end. They should be able to give reasons for the endings they choose, based upon the story so far and their knowledge of story structure.

Group discussion

Call together all members of section A. Representatives of each subgroup can describe/explain their story-endings. The entire section should then vote on the best ending. Teacher can then read the 'official ending' (see next page). *Is it better/worse than the pupils' version? Why?*

If activities below are to be used, this discussion should be kept secret from pupils in section B.

Repeat procedure for section B.

Individual reading/Storytelling/ Prediction

Pupils are now familiar with their group's story. They should now re-read it, with a view to re-telling it to a member of the other group, and asking him/her to predict the ending.

Pair off members of section A with members of section B. Each section A pupil tells the Baron Munchhausen story to his/her partner and asks partner to work out the ending. Each section B pupil does the same with 'Arion the Singer'.

Baron Munchhausen and the Basket from the Sky

Details about Rudolphe Raspe (1737–94), and another of his stories, are in **Worksheet 5f**.

Conclusion of story:

The balloon continued to drift closer to the sun. The scientist was by this time getting quite sunburned, and the poor sheep was so hot in its woolly coat that it died of heat exhaustion and hunger. This was very fortunate for the scientist, as he had eaten all his supplies and was feeling very hungry himself. He sheared the fleece from the sheep, and placed the carcass directly in the sun's rays (which he was being careful to avoid himself). He soon had enough roast mutton to sustain him for some time.

At this point in his story, the scientist looked at Baron Munchhausen gratefully. 'I suppose I should still be up there,' he said, 'if you had not released me by shooting your pistol at the balloon and puncturing it so that the gas escaped.'

The Baron realised that the silver globe he had seen had in fact been the balloon. He told the scientist that he was glad to have been of service, and invited him home to tell his amazing story to the Sultan of Turkey.

Books

Stories about Baron Munchhausen:
Baron Munchhausen and other comic tales from Germany, R E Raspe (Dent)
Stories about dolphins;
True Animal Stories, Margaret Davidson (Hippo)

He quickly ordered his servants to rescue the basket and bring him its contents. To his great surprise these turned out to be a man, and part of a sheep, which seemed to have been roasted. When the man had recovered from his fall from the skies, Baron Munchhausen asked him how he came to be floating in the air with a cargo of roast mutton.

The man's story had started several days before. He was a scientist, living near Land's End in Cornwall. He had managed to acquire a balloon – a new invention in those days – and had taken a sheep up in it to see how the animal was affected by being at a great height. It was a scientific experiment.

However, the balloon had no sooner taken off when the wind changed suddenly and, instead of drifting inland towards Exeter, the scientist and his sheep began to drift helplessly out to sea. The scientist tried to bring down the balloon by pulling a string and releasing the hot air which filled it. Unfortunately, however, the string was broken and the balloon continued to rise through the clouds.

Higher and higher they drifted, until eventually they were higher even than the moon, and so close to the sun that the scientist's eyebrows were getting scorched. Further and further they drifted too, for days and days and days . . .

What happened next?
(Concluded in Teacher's Notes)

Arion the Singer

Once long ago in the city of Corinth in Ancient Greece, there was a wonderful singer called Arion. The King of Corinth greatly admired Arion's singing. When he heard there was to be a singing competition on the island of Sicily, he urged Arion to enter it and win the competition for the honour of his city.

Arion set off for Sicily in one of the king's ships. On the way, he practised his singing every day, and his voice was so beautiful that all the dolphins in the sea came to swim beside the ship and listen to him.

16

Conclusion of 'Arion the Singer'

The wicked captain and crew sailed back home to Corinth, where the captain went straight to the king, and fell on his knees before him. 'Oh, your majesty,' he cried, 'I have sad news. The singer Arion has met a terrible end. On the way back from Sicily he was sitting on the deck of the ship when a freak wave washed him into the water. My men tried everything in their power to rescue him, but all in vain.'

'Really?' said the king. 'That is very sad news. It is also very surprising.' Then, to the captain's horror, the king threw back a curtain beside the throne, and there was Arion!

'But . . . how did you get here?' stuttered the captain.

'I had a very special form of transport,' replied Arion. 'During our time at sea, I often sat singing on the deck, and every time an audience of dolphins came to listen to me. As I sang my last song they gathered as usual – then when I leapt into the water, the largest dolphin took me on his back and carried me home to Greece. I was here long before you in your cumbersome ship.'

'And he has told me what happened, you treacherous dog,' said the King of Corinth. 'You will pay for your crimes!' So the wicked captain and crew were put to death, and Arion's treasure returned to him.

When they reached Sicily, Arion entered the competition and won it easily. The King of Sicily gave him the prize, a huge bag of gold, and many other admirers also showered him with gold and precious jewels. He went back to the ship a rich man, looking forward to telling the King of Corinth about his success.

Unfortunately, the captain and crew of the ship were dishonest. When they saw Arion's riches they wanted them for themselves, and they plotted to kill him. Once they were far out to sea, the captain told Arion what they had decided. "We are going to throw you overboard," he said, "and divide up your fortune between us. We shall tell the King of Corinth that you fell in the sea and we were unable to save you. Prepare yourself to die!"

Poor Arion realised that he would never persuade them to let him live. He nodded his head sadly. "I understand," he said. "But will you grant me one wish? I should like to sing one last song before I die." "Very well," the captain agreed grudgingly. "You may sing a last song. But as soon as you have sung the last note, you must throw yourself into the sea."

So Arion turned to face the sea and sang his last song. He sang more sweetly and hauntingly than he had ever sung before, and even the wicked captain and crew were moved by the beautiful music. However, they did not change their minds, and when Arion had sung his last note, they came towards him. Arion didn't hesitate for a moment – he took a great leap from the deck of the ship and tumbled down, down into the sea . . .

What happened next?
(Concluded in Teacher's Notes)

17

Language/spelling: adverbs

(brief definition in Glossary)
The adverb is a part of speech which has many functions, one of which is to tell more about a verb. There are **adverbs of time** (e.g. yesterday, now, never) and adverbs of place (e.g. here, abroad, somewhere). The most easy to identify are **adverbs of manner** (telling *how* something is done), which are usually formed by adding 'ly' to the end of an adjective, e.g.: **quick+ly**, **sad+ly**, **happy+ly**.

Hunt the adverb

There are 8 adverbs in 'Baron Munchhausen and the Basket from the Sky' (pages 15–16) and another 8 in 'Arion the Singer' (pages 16–17).
Pupils in pairs should race to find and note the adverbs down, along with their base adjectives, e.g. lazy+ly, immediate+ly.

Spelling: the 'ly' suffix

Changing an adjective to an adverb of manner depends on the addition of a **suffix** (see Glossary).
- Almost always the adjective is unchanged when 'ly' is added, e.g. quiet + ly, exact + ly.
- If the adjective ends in 'l', the adverb will have two 'l's, e.g. real + ly, usual + ly, awful + ly.
- If the adjective ends in 'y', this will change to 'i' before the 'ly' is added (according to the usual rule):
  e.g. happy + ly = happily, busy + ly = busily
- Where an adjective ends in 'e', this is not dropped when 'ly' is added: e.g. late + ly, secure + ly. (The only exceptions to the last rule are the 'le' words, like 'comfortable → comfortably', 'simple → simply', where 'ly' is substituted for 'le'.)

Language awareness/Drama

The Adverb Game

One member of the group/class is 'it', and leaves the room. The rest choose an adverb (e.g. happily, cleverly, generously). 'It' is called back in and has to guess the adverb by doling out tasks and watching pupils act them out 'in the manner of the adverb', e.g.: 'it' might ask: 'Pretend to clean your teeth/skip around the room/sing a song, etc. in the manner of the adverb.' Whoever is chosen must demonstrate the adverb by the way s/he performs the task.

Let the Train Take the Strain

Reading aloud

Groups/pairs/individual pupils prepare poems for reading. Allow a few readings of each poem before discussion.

Discussion: preferences

Which poems do pupils like best and why?

Discussion: rhythm

'The Song The Train Sang'

What different effects does the poet try to get in the three sections of this poem? How does the rhythm (see Glossary) help in each case? Is there a rhyme in the first section? What is the rhyme scheme in the second section? (AA, BB, etc.) Where does this rhyme scheme break down, and why do you think the poet does this? (to convey the jerking of the train as it slows down)

'From a Railway Carriage'

Robert Louis Stevenson (1850–94), born in Edinburgh, spent much of his childhood bedridden from illness, and loved the stories and poems with which his nurse entertained. When he later became an author, he wrote several stories and 'A Child's Garden of Verses' to pass on that pleasure to another generation of children.

When they have heard it a couple of times, pupils should try to tap out the rhythm of this poem without the words. How does this poem differ from 'The Song the Train Sang'? Why? Which of the two poems gives you stronger pictures of the view from the train window? Which rhythm sounds more like a train to you? etc.

Let the Train Take

The City Station

Here is an avenue of welcome,
Open arms and long embrace –
'How was the journey? My, you have grown!'
While each minute hides its face.

Here is an endless strip of sadness,
Find your handkerchief and cry –
'Don't forget us. Write soon. God bless –'
While the huge clock wipes its eye.

John Mole

The Song the Train Sang

Now
When
Steam hisses;
Now
When the
Coupling clashes;
Now
When the
Wind rushes
Comes the slow but sudden swaying,
Every truck and carriage trying
For a smooth and better rhythm.

This . . . is . . . the . . . one. . . .
That . . . is . . . the . . . one. . . .
This is the one,
That is the one,
This is the one, that is the one,
This is the one, that is the one. . . .

Over the river, past the mill,
Through the tunnel under the hill;
Round the corner, past the wall,
Through the wood where trees grow tall.
Then in sight of the town by the river,
Brake by the crossing where white leaves quiver.
Slow as the streets of the town slide past
And the windows stare
                              at the jerking of the coaches
Coming into the station approaches.

Stop at the front.
Stop at the front.
Stop . . . at the front.
Stop . . . at the. . . .
Stop.
              AHHHHHH!

Neil Adams

18

Discussion: arrivals and departures

'The City Station'

Who do you think is greeting whom in the first stanza? Why do you think that? Why should the minutes (or children being greeted) hide their faces? (embarrassment?) What's happening in the second stanza? Why should the clock wipe its eye? What do you think the 'avenue of welcome' and the 'endless strip of sadness' is? (the platform?) etc.

'The Ways of Trains'

The poet here makes her train seem like an animal – what sort? What words suggest that the train is a friendly creature? What similarities and differences can you find between this poem and 'The City Station'? etc.

(page 19)

the Strain

From a Railway Carriage

Faster than fairies, faster than witches,
Bridges and houses, hedges and ditches;
And charging along like troops in a battle,
All through the meadows the horses and cattle:
All of the sights of the hill and the plain
Fly as thick as driving rain;
And ever again, in the wink of an eye,
Painted stations whistle by.

Here is a child who clambers and scrambles,
All by himself and gathering brambles;
Here is a tramp who stands and gazes;
And there is the green for stringing the daisies!
Here is a cart run away in the road
Lumping along with man and load;
And here is a mill, and there is a river:
Each a glimpse and gone for ever!

Robert Louis Stevenson

The Ways of Trains

I hear the engine pounding
in triumph down the track –
trains take away the ones you love
and then they bring them back!

Trains take away the ones you love
to worlds both strange and new
and then, with care and courtesy,
they bring them back to you.

The engine halts and snuffs and snorts,
it breathes forth smoke and fire,
then snatches crowded strangers on –
but leaves what you desire!

Elizabeth Coatsworth

19

The Train

A green eye—and a red—in the dark,
Thunder—smoke—and a spark.

It is there—it is here—flashed by.
Whither will the wild thing fly?

It is rushing, tearing through the night,
Rending her gloom in its flight.

It shatters her silence with shrieks.
What is it the wild thing seeks?

Alas! for it hurries away
Them that are fain to stay.

Hurrah! for it carries home
Lovers and friends that roam.

(Mary E Coleridge)

Story books

Anna, Grandpa and the Big Storm,
Carta Stevens (Puffin)
The Railway Cat books, Phyllis Arkle
(Puffin)

Class presentation/ Group planning and organisation

These poems could be used as the basis of a presentation, perhaps as part of a school assembly.

All are suitable for reading aloud, and 'The City Station' is suitable for dramatisation.

Once the poems are familiar, groups of pupils should work on ways of presenting them as effectively as possible. Different presentations can be discussed, and the best version of each developed for presentation to an audience.

See also 'The Song of the Train' (back cover of Book 3), 'Night Mail' (Book 5, pages 16–17), and notes to both.

Discussion/Writing: prayers

What are the worst things about seeing someone off on a train journey? What sorts of worries do you have? etc.

Pupils could write prayers for the safety and speedy return of people departing on train journeys. See 'Prayer for a Pilot' (page 11 of Book 4) and prayers in school assembly books, etc, as models.

Language/Spelling links

- Train – **-ain** ending in two-syllable words, e.g.: again, certain, captain, mountain, bargain, Britain, maintain, explain.
- 'No job' final **-e** on engine, as in: **imagine**, **genuine**, **promise**.
- **Soft g** in engine. **G** is usually **soft** when followed by **e**, **i**, or **y** (as in **soft c** see notes to page 5), e.g.: **danger**, **magic**, **gymnastics**, **emergency**, **gorgeous**, **pigeon**.
- Station: **-tion** words.

How Do You Fill a Canal?

This page gives examples of a genuine draft letter from a Level 4 child, his finished letter, and the reply he received.

Discussion: drafting a letter

What are the main differences between the layout of Matthew's draft letter and the final version he posted? What are the main differences in the way the letter is expressed?

Spoken and written language

The draft is written much as Matthew would speak. His revised version is in the clearer, more explicit language of written English.

Why do you think such changes were needed? etc.

Drafting and editing

What spelling errors has Matthew corrected? What other changes has he made? etc.

Discussion: formal letter

Note the headed paper, layout, sign-off line: 'Yours sincerely'. Matthew uses 'Yours faithfully' because he begins his letter 'Dear sir'. Mr Gwatkin uses 'Yours sincerely' because he is addressing Matthew by name. *What part of speech are 'sincerely' and 'faithfully'?*

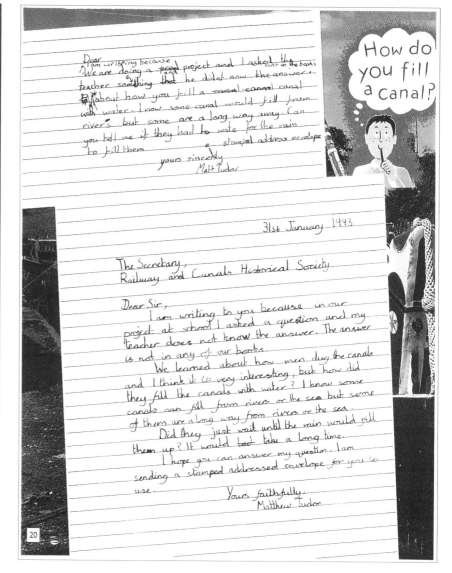

Letter writing

The best way to learn letter-writing skills is to write a letter. Those given here provide model drafting procedures/layout. Questions may arise as a result of pupils' work on the topic which could become written enquiries. Alternatively, pupils could devise questions on other topics of interest to them. If pupils have queries for which no appropriate address is given, three resources which can be found in the Reference section of a local library may be of use (the first is a fund of useful addresses, such as that of the Inland Waterways Association):

Directory of British Associations and Associations in Ireland, ed. Henderson and Henderson (CBD Research Ltd)

Kelly's Business Directory (Reed Information Services)

Key British Enterprises – Britain's top 50,000 companies (Dunn and Bradstreet International)

(page 21)

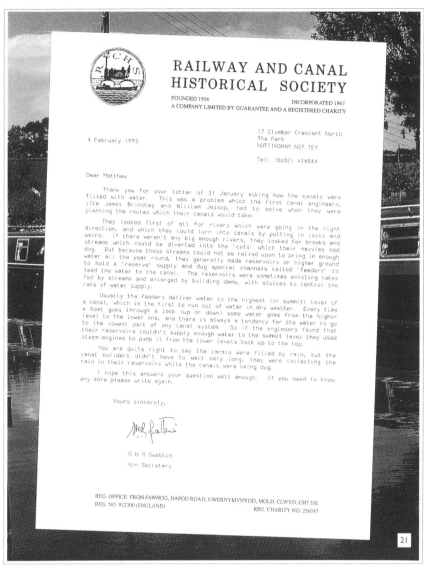

Books

About canals and canal boats for Level 4+ readers (or for reading to pupils):

The Butty Boy, Jill Paton Walsh (Puffin)

A Chance Child, Jill Paton Walsh (Puffin)

The Canal Children, Brian Wright (Heinemann)

Tom Tiddler's Land, John Rowe Townsend (Puffin)

Punctuation: capital letters

These letters feature many examples of the use of capital letters and may be used for summary/revision of this point.

Pupils (in class discussion or competitively in pairs) could find and explain examples of the various uses within the text, e.g.:

- a sentence (or a phrase if it stands independently)
- any proper noun, e.g. names and addresses
- the names of months
- initials in some abbreviations (e.g. RCHS).

Pupils should then collect other uses of capitals, using the rest of this book and other sources, e.g.:

- first letter of a line of poetry;
- words referring to God;
- days of the week, holidays and festivals;
- important words in a title.

Worksheet 4g

After discussion, as above, pupils should complete this worksheet individually or in pairs. (It is best done in pencil, as most pupils will find it necessary to correct their corrections.)

4g

River and Road

(page 22)

Play-reading

Plays are an ideal medium for group reading, providing opportunities for many readers to be involved at once. Several groups could read the play simultaneously if desired. There are parts for 5 actors, but the Otter does not have much to say and his part could therefore be doubled up with that of Toad (or the car horn).

Comprehension/Reading for detail/Writing in sentences

Questions about the play suitable for pupils' written answers can be found on **Worksheet 4b** (Section C).

Discussion/ Comprehension/ Inference/Deduction

What sort of a character would you say Mole is? Think of adjectives to describe him.
What sort of a character do you think Rat is? Think of adjectives to describe him.
What words and phrases on pages 22–23 suggest that Mole and Rat's life together was pleasant?
When Rat first describes Toad (before they meet Otter), what impression does he give of him?
How does Mole's impression change on the way to Toad Hall and why?
How would you describe Toad's character? Think of adjectives to describe him.
(Toad's own assessment of his character is given in a poem on page 82.)
How does Toad take his friends for granted? When he says his motto is 'Live for Others', do you believe him? Why/why not?
What reasons does Toad give for his enthusiasm for caravanning? Do you agree? Why/why not?
What do (a) Rat, and (b) Mole think about caravanning? Why does Toad change his opinion?
What effect does the sight of the car have on Toad's behaviour? on his mind?
What do you think will happen next? etc.

River and Road

Characters

Narrator   Otter
Mole   Toad
Rat   Car horn

Narrator	Once upon a time, there was a little mole who was fed up of life underground.
Mole	Oh bother! Oh blow! I want some adventure!
Narrator	So he left his home and went up into the world. As he was wandering along the banks of a river, he met a water rat.
Rat	Hello, Mole!
Mole	Hello, Rat!
Narrator	The rat took the little mole for a ride down the river in his rowing boat.
Rat	You know, my young friend, there is *nothing* – absolutely nothing – half so much worth doing as simply messing about in boats.
Narrator	And at the end of the day the two animals were getting along so well that the rat invited the mole to come and stay with him for a while.
Rat	Why don't you stay? I'll teach you to row, and to swim, and you'll be as handy on the river as any of the riverbank animals.
Narrator	The mole was very pleased and grateful, and he soon settled in with the water rat. They lived in Rat's comfortable little home, and messed about in boats, and Mole became friends with all the other animals on the riverbank. They never had any worries – until one day Mole asked his friend a favour.
Mole	Ratty, if you please, I want to ask you a favour.
Rat	Ask away, old chap. What can I do for you?
Mole	Well, would you take me to call on your friend Mr Toad? You've often talked about him, but I haven't met him yet. I do so want to meet him.

22

Rat Why, certainly. Get the boat out and we'll paddle up to Toad Hall at once. It's never the wrong time to call on Toad. Early or late, he's always the same fellow. Always good-tempered, always glad to see you, always sorry when you go!

Mole He must be an awfully nice animal.

Rat He is indeed the best of animals. So simple, so good-natured, and so friendly.

Narrator Mole and Rat rowed gently down the river in the spring sunshine. Other animals smiled and waved back from the banks as they passed – rabbits, hares, kingfishers, dabchicks, moorhens – and after a while a streak of bubbles on the surface of the water showed that someone was swimming along beside them.

Otter Hello there! It's only me. Where are you off to this morning?

Rat Oh, hello Otter. We're off to Toad Hall. I want to introduce my new friend Mole to dear old Toad.

Otter Are you sure you'll find him at home? He might be out *doing* things!

Rat That's a point. Oh well, we can but try!

Mole What sort of things do you mean?

Otter Oh, crazes, of course. Toad has crazes for different sorts of transport – one time it was nothing but sailing, then he tired of that and took to punting.

Rat Yes, nothing would please him but to punt all day and every day, and a nice mess he made of it too!

Otter Last year it was house-boating, and we all had to go and stay with him in his houseboat and pretend we liked it. He was going to spend the rest of his life in a houseboat. But it's all the same, whatever he takes up. He'll get tired of it, and start something fresh.

Rat That's true. He's such a good fellow, but so unsteady – especially in a boat!

23

Presentation/Drama

The play may be presented for other pupils, either dramatised by pupils in groups, or presented as a puppet play.

OR

Group work/Taped reading

The play is also suitable for presentation on tape as a 'radio play' with appropriate sound-effects and musical accompaniment.

Song:

Eton Boating Song by William Johnson (1823–1892)

Jolly boating weather
And a hay harvest breeze,
Blade on the feather,
Shade off the trees.
Swing, swing together,
With your backs between your knees,
Swing, swing together,
With your backs between your knees.

Literature: background
Kenneth Grahame (1859–1932) wrote *The Wind in the Willows* in 1908. The original was illustrated by Ernest Shepard, who also illustrated the Pooh stories. Pooh's creator, A A Milne, adapted the story for the stage in 1929 as 'Toad of Toad Hall', and another adaptation was made by Alan Bennett in 1992.
There have been many T V and video versions of the story, which pupils may have seen.
In what ways does this version (the language and illustrations of which are modelled on the originals) differ from video adaptations? etc.

Otter	It was a rowing-boat last time I heard. New togs, new everything. But he's probably tired of that by now. Oh – just a minute!
Narrator	At that moment a mayfly flew past. There was a swirl of water and a "cloop", and the mayfly had disappeared. So had the Otter.
Mole	Where's he gone?
Rat	Dinner, I think, old chap. Anyway, he's kept us company as far as Toad Hall. Look, there it is – up on the hill.
Narrator	Mole looked up and saw a handsome old house of red brick, with well-kept lawns reaching down to the water's edge.
Mole	I say. Toad must be rather rich.
Rat	Yes, he is, rather. This is really one of the nicest houses in these parts, though we never admit as much to Toad. He's a bit conceited, you know.
Narrator	Mole was beginning to wonder whether he really wanted to meet Toad after all – rich, conceited, always having crazes – he didn't sound as nice as Rat had made him out to be. But they got out of the boat and made their way across the gardens to Toad Hall, and as they neared the stables they heard a cry.
Toad	Ratty! Hooray! This is splendid!
Rat	Ah, there you are, Toad. I've brought someone to meet you. This is my friend Mole.
Toad	Wonderful! Wonderful!
Mole	Pleased to meet you.
Toad	Wonderful! Marvellous! You know, I was just going to send a boat down the river for you, Ratty, with strict orders that you were to be fetched up here at once, whatever you were doing. I want your help. It's most important.
Rat	Oh, about your rowing, I suppose. We heard you'd got a new boat. I suppose you are splashing a fair bit. Well, I'll give you a few lessons if you like.
Toad	Oh, pooh! Boating! Silly boyish amusement. I've given that up long ago. Sheer waste of time, that's what it is. No, I've discovered the real thing – the only genuine occupation of a lifetime. I mean to devote the rest of my life to it. Come Ratty and . . . your friend here, come just as far as the road outside Toad Hall and you shall see what you shall see.

24

Poem

Toad's poem about himself from *The Wind in the Willows:*

'It was perhaps the most conceited song that any animal ever composed:

The world has held great Heroes,
    As history-books have showed;
But never a name to go down to fame
    Compared with that of Toad!

The clever men at Oxford
    Know all that there is to be knowed.
But they none of them know one half as much
    As intelligent Mr Toad!

The animals sat in the Ark and cried,
    Their tears in torrents flowed.
Who was it said, "There's land ahead"?
    Encouraging Mr Toad!

The Army all saluted
    As they marched along the road.
Was it the King? Or Kitchener?
    No. It was Mr Toad.

The Queen and her Ladies-in-waiting
    Sat at the window and sewed.
She cried, "Look! who's that *handsome* man?"
    They answered, "Mr Toad."

The motor-car went Poop-poop-poop,
    As it raced along the road.
Who was it steered it into a pond?
    Ingenious Mr Toad!

(page 25)

Narrator	Toad led a bewildered Ratty and Mole round his great house and down the drive to the road. And there, outside the gates of Toad Hall, they saw . . .
Rat	A gypsy caravan! Oh no, not another craze!
Toad	Isn't she gorgeous?
Mole	Oh yes – so shiny and new. Yellow and green, and with red wheels!
Toad	That's right, old chap – I can see you appreciate her. There's real life for you, in that little caravan! The open road, the dusty highway, the heath, the common, the rolling downs! Camps, villages, towns, cities! Here today, up and off to somewhere else tomorrow! The whole world before you and a horizon that's always changing!
Mole	How marvellous you make it sound.
Toad	Come inside and look at the arrangements. Planned them all myself, I did!
Narrator	Toad took Mole by the hand and led him into the caravan, with Rat following doubtfully behind. Inside were sleeping bunks, a little table that folded up against the wall, a cooking stove, lockers, bookshelves, a birdcage with a bird in it, and everything you could need for a life on the road.
Mole	Why, there are jugs and pots and pans. And biscuits and sardines and bacon and jam.
Toad	Of course! You'll find nothing has been forgotten when we make our start this afternoon.
Mole	Oh my goodness!

25

Language/Discussion/Punctuation of direct speech

Pupils reared in the video-age often have difficulty distinguishing between narrative and dialogue. A playscript provides a useful vehicle for discussion of this issue, and of the related question of punctuation of direct speech.

In this play, the Narrator tells some of the story, and a few stage directions tell what the characters do. Otherwise, however, the plot is carried almost entirely through the speeches made by the characters.

This should not be the case in most written stories, where the writer acts as a narrator, filling in the context and explaining who is speaking at any one time.

Worksheet 4h

4h

Demonstrate to pupils by comparing the relevant section of the play on page 25 with Section A of Worksheet 4h.
What words have been added in the story version? Why is this necessary in a story?

(phrases like 'said Otter' are known as **dialogue carriers**)
What part of speech are 'anxiously' and 'cheerfully'? Why do you think they have been added?
What punctuation has been added in the story version?
Why is this necessary?
(We refer to ' ' as **speech marks** – see Glossary.)
Apart from punctuation, how does the writer make it clear that a new person has started to speak?

Pupils can then complete Worksheet 4h by filling in the missing dialogue in Section B.

Pupils nearing Level 4 could discuss whether the story versions would benefit from the addition of further details (e.g. descriptions of people's feelings, of the surroundings, etc.).

Punctuation of direct speech

Pupils who are nearing independent level may be able to convert sections of the play into narrative/direct speech for themselves, using the material on **Worksheet 4h** as a model.

Revise the rules:

- Every new speaker gets a new paragraph.
- Speech marks around the words actually spoken.
- Punctuation which is part of that speech goes inside the speech marks.

At this stage, the first two rules are the most important features to stress. Teaching of the third rule can become very complex and confusing, and should be kept to a minimum.

Pupils in pairs could rewrite and punctuate:

- page 22 – **Mole:** Ratty, if you please …
  Ratty: … paddle up to Toad Hall at once.
- page 24 – **Toad:** Ratty! Hooray! …
  Ratty: … a few lessons if you like.

From this point, teaching will relate to individual pupils' errors.

Rat   I beg your pardon – but did I hear you say something about "we" and "start" and "this afternoon"?

Toad   Now, you dear good old Ratty. Don't begin talking in that stiff and sniffy sort of way, because you know you've *got* to come. I can't possibly manage without you, so please consider it settled.

Mole   But . . . but . . .

Toad   No buts. You surely don't mean to stick to your dull fusty old riverbank all your life do you, and just live in a hole in a bank and a *boat*?

Rat   Yes, I do!

Toad   Nonsense! I want to show you the world! I'm going to make an *animal* of you, my boy.

Rat   I don't care. I'm not coming and that's flat. I *am* going to stick to my old river, *and* live in a hole and *boat*, as I've always done. And what's more, Mole's going to stick with me and do as I do, aren't you Mole?

Narrator   Mole looked at the caravan longingly, but he was a loyal little creature.

Mole   Of course I am. I'll always stick with you, Rat, and that's that. . . . But, all the same, it sounds as if it might have been – well, rather fun, you know!

Toad   Of course it will be fun. Rat will change his mind. We'll have some lunch and talk it over. We needn't decide anything in a hurry. Of course, *I* really don't care. I only want to give pleasure to you fellows. "Live for others!" That's my motto!

Narrator   Toad led the two animals down the steps of the caravan and turned to take them into the Hall for lunch, but at that moment they heard a faint hum from far away along the road. A warning hum, like the drone of a bee.

Toad   I say, what's that noise?

Mole   There's a small cloud of dust back there along the road – look!

Rat   Whatever can it be?

Car   (*Faintly*) Poop poop.

Toad   Can't imagine, old man.

Narrator   But before they could say any more the faint hum turned into a loud whirl of sound . . .

Car   Poop poop!

26

Books

Related to the extract:

The Wind in the Willows, Kenneth Grahame (Puffin)

Toad of Toad Hall, A A Milne – play (Samuel French)

Wild Wood, Jan Needle (Gryphon) – sequel written from the point of view of the stoats and weasels

Narrator	and a blast of wind . . .
Car	Poop poop!
Narrator	and it was on them!
Rat	Argh!
Mole	Oh!
Toad	Eek!

Narrator They had a moment's glimpse of plate-glass and shining steel. A magnificent motor car, immense, breath-snatching, passionate, flung them headlong into the ditch!

Car Poop poop!

Narrator A cloud of dust blinded them, and then, as quickly as it had appeared, the car was gone – it had dwindled into a speck in the distance, changing back to a droning bee once more.

Car (*Faintly*) Poop poop.

Rat Well! I say! (*Pulling himself up*) You villains! You scoundrels! You highwaymen! You – you – roadhogs! I'll have the law on you! I'll report you to the courts!

Mole Oh, Ratty, take care. It might come back.

Toad (*Faintly*) Poop poop.

Rat Just let it dare! I'll teach it to rush past fellows, like that, knocking them off their feet!

Mole Oh dear!

Toad (*Louder*) Poop poop.

Rat I say, what's the matter with Toad?

Mole I don't know. His eyes look all glassy.

Rat Did that thing hurt him? Is he damaged?

Toad Poop poop!

Rat Toad, old man, are you all right? What's the matter?

Toad What? Oh hello, Ratty. Wasn't it wonderful?

Rat Wonderful? What are you talking about?

27

Suffixes
(see Glossary)
A suffix would not usually stand as a complete word on its own.
- We have already met the suffix **-ly** (usually associated with adverbs). It occurs in the play in:

absolutely	simply
awfully	longingly
doubtfully	really

- Another common suffix featuring in the play is **-ful** (usually associated with adjectives), e.g. grateful, awful, doubtful.
- **–ing** is usually associated with verbs, e.g. rowing, sailing, punting.
- **–ment** is usually associated with nouns, e.g. amusement, arrangement.

Pupils can think/of collect other examples of **-ful**, **-ing**, **-ment** words, and check whether they are nouns, adjectives, verbs.
Note: The complete word 'full' becomes 'ful' when used as a suffix.
Can pupils think of further examples of suffixes?
(NB Prefixes – see notes to page 31)

Language awareness/ Spelling links: word-building
Many types of word-building feature in the vocabulary of the play. We focus on two: compound words and suffixes.

Compound words
Words created by placing two or more complete words together (not including prefixes or suffixes) to create a composite meaning. (True compound words do not require a hyphen), e.g. on pages 25–28:

under + ground
river + bank
sun + shine
dab + chicks
king + fishers
moor + hens
no + thing
house +boat
some + thing
every + thing
may + fly
any + way
(hand + some originally meant 'convenient' or 'handy', then came to mean 'suitable', and from there to 'good-looking')
Can pupils find and explain the meaning of 14 examples from the point at which Mole and Ratty arrive at Toad Hall on page 24 to the end?
what + ever
life + time
out + side
high + way
some + where
book + shelves
bird + cage
after + noon
any + thing
motor + car
head + long
high + way + men
road + hogs
some + body
Can pupils think of/collect further examples in their reading?

Toad	Glorious, stirring sight! The poetry of motion! The real way to travel. The only way to travel! Here today – in next week tomorrow! Villages skipped, towns and cities jumped – always somebody else's horizon! Oh bliss! Oh poop-poop! Oh my, oh my!
Mole	Oh, stop being an ass, Toad!
Toad	And to think, I never knew! All those wasted years that lie behind me, I never knew, I never even dreamed! But now, now that I know, oh what a flowery track lies before me from now on! Poop poop!
Mole	What are we to do with him?
Rat	Nothing at all, Mole. Because there really is nothing to be done. You see, I know him from old. He has got a new craze, and it always takes him this way. He'll go on like this for days now, like an animal in happy dream.
Mole	Oh dear!
Rat	Then he'll start looking for one of those poop-poop machines.
Mole	Oh dear, oh dear.
Rat	And goodness knows what scrapes he'll get into. Well, there's nothing to be done about it. There never is anything to be done about Toad. At least we can get back to the riverbank while he's still in a dream. Let's get him home.
Narrator	Slowly, Toad allowed himself to be led back into the Hall.
Toad	Poop poop!
Narrator	And Ratty and Mole sadly rowed back down the river. That evening they were back in their own cosy riverside parlour, with the usual peaceful riverside life going on all round them. But now they had something to worry about – how long would it be before Toad went up to town and ordered a large and very expensive motor car? And what trouble would he get into then?

28

Books

About road transport for readers approaching Level 4:

Professor Branestawm's Pocket Motor Car, Norman Hunter (Puffin)

Follow That Bus, Pat Hutchins (Lions)

The Demon Bike Rider, Robert Leeson (Lions)

Hairy and Slug, Margaret Joy (Puffin)

The Bus Under the Leaves, Margaret Mahy (Puffin)

The Mouse and the Motorcycle and other books, Beverley Cleary (Puffin)

Vera Pratt books, Brough Girling (Puffin)

Ride to the Rescue (about horses), June Crebbin (Puffin)

Tardis (page 29)

Reading/Discussion

The comic strip may be read like a play, with a narrator and three actors. *Has anyone seen 'Dr Who' on TV/video?* (The appearance of the doctor here is based on his first incarnation in 1963.)
What is particularly strange about the policebox? Do you know why it's called the Tardis? (an acronym of Time And Relative Distance in Space)
What sort of thing do you think they will see when the doors are open? – e.g. outdoor scene? indoor scene? people? clothing? buildings? transport? etc.

Discussion: comic strips

The TV Comic was published throughout the 1960s at 6d an issue.
What is your favourite comic strip? Where does it appear? Do you like/dislike comics? Why/why not? If yes, what particular aspects of comics do you think make them easier to read than normal text? What do you think of the drawing of this one? Who was the artist? etc.

Writing/Comic strip/Drama

Pupils (individuals or pairs) devise their own continuation of the story. Various possibilities, e.g.:
• prose narrative
• comic strip
• improvise and develop a short play, which could later become the basis for prose narrative or a comic strip.

Language/Poetry: acronyms and acrostic poems

What other acronyms do you know? (e.g. radar – Radio Detection And Ranging; laser – Light Amplification by Stimulated Emission of Radiation)
Pupils could attempt acrostic poems on some type of transport, e.g.:

Piercing the clouds
Like a tiny ripping
Arrowhead
New, gleaming, soaring,
Escaping the pull of the earth.

Fiction

The Planet of Terror, adventure game book (Walker)

Transported to Other Worlds

Reading aloud
Groups/pairs/individual pupils prepare poems for reading. Allow a few readings of each poem before discussion.

Discussion: preferences
Which poems do pupils like best, and why?

Poetry/Discussion
All these poems make us look at some aspect of transport with fresh eyes:

'Southbound on the Freeway'
*Where do you think Orbitville is? What is the tourist describing? (cars) What are the cars' guts? feet? eyes? What are the measuring tapes? Which cars have an extra eye? How do you know? Are the descriptions good ones – why/why not? Which **are** drivers – the cars' guts or their brains? etc.*

'Submarine'
Which words and phrases here describe the undersea world? Which describe the interior of the submarine?
(note contrasts: 'hard/harsh' versus 'soft' language)
Why can't the crew see outside? What must it feel like in a submarine? How do you feel for the crew? etc.

'Fuelled'
What is fuel? Why should something with man-made fuel get more applause than something with natural fuel? Which do you think is more amazing – the rocket or the seedling, and why? etc.

General
Look at the title of the page – which is the 'other world' in each case? Which of the three seems strangest to you? Which are not usually 'other worlds' to you? Do the poems make them seem strange – if so, why? etc.

Southbound on the Freeway

A tourist came in from Orbitville,
parked in the air, and said:

The creatures of this star
are made of metal and glass.

Through the transparent parts
you can see their guts.

Their feet are round and roll
on diagrams or long

measuring tapes, dark
with white lines.

They have four eyes.
The two in back are red.

Submarine

This is the world of the submarine
A wavering jungle, dark and green,
That sailormen glide through;
They eat and sleep in their steel case
For weeks before going back to base,
And never see the view.

And it is magical, this world,
With restless foliage and curled
Serpents of the deep;
Small living submarines swim near
With goggle eyes, then disappear
Like images in sleep.

The crew lives in eternal night,
Lit by harsh electric light,
Like travellers who ride
In coach or carriage through superb
Scenery, yet can't disturb
The blinds to look outside.

Vernon Scannell

Discussion/Writing
(See poem 'Submarine' in Book 3, page 20.)
Choose an everyday journey or form of transport you know well. Think of a point of view other than your own from which you could describe that transport (e.g. as an alien/a baby/an animal/the transport itself/the road).
Discuss pupils' ideas and help develop them (brainstorming, drafting and editing) into short passages or poems.

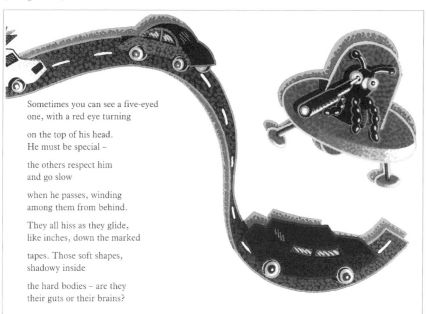

Sometimes you can see a five-eyed
one, with a red eye turning

on the top of his head.
He must be special –

the others respect him
and go slow

when he passes, winding
among them from behind.

They all hiss as they glide,
like inches, down the marked

tapes. Those soft shapes,
shadowy inside

the hard bodies – are they
their guts or their brains?

May Swenson

Fuelled

Fuelled
by a million
man-made
wings of fire –
the rocket tore a tunnel
through the sky –
and everybody cheered.

Fuelled
only by a thought from God –
the seedling
urged its way
through the thicknesses of black –
and as it pierced
the heavy ceiling of the soil –
and launched itself
up into outer space –
no
one
even
clapped

Marcie Hans

31

Class presentation/ Group planning and organisation

The three poems and pupils' own work could be used as the basis of a presentation, perhaps as part of a school assembly.

Discussion/Writing: a fresh eye

We often take our environment for granted or fail to notice what is going on as we travel through it – why does this happen? Why can it be a bad thing? (Pupils think of examples, e.g. destruction/pollution of environment; failures in conservation – 'you don't miss what you've got till it's gone')
How could we try to avoid taking things for granted? etc.
Pupils could write prayers about the importance of keeping a 'fresh eye' when travelling.
Use the poem on page 11 or prayers in school assembly books as models.

Language: prefixes
(see Glossary)
Can you find another word with the 'trans' prefix on these pages? What does it mean? etc.

Worksheet 4i
This worksheet contains work on prefixes which may be completed by individuals or pairs of pupils.

4i

Books about space travel
Halfway Across The Galaxy, Robin Klein (Puffin)
Harvey's Ark, Robin Kingsland (Puffin)
Mr Browser and the Brain Sharpeners, Philip Curtis (Puffin)

The Stowaways

(page 32)

The Stowaways is published as a short novel by Puffin, as is another story by Roger McGough, *The Great Smile Robbery*. He is better known for his poetry, of which several collections for children are published by Puffin:
An Imaginary Menagerie
Nailing the Shadow
Sky in the Pie

Reading aloud
Split the story into sections for individual children to prepare and read aloud while the rest of the class follow in their books.

Discussion: preferences
Do you like/dislike the story? Why?

Discussion/ Comprehension/ Inference/Deduction
For example: *How can you tell from the first paragraph that this is going to be a light-hearted story? Find an example of a **pun** (see Glossary) in the first paragraph.*
How old do you think the writer and Midge were when this story happened? Why do you think that?
Why didn't the writer like Wednesdays? Which days do you like/dislike, and why?
List all the things that went wrong that Wednesday, to make them decide to run away.
Why did the policeman stop the boys? Do you think he believed them? Why/why not? How did the boys manage to sneak on to the ship? Did they divide the supplies fairly? What happened to Midge, and why? Why did they decide to give themselves up? What told them that they were not on a seagoing ship? What is a ferry? Why weren't the writer's parents worried when he told them where he'd been? etc.
How effective are the characters/setting/plot of this short story?
(See notes with pages 12–13.)

When I lived in Liverpool, my best friend was a boy called Midge. Kevin Midgeley was his real name, but we called him Midge for short. And he was short, only about three cornflake packets high (empty ones at that). No three ways about it. Midge was my best friend and we had lots of things in common. Things we enjoyed doing like . . . climbing trees, playing footy, going to the pictures, hitting each other really hard. And there were things we didn't enjoy doing like . . . sums, washing behind our ears, eating cabbage.

But there was one thing that really bound us together, one thing we had in common – a love of the sea.

In the old days (but not so long ago) the River Mersey was far busier than it is today. Those were the days of the great passenger liners and cargo boats. Large ships sailed out of Liverpool for Canada, the United States, South Africa, the West Indies, all over the world. My father had been to sea and so had all my uncles, and my grandfather. Six foot six, muscles rippling in the wind, huge hands grappling with the helm, rum-soaked and fierce as a wounded shark (and that was only my grandmother!). By the time they were twenty, most young men in this city had visited parts of the globe I can't even spell.

In my bedroom each night, I used to lie in bed (best place to lie really), I used to lie there, especially in winter, and listen to the foghorns being sounded all down the river. I could picture the ship nosing its way out of the docks into the channel and out into the Irish Sea. It was exciting. All those exotic places. All those exciting adventures.

Midge and I knew what we wanted to do when we left school . . . become sailors. A captain, an admiral, perhaps one day even a steward. Of course we were only about seven or eight at the time so we thought we'd have a long time to wait. But oddly enough, the call of the sea came sooner than we'd expected.

It was a Wednesday if I remember rightly. I never liked Wednesdays for some reason. I

Comprehension/ Reading for details/ Writing in sentences
Questions about the story for pupils to answer in writing can be found on **Worksheet 4b** (Section D). This exercise gives pupils practice in scanning a text for information and writing in complete sentences.

Poem
See also: Roger McGough's poem 'No More Ferries' in *Sky In The Pie* (Puffin).

(page 33)

could never spell it for a start and it always seemed to be raining, and there were still two days to go before the weekend. Anyway, Midge and I got into trouble at school. I don't remember what for (something trivial I suppose like chewing gum in class, forgetting how to read, setting fire to the music teacher), I forget now. But we were picked on, nagged, told off and all those boring things that grown-ups get up to sometimes.

And, of course, to make matters worse, my mum and dad were in a right mood when I got home. Nothing to do with me, of course, because as you have no doubt gathered by now, I was the perfect child: clean, well-mannered, obedient . . . soft in the head. But for some reason I was clipped round the ear and sent to bed early for being childish. Childish! I ask you. I *was* a child. A child acts his age, what does he get? Wallop!

So that night in bed, I decided . . . Yes, you've guessed it. I could hear the big ships calling out to each other as they sidled out of the Mersey into the oceans beyond. The tugs leading the way like proud little guide dogs. That's it. We'd run away to sea, Midge and I. I'd tell him the good news in the morning.

The next two days just couldn't pass quickly enough for us. We had decided to begin our amazing around-the-world voyage on Saturday morning so that in case we didn't like it we would be back in time for school on Monday. As you can imagine there was a lot to think about – what clothes to take, how much food and drink. We decided on two sweaters each and wellies in case we ran into storms around Cape Horn. I read somewhere that sailors lived off rum and dry biscuits, so I poured some of my dad's into an empty pop bottle, and borrowed a handful of half-coated chocolate digestives. I also packed my lonestar cap gun and Midge settled on a magnifying glass.

33

Discussion/Writing: running away

Do you think there were good reasons for the writer to run away? Why/why not? How did he and Midge prepare? Were their preparations adequate? Why/why not? If you were running away, what sort of preparations would you make? What you would need? What precautions you would have to take? What destination? etc. What sorts of transport could a boy/girl use for running away? etc.

Pupils invent one or more characters (see notes with page 4); devise setting (see notes with page 11) and reason for characters to run away; work out plans, transport, destination; devise plot (see notes to page 11 – problem/solution).

Pupils attempt their own short story, modelled on 'The Stowaways'.

Reading/ Dramatisation

Groups of 4 practise reading the second half of the story (from 'Hardly anyone was about' on page 34 to the end), using a main narrator and other voices for the speeches of the two boys, the policeman and the writer's parents. They should read the story like a play, using punctuation to guide phrasing, and paying particular attention to intonation and expression.

Language: paragraphs
(See Glossary, on page 40 of Book 4.)

Show pupils Worksheet 4j, in which a short story is written without paragraphs. Do not attempt to read it at present. Compare its layout to that of 'The Stowaways'.

Which looks easier and more pleasant to read? Why?

Help children identify the rules for paragraphing:

- a new paragraph each time anyone speaks;
- each paragraph groups facts/events together to make a 'unit of sense';
- the writer uses paragraphs to influence the way his/her readers read the story – they make his meaning clear by presenting the story to the reader in suitable chunks;
- breaks between paragraphs can show time passing;
- the first word of each new paragraph is **indented** (see Glossary);
- paragraphs can be of different lengths.

On Friday night we met round at his house to make the final plans. He lived with his granny and his sister, so there were no nosy parents to discover what we were up to. We hid all the stuff in the shed in the yard and arranged to meet outside his back door next morning at the crack of dawn, or sunrise – whichever came first.

Sure enough, Saturday morning, when the big finger was on twelve and the little one was on six, Midge and I met with our little bundles under our arms and ran up the street as fast as our tiptoes could carry us.

Hardly anyone was about and the streets were so quiet and deserted except for a few pigeons straddling home after all-night parties. It was a very strange feeling, as if we were the only people alive and the city belonged entirely to us. And soon the world would be ours as well – once we'd stowed away on a ship bound for somewhere far off and exciting.

By the time we'd got down to the Pier Head, though, a lot more people were up and about, including a policeman who eyed us suspiciously. ''Ello, 'Ello, 'Ello,' he said, 'and where are you two going so early in the morning?'

'Fishing,' I said.

'Train spotting,' said Midge and we looked at each other.

'Just so long as you're not running away to sea.'

'Oh no,' we chorused. 'Just as if.'

He winked at us. 'Off you go then, and remember to look both ways before crossing your eyes.'

We ran off and straight down on to the landing stage where a lot of ships were tied up. There was no time to lose because already quite a few were putting out to sea, their sirens blowing, the hundreds of seagulls squeaking excitedly, all tossed into the air like giant handfuls of confetti.

Then I noticed a small ship just to the left where the crew were getting ready to cast off. They were so busy doing their work that it was easy for Midge and me to slip on board unnoticed. Up the gang-plank we went and straight up on to the top deck where there was nobody around. The sailors were all busy down below, hauling in the heavy ropes and revving up the engine that turned the great propellers.

34

4j

Worksheet 4j: **Paragraphing**
('Sheik Chilli Takes the Train': a story from Utter Pradesh)

The teacher should read the whole of this story to pupils to make sure they understand it before beginning work on it.

Pupils work in pairs: read the story carefully, working out where they think paragraph breaks should come; mark these in pencil.

Each pair should compare their effort with that of another pair, discuss which is more effective and alter their paragraphing as necessary. Finally, pupils should cut up the story into individual paragraphs and paste it up on paper as shown.

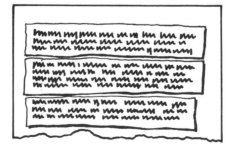

There is no single 'correct' method of paragraphing the passage. Anything which works is acceptable.

(NB It is particularly effective if the passage can be transferred to a word-processor, so that different layouts can be tried out on screen.)

We looked around for somewhere to hide. 'I know, let's climb down the funnel,' said Midge. 'Great idea,' I said, taking the mickey. 'Or better still, let's disguise ourselves as a pair of seagulls and perch up there on the mast.'

Then I spotted them. The lifeboats. 'Quick, let's climb into one of those, they'll never look in there – not unless we run into icebergs anyway.' So in we climbed, and no sooner had we covered ourselves with the tarpaulin than there was a great shuddering and the whole ship seemed to turn round on itself. We were off! Soon we'd be digging for diamonds in the Brazilian jungle or building sandcastles on a tropical island. But we had to be patient, we knew that. Those places are a long way away, it could take days, even months.

So we were patient. Very patient. Until after what seemed like hours and hours we decided to eat our rations, which divided up equally. I gave Midge all the rum and I had all the biscuits. Looking back on it now, that probably wasn't a good idea, especially for Midge.

What with the rolling of the ship, and not having had any breakfast, and the excitement, and a couple of swigs of rum – well you can guess what happened – woooorrppp! All over the place. We pulled back the sheet and decided to give ourselves up. We were too far away at sea now for the captain to turn back.

The worst he could do was to clap us in irons or shiver our timbers.

We climbed down on to the deck and as Midge staggered to the nearest rail to feed the fishes, I looked out to sea hoping to catch sight of a whale, a shoal of dolphins, perhaps see the coast of America coming in to view. And what did I see? The Liver Buildings.

Anyone can make a mistake can't they? I mean, we weren't to know we'd stowed away on a ferryboat.

One that goes from Liverpool to Birkenhead and back again, toing and froing across the Mersey. We'd done four trips hidden in the lifeboat and ended up back in Liverpool. And we'd only been away about an hour and a half. 'Ah well, so much for running away to sea,' we thought as we disembarked (although disembowelled might be a better word as far as Midge was concerned). Rum? Yuck.

We got the bus home. My mum and dad were having their breakfast. 'Aye, aye,' said my dad, 'here comes the early bird. And what have you been up to then?'

'I ran away to sea,' I said.

'Mm, that's nice,' said my mum, shaking out the cornflakes. 'That's nice.'

Roger McGough

Books

Short stories for Level 4 readers, with a Transport theme:
'Daddy's New Car' in *Getting Rich With Jeremy James*, David Henry Wilson (Piccolo)
How To Stop A Train With One Finger, David Henry Wilson (Piccolo)
Friends and Brothers, Dick King-Smith (Mammoth)
'The Crocobus' in *Rough and Tumble*, ed. Anne Wood and George English (Puffin)
'Sir's New Car' in *I'm Trying To Tell You,* Bernard Ashley (Puffin)

Language/Spelling

- *'Stowaway'* is a compound word – *what does it mean?*
- Plural – **stowaways**, gives an example of the rules for adding endings **to words ending in y**. Where the **y** is preceded by a vowel, the two letters work together, e.g.:
  stow<u>ay</u>, qu<u>ay</u>, st<u>ay</u>
  k<u>ey</u>, vall<u>ey</u>, monk<u>ey</u>, journ<u>ey</u>
  b<u>oy</u>, destr<u>oy</u>
  b<u>uy</u>, <u>guy</u>
  and endings may be added without making any changes to the **y**, e.g.:
  stowaways, quays, stayed
  keys, monkeyed, journeyed
  boys, destroyer
  buyer, guys
  (NB no words end in iy)
This contrasts with words ending in **consonant + y**, where **y** changes to **i** before an ending is added:

y → i when adding an ending
- in nouns, e.g. **fly/flies**; **sky/skies**; **reply/replies**; **baby/babies**; **lady/ladies**; **story/stories**, etc.
- in verbs, e.g. **hurry/hurries/hurried**; **carry/carries/carried**; **reply/replies/replied**, etc.
  (Note: if the change would mean two i's together, the y is retained, e.g. **carrying, flying, applying**.)
- in adjectives, e.g. **happy/happier/happiest**; **dry/drier/driest**
- in a pronoun: **my/mine**

Discussion/Dialect
(See Glossary for definition)
Share the page with pupils and discuss where speakers come from/what they mean, etc.
Dialect words in examples:
right good (Yorks) = very good
puddenhead (Cornwall) = fool
guider (Yorks)/**cartie** (SE Scotland)/**bogie** (Newcastle)/**dilly** (Cornwall) = home-made, 4-wheeled vehicle.

The dialect words for a **sledge** at the top of the page and for a **two-wheel cart** and **wheel hubs** at the bottom of the page are from across the British Isles.
Do you have any other dialect words for any of these things? Other things to do with transport? Local/ethnic dialect words in general?

Dialect words/ Spoken English
Interest in one's own native dialect and how it differs from Standard English is an excellent introduction to the study of language.
Pupils may know dialect words from their own area/ethnic group; or they may be able to collect them from adults.
Opportunity for interviewing/taping.

Non-chronological writing
Pupils might compile a 'dialect dictionary'.

Discussion: accent
(See Glossary)
Can pupils 'do' different accents (e.g. Coronation Street/East Enders/American)? What is the difference between accent and dialect? etc.

Discussion/Dialect grammars
The examples in the pupil's book focus on dialect words, but more important for teaching purposes are **dialect grammars**, e.g. 'We was talking' for 'We were talking'. Pupils must recognise how the grammar of their native dialects differs from that of Standard English (see page 39 and Glossary). The teaching required in this respect will differ from one part of the country to another, and should arise from a consideration of pupils' and others' dialect variations.

Short story
To read to pupils: 'Spit Nolan' in *The Goalkeeper's Revenge*, Bill Naughton (Puffin)

We do not usually *write* in local or ethnic dialects. It is important that written English should be easy for *all* English speakers to read and understand, no matter where they come from. For this reason, there is one English dialect which should generally be used for written English. It is called "Standard English".

Many people speak in a Standard English dialect too. The newsreaders on T.V. and radio always speak Standard English, so that everyone can understand, all over the country.

You can speak Standard English in any accent at all. It doesn't have to be spoken in a "posh" voice!

Standard English is the dialect of English used for writing. However, local or ethnic dialects are sometimes used in poems, rhymes and songs, like these two from different parts of Scotland:

Oh, yee cannae shove yer granny aff a bus,
Oh, yee cannae shove yer granny aff a bus,
Oh yee cannae shove yer granny,
For she's yer mammy's mammy,
Oh yee cannae shove yer granny aff a bus!

In ma wee red motor
I can gang for miles –
Up and doon the garden,
Through the lobby whiles.
Mony another motor
Gangs to toons afar –
None can gang where I gang
In ma wee red car!

Rhymes/Language

The first rhyme should be sung to the tune of 'She'll be coming round the mountain when she comes'. The second is best read in a refined Scottish accent, if possible.
What do these rhymes mean? Which words are dialect words? If they were written in Standard English, how would they sound– which words or phrases would change and how? Which do you think fits the poem best – Standard English or the Scottish dialect? Why?

Discussion/Language awareness

Standard English

(See Glossary)
Standard English is merely a dialect of the English language (originally the dialect of the educated classes in SE England), and of no greater or lesser worth than other dialects. It has, however, been adopted as the dialect in which written English is to be presented. It is also used for speech in formal situations.
What does 'Standard' mean? Why do you think we have a 'standard' form of English? What might happen if everyone wrote in their own dialects? When might you need to speak in Standard English? (When might you speak in your own dialect?)

Accent

The accent which is usually associated with Standard English is known as Received Pronunciation (RP), but nowadays any accent is accepted with Standard English.
Can pupils read aloud the newsreader's speech in accents other than RP? Do you know any Standard English speakers with regional/ethnic accents? (Perhaps some of their teachers?)

The Kids' Good Car Guide

(page 38)

The Programmes of Study for Level 4 recommend the compilation of anthologised material by groups of pupils, especially on computer. This page from a 'rear-seat passengers' good car guide' is provided as a model of an anthology related to the Transport theme.

Other themes include:
– 'Good Bus Guide' to local services
– 'Good Bike Guide'
– Holiday transport reports
– Safety reports on local roads
– Travel games and pastimes (for brightening long car journeys)
– Rhymes about transport (e.g. nursery rhymes, playground rhymes and games, etc.)

Discussion

Preliminary discussion should centre on:

Content of entries

For example: *What sorts of information/material do we want to include and what is the best way to organise this? How can we get the information concerned?* etc.

Format of entries

For example: *How are we going to set it out? What headings/subheadings, etc. are necessary? Can we create a 'template' which everyone can use as a basis? Can we use symbols in any way?* etc.

Organisation of anthology

For example: *Do we want to organise the whole thing in any way (e.g. alphabetically? geographically?)* etc.

Research/Non-chronological writing

Each pupil/pair of pupils can then research a chosen item to find all the information required.

Information Technology/Data-banks

If possible, this is an ideal opportunity for using word-processing facilities: a basic template can be made up, and each pupil/pair fill their entry into it. The group would thus be creating a mini-databank.

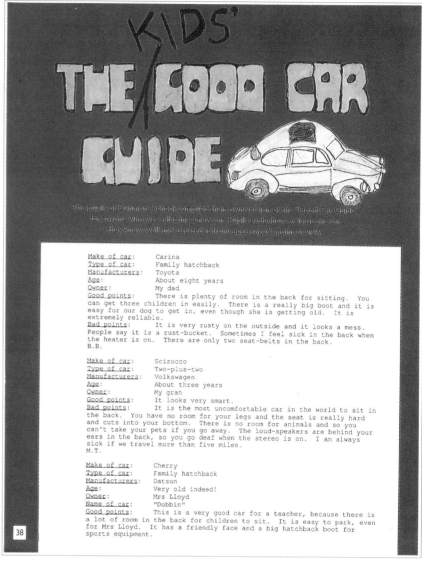

THE KIDS' GOOD CAR GUIDE

The pupils of Dunmore School compiled their own version of the "Good Car Guide" for anyone who was selecting a new car. Pupils each chose at least one car they knew well and assessed it from a passenger's point of view.

```
Make of car:     Carina
Type of car:     Family hatchback
Manufacturers:   Toyota
Age:             About eight years
Owner:           My dad
Good points:     There is plenty of room in the back for sitting.  You
can get three children in easily.  There is a really big boot and it is
easy for our dog to get in, even though she is getting old.  It is
extremely reliable.
Bad points:      It is very rusty on the outside and it looks a mess.
People say it is a rust-bucket.  Sometimes I feel sick in the back when
the heater is on.  There are only two seat-belts in the back.
B.B.

Make of car:     Scirocco
Type of car:     Two-plus-two
Manufacturers:   Volkswagen
Age:             About three years
Owner:           My gran
Good points:     It looks very smart.
Bad points:      It is the most uncomfortable car in the world to sit in
the back.  You have no room for your legs and the seat is really hard
and cuts into your bottom.  There is no room for animals and so you
can't take your pets if you go away.  The loud-speakers are behind your
ears in the back, so you go deaf when the stereo is on.  I am always
sick if we travel more than five miles.
M.T.

Make of car:     Cherry
Type of car:     Family hatchback
Manufacturers:   Datsun
Age:             Very old indeed!
Owner:           Mrs Lloyd
Name of car:     "Dobbin"
Good points:     This is a very good car for a teacher, because there is
a lot of room in the back for children to sit.  It is easy to park, even
for Mrs Lloyd.  It has a friendly face and a big hatchback boot for
sports equipment.
```

38

Maps (page 39)

MAPS

High adventure
   And bright dream –
Maps are mightier
   Than they seem:

Ships that follow
   Leaning stars –
Red and gold of
   Strange bazaars –

Ice floes hid
   Beyond all knowing –
Planes that ride where
   Winds are blowing!

Train maps, maps of
   Wind and weather,
Road maps – taken
   Altogether

Maps are really
   Magic wands
For home-staying
   Vagabonds!

Dorothy Brown Thompson

39

Reading poetry
Give the poem to a pupil to prepare before reading it to the rest of the class/group.

Discussion
What does the poet mean when she refers to ships following stars? What are bazaars? ice floes?
What different types of maps are mentioned? What other types can you think of?
What is a vagabond?
In what ways could a map be a magic wand?
What sort of things might you see in your imagination if you travelled around the map shown here? How would you travel? etc.

Group/Individual work: maps
Pupils collect as many sorts and examples of maps as possible.

Discussion
Discuss/compare elements such as scale, keying devices, reading the maps, etc.
Each pupil chooses a map, and plans a journey within it – route, transport, any other relevant details, etc.
Each pupil imagines taking his/her journey, using the map as a stimulus.

Speaking/Writing
Pupils either describe their journeys or write accounts of them. Written accounts should be displayed with the maps to which they refer.

Discussion: poetry and transport
Pupils should look back over the poems in the book.
Which do you like best/least? Why? What does the word 'transport' mean? In what way could poems be described as a form of transport? Which of the poems in this book transport you furthest? Which do not transport you very far at all? etc.

Glossary

The glossary is provided so that the vocabulary needed for Level 4 work is available to the pupils. Definitions are, as far as possible, in language appropriate to the age-group, and are therefore somewhat simplistic.

For reasons of space, we have not usually included terms which are defined in earlier books.

All definitions require plenty of discussion with the teacher. Pupils must then experience the concept concerned within the context of real language before they can be expected to grasp the meaning. Wherever possible, vocabulary has been introduced in the teacher's notes to individual pages, often with a follow-up activity or worksheet. By the time pupils have finished the book they should be familiar with most of the terms.

◆ **abbreviation** (n.)
A short way of writing something, often using initials,
e.g. *e.g. = for example*
i.e. = that is
Mr = Mister

◆ **accent** (n.)
The way a person pronounces words – it is affected by tone of voice and speech rhythms. Accents vary from one part of the country to another, and the same words can sound different if spoken in different accents.
Particular accents sometimes go with particular dialects of English.

◆ **adverb** (n.)
[See also part of speech]
A word which describes an action
e.g. *quickly, slowly, noisily*

◆ **apostrophe** (n.)
A punctuation mark like a flying comma. It shows
1. where letters have been missed out of a word or words,
    e.g. *it'll = it will; can't = cannot*
2. ownership,
    e.g. *the car's voice*
    Toad's caravan

◆ **catalogue** (n.)
A list of items arranged in a special order so that they can be found quickly.
[See also: index, classification, databank]

◆ **to classify** (v.)
To arrange items in order.
classification (n.)
A system for arranging items in order, e.g. *the Dewey Decimal Classification System.*

◆ **comma** (n.)
A punctuation mark used between the items in a list, or to separate parts of a sentence.

◆ **databank** (n.)
Information about a particular subject classified and stored for reference on a computer.

◆ **dialect** (n.)
A way of speaking the language which is particular to one part of the country or ethnic group. There are dialect words (such as *drag* for *sledge*) and dialect grammars (such as *We was there* for *We were there*). Dialects often have an accent which goes with them.
[See also Standard English]

◆ **direct speech** (n.)
The actual words someone speaks, as shown in a piece of writing.
[See also speech marks]

◆ **encyclopaedia** (n.)
A book or set of books giving information on many subjects.

◆ **exclamation mark** (n.)
A punctuation mark (!) which shows that a phrase or sentence
1. should be spoken in a raised voice
    e.g. *"Help! Fire!"*
or
2. is used in a joking or unusual way
    e.g. *"Here today – in next week tomorrow!"*

◆ **folktale** (n.)
A story which has been handed down from one generation to another. Folktales are usually a spoken tradition, i.e. they are told, not written down.

◆ **to indent** (v.)
    Begin your writing a little way in from the margin, to show that you are starting a new **paragraph** (as we have done in the first line of this definition).

◆ **index** (n.)
An alphabetical list, which shows the subjects dealt with in a book, a set of encyclopaedias, or a whole library.
[See also catalogue]

◆ **italic print** (n.)
A type of print which leans towards the right. It is used to draw attention to particular words. The most common reasons for the use of italic print are:
1. for the titles of books, films, etc.
2. to show that a word should be *stressed* when read aloud.

◆ **joining word** (n.phr.)
[See also part of speech]
A word which joins words or groups of words together, e.g. *and, but when, so, as, while, because, although.*

◆ **limerick** (n.)
A type of verse (usually funny), which has two rhyming lines, then two shorter rhyming lines, and a last line which rhymes with the first two.

◆ **noun phrase** (n.phr.)
A phrase of two or more words which act together as the name of something (i.e. like a noun).

40

♦ **onomatopoeia** (n.)
A word which sounds like the thing it refers to, e.g. *chug, whirr, click.*

♦ **paragraph** (n.)
A chunk of writing, usually several sentences long, dealing with one main idea or topic. Each new paragraph starts on a new line, and the first line is indented.

♦ **part of speech** (n.phr.)
The way a word is being used in a phrase or sentence, e.g. *noun, verb, adjective, adverb, pronoun.*

♦ **plot** (n.)
The story-line in a book or piece of writing.

♦ **phrase** (n.)
A group of words which go together to make sense, but do not make a complete sentence.

♦ **prefix** (n.)
A group of letters at the beginning of a word, which hold a unit of meaning,
e.g. *trans* meaning *across* (as in *transport, transfer, transform*)
e.g. *sub* meaning *under* (as in *subway, submarine*)

♦ **proverb** (n.)
A wise saying, which has been handed down from generation to generation.

♦ **pun** (n.)
A joke using words with a similar sound but different meanings,
e.g. *What kind of ears does have a train have? Engineers!*

♦ **punctuation marks** (n.phr.)
In general, these are to help the reader make sense of a piece of writing. They show how words are grouped together in phrases and sentences to make sense. Some also show what tone of voice is needed to read the words (? !).
The apostrophe is an exception (see above).

♦ **reference book** (n.phr.)
A book which you use to look up particular bits of information, without reading the whole book.

♦ **rhythm** (n.)
A regular pattern of sounds or beats.

♦ **speech marks** (n.)
Punctuation marks that look like this " ". They are placed around passages of direct speech to show the exact words which someone has spoken.
e.g. *"Where are you going?" asked Otter.*
"We're off to Toad Hall," said Rat.

♦ **Standard English** (n.phr.)
The dialect of English which is used in written language. It is also the dialect spoken by many people (such as newsreaders) who wish to be understood by all groups of English speakers, wherever they come from.

♦ **suffix** (n.)
A group of letters at the end of a word and holding a unit of meaning, e.g. *-ly* at the end of adverbs, meaning *in this way* (as in *"heavily"*, *"loudly"*).

♦ **word-family** (n.)
A group of words that come from the same root:
e.g. *flew, flight.*

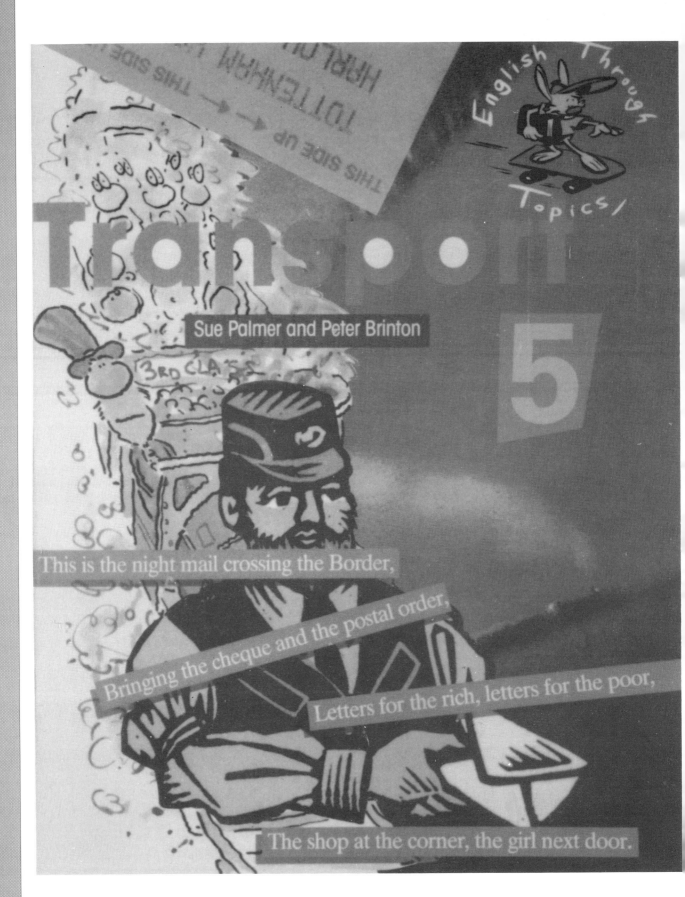

Book 5

For pupils working towards Level 5

PUPIL'S BOOK 5: resource material, linked to the theme of Transport:
- *reading for pleasure:* poems; extracts from children's and classic fiction; a short story; a play based on Greek mythology
- *reading for information:* researching from information books; advertisements; information leaflets; article on language
- *stimuli for writing in various genres:* stories and sketches; poetry; factual writing; note-making; information-writing; letters; reports; playscripts; articles
- *stimuli for spoken language activities:* class and group discussion; debates; reports; formal and informal presentations.

THE TEACHER'S NOTES:
- suggestions (accompanying each page of Book 5) for using the resource materials to cover the Level 5 English requirements.
  (A guide to the layout of the Teacher's Notes – page 8.)
- background information on resource material
- further extracts or stories and suggestions for pupils' further reading, related to the topic or to the material provided in the pupil's book.
- details of non-fiction books at an appropriate level, related to the topic.

WORKSHEETS: practice work on:
5a	Comprehension questions	Section A: pages 3–6 (note on page 3)
		Sestion B: pages 10–12 (note on page 10)
		Section C: pages 13–15 (note on page 13)
5b	Commas	(see notes to page 5)
5c	Simple and complex sentences	(see notes to pages 5–6)
5d	Standard English	(see notes to page 12)
5e	Reading a train timetable	(see notes to page 15)
5f	Chunking for meaning	(see notes to page 15)
5g	Fact and opinion	(see notes to page 23)
5h	Punctuation of direct speech	(see notes to page 38)
5i	Apostrophe to show ownership 1	(see notes to page 39)
5j	Apostrophe to show ownership 2	(see notes to page 40)

While detailed suggestions for the use of the resource material are provided, individual teachers have their own preferred methods of working, and should use the materials as is most appropriate to their own teaching styles and their pupils' needs.

Covering the English Curriculum

The material is intended to **supplement** the ongoing language work of a class of children working towards Level 5, and link it to the theme of Transport.

Pupil's Book 5 has been designed to provide:
- stimuli for large and small group discussion; drama; formal and informal presentations and reports by individuals and groups; organised debates;
- opportunities to discuss poems and stories, develop ideas and express points of view formally and informally;
- opportunities for group planning and making of presentations;
- stimuli for discussion of dialect variations and specialist terms relating to transport;
- opportunities to read and respond to a wide range of literature: fiction, poetry, mythology, classic English literature, a complete short story, a play;
- opportunities to explore and justify opinions about the above;
- examples of written and broadcast material designed to influence opinions, and opportunities to distinguish between fact and opinion, and to recognise bias;
- a model of the process of information search and research reading;
- opportunities to discuss a wide variety of language use in written material of various kinds, including word-play and different styles of writing;
- stimuli to write in a variety of forms, including letters, instructions, stories and poems;
- practice in organisation of text using punctuation, including the comma, and layout to increase clarity;
- further help with the setting out of direct speech;
- information on and a model of note-taking procedures, opportunities to draft and revise;
- information about word origins, and some links to spelling (although it is recommended that the systematic teaching of spelling continues alongside ETT);
- technical vocabulary in which to discuss language use and the mechanics of reading and writing.

NB Only spelling points which arise from the resource material are covered: further systematic spelling instruction will be required.

Keeping track

The Record-keeping checklist on page 103 correlates the National Curriculum Attainment Targets for Level 5 with the activities suggested in these notes. The numbers used to record the correlations are the page numbers of the Pupil's Book against which activities are recommended in the Teacher's Notes.
Please see also the notes on page 11 about record-keeping.

Record-keeping checklist

Opportunities for covering Level 5 NC English Attainment Targets

See activities suggested to accompany the pages given below in Pupil's Book 5:

	2	3-6	7-9	10-12	13-15	16-17	18	19	20-21	22-23	24	25-30	31	32-41	42/43	44/45	46/47
Speaking and Listening																	
Deliver organised, sustained account	2			10-12	13-15												
Contribute/justify point of view in discussion	2	3-6	7-9		13-15				20-21	22-23				32-41			46/47
Use transactional language		3-6	7-9		13-15				20-21	22-23							46/47
Plan/participate in presentation	2				13-15	16-17	18	19					31	32-41		44/45	46/47
Discuss variations in dialect/vocabulary		3-6	7-9	10-12	13-15	16-17			20-21				31	32-41		44/45	
Reading																	
Read range of stories/poems	2	3-6	7-9	10-12	13-15	16-17	18				24		31	32-41			46/47
Explain preferences		3-6	7-9	10-12	13-15				20-21	22-23		25-30	31				
Develop views and support by ref. to text	2	3-6	7-9	10-12	13-15					22-23		25-30		32-41	42/43		
Recognise fact/opinion			7-9		13-15				20-21	22-23		25-30			42/43		
Select ref. books, etc.: read for research			7-9		13-15					22-23		25-30			42/43		
Recognise/discuss word-play and imaginative use of language	2		7-9	10-12					20-21					32-41			
Writing																	
Use variety of forms for variety of purposes		3-6			13-15	16-17	18		20-21			25-30					
Use organisational devices for clarity		3-6			13-15				20-21	22-23		25-30					
Use paragraphing and punctuation for clarity		3-6	7-9	10-12		16-17				22-23	24	25-30		32-41			
Punctuate direct speech		3-6		10-12	13-15									32-41			
Use Standard English forms in writing		3-6		10-12	13-15	16-17				22-23		25-30		32-41			
Recognise and discuss use of dialect grammars		3-6		10-12	13-15												
Assemble ideas, draft, revise		3-6		10-12	13-15					22-23	24	25-30					
Discuss variations in vocabulary/style		3-6		10-12	13-15	16-17	18			22-23		25-30					
Presentation																	
Spell complex words		3-6		10-12	13-15	16-17					24	25-30			42/43		
Check drafts		3-6		10-12	13-15	16-17					24	25-30					
Clear legible printed and joined writing		3-6		10-12	13-15	16-17					24	25-30					

s checklist refers to the National Curriculum in English at the time of going to press (Spring 1993). An updated sheet for the revised
riculum, when known, is available free to purchasing schools, from Oliver & Boyd, Longman House, Burnt Mill, Harlow, Essex CM20 2JE.

Assessing and teaching children using ETT Book 5

(See notes on assessment in General introduction, page 11 and *Copymasters*, page ix)

The resource material is pitched for teaching purposes roughly halfway between a Level 4 and a Level 5 standard. Teacher input will, of course, vary to accommodate children's needs as they progress along the developmental continuum between Levels 4 and 5. Progress can be informally assessed by observation of a child's performance when using the resource material and carrying out activities. For example:

	Just above Level 4 (beginner)	**Between Levels 4 and 5** (midway)	**Nearing Level 5** (independent)
Spoken English	Brief, loosely organised spoken accounts; needs teacher support for large-scale group activities; aware of major differences between Standard English and local dialect forms.	Spoken accounts better organised and gaining in depth; participates in large-scale group activities with less support; developing awareness of a variety of dialect forms.	Sustained, organised spoken accounts; able to complete large-scale group activities with little support; able to discuss dialect variation in spoken and written language.
Reading	Able to express but not justify preferences; not able to distinguish between fact and opinion; unable to conduct a simple research project; unsure why writers use particular words, styles, techniques.	Beginning to justify literary preferences; starting to recognise fact and opinion; able to undertake a simple research project with support; beginning to recognise why writers have selected particular words, styles, techniques.	Able to justify some literary preferences; able to distinguish between fact and opinion; able to undertake a simple research project independently; able to comment on writers' choice of words, use of techniques and styles.
Writing	Style of written work not varying according to purpose; use of organisational devices limited and punctuation still incorrect; sometimes using Standard English instead of local dialect grammar in written work; unaware of various registers of writing.	Beginning to use a variety of forms/styles according to purpose of writing; use of organisational devices and punctuation occasionally incorrect; using local dialect forms in written work only occasionally; growing in awareness of a variety of registers of writing.	Varying writing style according to purpose; use of organisational devices and punctuation usually correct; almost always using correct Standard English grammatical forms; aware that there is a range of registers in writing and sometimes using examples appropriately.

Contents

Let's go Ride

Reading poetry

Several groups of 3 pupils should prepare the poem for presentation to the rest of the class/group.

Presentation/ Discussion

Each group should present their version of the poem.
Discuss variations in presentation and why pupils chose particular techniques – how appropriate to the poem? etc.

'Let's Go Ride'

The poem sums up the romance of travel and transport.
Who do you imagine is speaking? Who is Johanna? In which country do you think they are, and why? What does the poet do in the first stanza?
(sets the scene; sets up the shape of the poem – rhyme, rhythm and repetition)
From what perspective is the sleighride viewed in the second stanza? (we're in the sleigh: immediate visual and tactile images)
How does the perspective change in the final stanza? (wider, grander – the sights and sounds around them: time is flying and the poet wants to experience these things 'while he may')
What is the effect of the final line of each stanza? (a reminder that romance does not come free of charge; but it's worth the price: 'only five dollars')
In what ways is the poem like a song?

Let's go ride in a sleigh, Johanna,
Let's go ride in a sleigh,
Through the mountains,
Under the trees,
Over the ice
On Lake Louise.
Let's go ride in a sleigh, Johanna,
    – There's only five dollars to pay.

Let's go ride today, Johanna,
Let's go ride today,
The horses shaking
Their silver traces,
The branches flaking
Snow on our faces.
Let's go ride today, Johanna,
    – There's only five dollars to pay.

Let's go ride while we may, Johanna,
Let's go ride while we may,
By the tall ice-fall
And the frozen spring
As the frail sun shines
And the sleigh-bells ring.
Let's go ride while we may, Johanna,
    – There's only five dollars to pay.

Charles Causley

Language: descriptive techniques

Does the poem make you want to go on the sleighride? Why/why not? Which words and phrases do you think are most evocative (i.e. bring the sleighride to life?) and why? Poetry and advertisements are often said to have a lot in common – in what ways is this poem like an advert for sleighrides?
Taking information from the poem, some pupils could make advertising posters for the sleighride.
What other sorts of transport sound romantic and exciting? Think of words and phrases which convey the beauty/power/glamour of other sorts of transport.
Using the best words and phrases, pupils could devise advertising posters for the form of transport in which they would most like to 'go ride'.

The Wild Ride in the Tilt Cart *(page 3)*

There was a lad named Tommy Hayes and a more likeable lad, you'd never hope to see, for all that he was a Sassenach born and bred. Tommy was the sort to take his fishing very seriously, so when a Scottish friend wrote to him and invited him to come up to his place in the Highlands for a visit and be sure to bring his fishing gear, Tommy was delighted. He'd always heard the fishing up where his friend lived was extra fine but he'd never had a chance to try it before. So immediately he sent a telegram to his friend to say he was coming and what time they could expect him to get there. Then he packed up his fishing gear and a few clothes in his bag, and off he went.

He stepped off the train just about nightfall into the midst of teeming rain with the water coming down in bucketsful and sloshing all over the place. The very first thing he discovered was that nobody had come to meet him. The station was on the edge of a small village, and there wasn't a soul in sight except for the stationmaster, and he was inside the station keeping out of the rain.

Tommy couldn't understand it for he'd sent the telegram in plenty of time. He went in and asked the stationmaster if he had seen anyone in the village from his friend's place, thinking maybe they'd had an errand to do and would be coming along for him later. But the stationmaster said that nobody at all had come over from that way for as good as a week. Tommy was surprised and maybe a little bit annoyed but he settled down in a corner of the station to wait for somebody to come and fetch him. He waited and waited and waited but nobody came at all, and after a while he found out why. The stationmaster came out of his bit of an office with a telegram in his hand. 'This is for the folk up where you're going,' he told Tommy. 'Maybe you'd not mind taking it along, since you're going there yourself.'

Tommy didn't have to read the telegram to know that it was the one he had sent to his friend. Well, that explained why nobody had come to meet his train. And what was more, nobody was going to come. Since the telegram hadn't been delivered, they wouldn't know at all that he was there.

'Och, well, 'tis a pity,' said the stationmaster. ''Twas early this morn I got it, and I'd have sent it along had anyone been passing by that was going in that direction. But what with the weather and all, there's few been out this day, and what there was, was bound the other way.'

Well, being a good-natured lad, Tommy couldn't see any sense in making a fuss about it. He'd just have to find a way for himself to get where he wanted to go.

The stationmaster was sorry for Tommy, but he could give him no help. There was nobody in the village who'd be able to take Tommy to his friend's house that night. Two or three folk had farm carts, but the beasts were all put up for the night and people were all in their beds. They wouldn't be likely to take it kindly if Tommy woke them out of their sleep.

'You could stay in the station o'ernight,' the man said. 'You'd be welcome to do so, if you liked to. Happen there'll be someone along on the morrow going the way you want to go.'

3

Ghost stories

With a transport theme:
'The Ghost Train' in
A Shriek of Spooks, ed.
Marks and Maynard
(Armada)
Other collections of ghost stories for Level 5 readers:
Ghost Stories, Robert Westall (Kingfisher)
Ghosts and Journeys, Robert Westall (Piper)
The Shadow Cage, Philippa Pearce (Puffin)
Ghosts That Haunt You, Aidan Chambers (Puffin)
The Shirt off a Hanged Man's Back, Dennis Hamley (Lions)

Reading/Comprehension/Interpretation

5a

Questions about the short story for pupils to answer in writing are provided on **Worksheet 5a** (Section A).

These may be tackled either before or after shared reading of the short story and oral discussion.

Reading aloud/Discussion

This story, by a Scottish writer, is told in colloquial style, with the rhythms of Highland speech, indications of accent in the spelling and occasional examples of dialect vocabulary. (Ideally it should be read in a West Highland Scots accent.)

A group of pupils should divide the story between them and prepare it for reading to the rest of the group/class. Other pupils should follow in their books as it is read.

Discussion/Interpretation

For example: *When do you think this story was set? Why? From the text, what do you think a tilt cart was?* (a covered wagon) etc.

Discussion: style and accent/dialect

(See Glossary definitions at back of Book 5, and notes to Book 4, pages 36–37.)
What sort of style has the writer used here (formal or informal)? Which turns of phrase suggest this to you? Can you express the same ideas in a more formal style?
Which words and expressions show you the story is told by a Scot? Find examples of: dialect words (e.g. Sassenach; glen); *spellings which indicate accent* (e.g. auld, de'il). *What would be their equivalents in Standard English?*

Discussion → writing: ghost stories

Transport and the supernatural often go together, e.g. ghost trains, phantom stagecoaches, the ferryman over the Styx, etc. Can pupils think of any other examples?

On first reading of 'The Wild Ride in the Tilt Cart' did you realise it was going to be a ghost story? If so, when and why? etc. Ghost stories, like all stories, require a **setting**, **characters** and **plot**. They also require a ghostly atmosphere, which the author must produce by the way he/she treats these three elements.

How does the author make his setting appropriate for supernatural happenings? (weather, isolation, darkness)

How does he make Rabbie MacLaren seem sinister? What is the basic plot? How is the story constructed so we don't find out who Rabbie is until the end? Which words and phrases contribute most to the creation of a ghostly atmosphere? What elements of the setting and language in the poems opposite produce a ghostly atmosphere?

Writing: a short story

Pupils each choose a form of transport and plan their own short stories with a 'ghostly transport' theme, first devising appropriate setting/characters/plot. During drafting and editing, attention should be paid to creating atmosphere with descriptive language.

108

'And maybe not,' said Tommy, not feeling very hopeful. 'No, if I'm going to get there at all, I can see I'll have to walk.'

'Aye,' the stationmaster agreed. ''Tis a matter of five miles.'

'That's not too bad,' said Tommy, determined to be cheerful.

'Mostly up and down hill,' said the stationmaster glumly. 'The road is rough, forbye. And 'tis raining.'

'It can't be helped,' said Tommy. 'I'll just have to make the best of it.' He picked up his bag and started out into the rain. The stationmaster came to the door and pointed out the road Tommy was to take. Tommy had gone a little way when the man called out after him. 'Have a care for auld Rabbie MacLaren! I doubt he'll be out on the road the night.'

That didn't mean a thing to Tommy, so he just plodded along through the rain.

The stationmaster had told him no lies about the road. Tommy couldn't remember having trod a worse one. It was up and down hill all right. Tommy toiled along, splashing through the puddles and slipping on loose pebbles, with the rain pouring from the back of his hat brim down inside the collar of his coat. He was beginning to wonder if the fishing was going to be fine enough to pay for all the trouble he was going through to get it when he heard the sound of cart wheels rolling up the hill behind him.

He stopped and turned to look, and although it was growing dark he could make out the shape of a tilt cart coming towards him. It had a canvas top stetched over some sort of framework, and Tommy thought to himself that if he could get a lift he'd be out of the rain at any rate. He set his bag down and stood in the middle of the road, waving his arms and shouting.

'Will you give me a lift up the road?' called Tommy.

The driver did not answer but the cart came on swiftly, bumping along over the ruts in a heedless way. As it came up to him, Tommy

called out again, 'Will you give me a lift?'

The man in the cart didn't say 'Aye', but he didn't say 'Nay'. The cart kept on rolling along and Tommy had to pick up his bag and jump to the side of the road to keep from being run down.

'I'll pay you well,' cried Tommy as he jumped. He felt rather desperate. The tilt cart was his only hope, for he doubted if he'd have another chance to get a lift that night. 'I'll pay you well!' said Tommy again.

The driver did not answer, but it seemed to Tommy that the horse that was drawing the cart slowed down a little. Tommy took that as a sign that his offer had been accepted. He picked up his bag and ran after the cart and hopped in beside the driver without waiting for the cart to come to a full stop.

As soon as Tommy was in the cart the horse picked up speed again. The creature didn't seem to be minding the roughness of the road in the least. It brought the cart up to the crest of the hill at a good round pace and, when they started down the other side, the horse stretched its legs and fairly flew. The cart bounced and bumped and jolted over the ruts and Tommy's teeth chattered with the shaking he was getting. All he could do was hold fast to the side of the cart and hope for the best. The cart wheels threw out sparks as they hit the stones that strewed the road, and every now and then a big one sent the cart a foot or more in the air. Uphill and downhill went Tommy with the cart, hanging on for dear life and expecting to land any minute in a heap in the ditch with horse, cart, and driver piled on top of him.

4

The Way Through The Woods

They shut the way through the woods
Seventy years ago.
Weather and rain have undone it again,
And now you would never know
There was once a way through the woods
Before they planted the trees.
It is underneath the coppice and heath
And the thin anemones.
Only the keeper sees
That, where the ring-dove broods,
And the badgers roll at ease,
There was once a road through the woods.

Yet, if you enter the woods
Of a summer evening late,
When the night-air cools on the trout-ringed pools,
Where the otter whistles his mate
(They fear not men in the woods
Because they see so few),
You will hear the beat of the horse's feet
And the swish of a skirt in the dew,
Steadily cantering through
The misty solitudes,
As though they perfectly knew
The old lost road through the woods...
But there is no road through the woods.
(Rudyard Kipling)

The Flying Dutchman

We met the *Flying Dutchman*,
By midnight he came,
His hull was all of hell fire,
His sails were all aflame;
Fire on the main-top,
Fire on the bow,
Fire on the gun-deck,
Fire down below.

Four-and-twenty dead men,
Those were the crew,
The Devil on the bowsprit,
Fiddled as she flew.
We gave her the broadside,
Right in the dip,
Just like a candle,
Went out the ship.
(Charles Godfrey Leland)

(page 5)

He plucked up enough courage after a while to attempt to implore the driver to slow down. He turned to look at the man beside him. What he saw took the words out of his mouth. It wasn't so much the sight of him, although that was bad enough. He was the hairiest creature Tommy had seen in his life. A wild thatch of hair grew over his head and down over his ears, and was met by a long grizzled beard that almost covered his face and blew in the wind as if it had life of its own. But that wasn't what struck Tommy dumb. With all that hair in the way Tommy could not be sure of it, yet he'd have sworn the man was grinning at him. Tommy didn't like it.

He felt that grin was full of a peculiar sort of evil, and it gave Tommy such a queer feeling that he hurriedly turned away without saying a word.

Just at the moment the road made a turn and he saw at the side of it, a little distance ahead, a great stone gateway. Tommy knew from the stationmaster's description that it was the entrance to his friend's place.

He gave a great sigh of relief. 'Pull up!' he cried to the driver. 'This is where I get out.'

But the driver made no sign of stopping, and the horse went racing past the gate. Tommy rose in his seat, shouting, 'Stop!' Just then the cart-wheels hit some obstruction in the road and Tommy, taken unawares, lost his balance. Over the side of the cart he flew and landed in the road on his hands and knees. By the time he pulled himself together and got to his feet, the cart was

out of sight, although he could still hear the horse's hooves pounding down the other side of the hill.

Tommy would have liked to have had a chance to tell the fellow exactly what he thought of him, but it was too late for that. The cart was gone, and Tommy's bag had gone with it, but at least he hadn't paid the driver. Taking what comfort he could from that, Tommy limped back to the gateway, and up the drive to the door of his friend's house.

Tommy's friend was terribly surprised when he opened the door at Tommy's knock, and saw him standing there on the door-stone. But when he saw the plight Tommy was in he asked no questions. He hurried Tommy up to his room and saw that he had a good hot bath and found him some dry clothes to put on.

When Tommy came downstairs again, warm and dry and feeling a hundred times better, he was so relieved to have arrived safely that he was prepared to treat his whole experience as a joke. He handed over the telegram and told his friend he didn't think much of the telegraph service in the Highlands.

Tommy's friend had several other guests staying with him and they all gathered around Tommy now to hear the story of his mishap.

'Och, Tommy lad,' said his friend. "Tis a long road and a bad night for walking."

'Did you walk all the way?' asked one of the guests.

'Well, no,' said Tommy. 'But I wish that I had. I got a lift from one of your wild Highlanders. I never had such a ride in my life before and I hope that I never shall again. And to top it all, the fellow went off with my bag.'

'I wonder who it would be?' asked Tommy's friend. 'Not many would be travelling in weather the like of this at night. The road is bad enough at best. A bit of rain makes it terrible.'

'I'll grant you that,' said Tommy. 'The fellow was driving a tilt cart.'

'A tilt cart!' exclaimed another man. 'Och,

5

Punctuation: use of the comma

The comma is used for:
- separating the items in a list
- separating **tag words or phrases** from the main sentence, e.g.:
  > Well, being a good-natured lad…
  > 'The road is rough, forebye.'
  > 'What sort of man was he to look at, Tommy?'
- showing how words within a sentence should be chunked together to help convey the sense.

Alert pupils to examples in 'The Wild Ride in the Tilt Car' and discuss the function of the comma. Pupils' reading aloud of sentences with particular attention to commas helps sensitise them to their use.

Worksheet 5b: commas
When pupils understand the three above uses of the comma, Worksheet 5b can be completed by individuals or pairs.

5b

Language: simple and complex sentences
The comma is of particular importance in complex sentences, where it is often used between clauses, clarifying the meaning.

Worksheet 5c
This gives practice in the forming and analysis of complex sentences, e.g.:

5c

> *As the car drove down the road which led to London, the driver sighed because he had been travelling for hours.*
> or
> *The car drove down the road to London, and the driver sighed, as he had been travelling for hours.*

There are many possible ways of combining or separating sentence elements, so there is no single 'correct' answer to each question. All grammatical and complete answers are acceptable.

After discussion and preparation as necessary, pupils should complete the worksheet individually or in pairs.

Language: sentence structure
Worksheet 5c, once completed, provides the focus for discussion on **clauses** (see Glossary and notes on next page) as a feature of sentence structure. Familiarity with the concept of clauses can be helpful to pupils when reading complex material, or when composing their own more complex written texts.

Discussion: clauses

Worksheet 5c

5c

In Section A of Worksheet 5c, the sentences provided are all **single-clause sentences** with **one verb**, e.g.:

The car <u>chugged</u> down the road. = 1 clause

The road <u>led</u> to London. = 1 clause

The driver <u>sighed</u>. = 1 clause

He <u>had been travelling</u> for hours. = 1 clause

Pupils should have converted these four simple sentences into a complex sentence, composed of several clauses, each with a verb, e.g.:

a 4-clause sentence:

As the car <u>chugged</u> down the road which <u>led</u> to London, the driver <u>sighed</u> because he <u>had been travelling</u> for hours.

or a 3-clause sentence:

While the car <u>chugged</u> down the road to London the driver <u>sighed</u>, as he <u>had been travelling</u> for hours.

Discuss the variety of ways in which pupils have converted the simple sentences in Section A into complex sentences. Using verbs as an indicator, can they tell how many clauses each of their complex sentences contains?

Discussion: main clauses and subordinate clauses

In most complex sentences, one clause acts as an 'anchor', upon which the others depend. This is known as the **main clause** (see Glossary), and its verb is the **main verb**, e.g.:

As the car chugged down the road to London, **the driver <u>sighed</u>** because he had been travelling for hours.

or

The car <u>chugged</u> along the road to London, while the driver sighed because he had been travelling for hours.

The clauses which depend on the main clause are known as **subordinate clauses**. They usually begin with a **joining word**, such as 'as' or 'while'. Can pupils identify main and subordinate clauses in the sentences in Section B of **Worksheet 5i**, and their own complex sentences for Section A?

NB In sentences joined with 'and', 'but' or 'or', there may be two or more clauses of equal weight, rather than a main clause and a subordinate clause.

---

they're none so common hereabouts. The only one I call to mind is the one belonging to auld Rabbie MacLaren.'

'Now that you mention it, I remember,' said Tommy. 'That was the name of the man the stationmaster told me to have a care for. I suppose he meant that I was to keep out of his way. How I wish I had!'

There was a dead silence for all of five minutes. Then Tommy's friend asked, 'What sort of man was he to look at, Tommy?'

'An old man, I'd say,' Tommy told him. 'He had more hair on his head and face than I've ever seen on a human being before. It probably looked like he meant than there really was of it, because it was so tangled and matted. Of course it was too dark for me to see much of him.'

'What was the horse like, Tommy?' asked his friend.

'Not what you'd call a big beast,' Tommy answered. 'In fact he was somewhat on the small side. But how he could go! That horse would make a fortune on a race track. We bumped and thumped along at such a pace that I expected both wheels to fly off at any minute.'

''Twas auld Rabbie MacLaren, to be sure!' said the guest who had asked about the tilt cart. 'He was always one to be driving as if the de'il himself was after him. There's a bad spot a mile further on, over the hill. If you miss the road on the turn there, over the cliff you go to the glen below. Auld Rabbie came tearing along hell-bent one stormy night and missed the turn and went over.'

'Went over!' Tommy exclaimed. 'It's a wonder he wasn't killed!'

'Killed?' repeated the other man. 'Of course he was killed. Auld Rabbie's been dead for a dozen years.'

It took Tommy a minute or two to get through his head what he was being told. Then all of a sudden he understood.

'Dead!' screeched Tommy. *'Then I've been riding with a ghost!'* and he fainted dead away.

6

The next morning one of the gillies brought Tommy's bag up to the house to see if it belonged to anyone there. He'd found it lying in the glen at the foot of the cliff, below the road. It was the good stout sort of bag that is strapped as well as locked, so all the harm that had come to it was a scratch here and there.

Tommy had recovered from his fright by that time, so they took him out and showed him the place where auld Rabbie went over. They told Tommy he was lucky that he left the cart where he did, for when it got to the bad spot the tragedy was always re-enacted and over the cliff again went the old man with his cart and his horse. There had been some folk who got a ride with auld Rabbie, expecting to reach the village over beyond the next hill, who had found themselves below the road in the glen instead. A number of them had been badly hurt, and two or three had never lived to tell the tale.

Tommy suffered no ill effects from his experience. To tell the truth, he was rather proud of it. And as he took his fishing seriously, he didn't let the ride with auld Rabbie spoil his holiday. He stayed on to the end and fished all the streams in the neighbourhood, and had a wonderful time.

But for a long time after he went home to London he couldn't sleep well on stormy nights. As soon as he turned out the light and closed his eyes he started to dream that he was riding wildly over that rough stony road in the tilt cart with the ghost of auld Rabbie MacLaren.

Sorche Nic Leodhas

Pioneers of Air Travel *(page 7)*

PIONEERS OF AIR TRAVEL

To an Aviator

You who have grown so intimate with stars
And know their silver dripping from your wings,
Swept with the breaking day across the sky,
Known kinship with each meteor that swings –

You who have touched the rainbow's fragile gold,
Carved lyric ways through dawn and dusk and rain
And soared to heights our heavy hearts have only dreamed –
How can you walk earth's common ways again?

Daniel Whitehead Hicky

END OF THE GREAT FLIGHT.

By LOUIS BLERIOT.

Dover, Sunday.

It is more important to be the first to cross the Channel by aeroplane than to have won a prize of £1,000. Nevertheless, I must first acknowledge the enterprise of *The Daily Mail* and its recognition of the importance of aviation in the offer of the prize which I have had the honour to win.

I am glad I have won it. I am more than happy that I have crossed the Channel. At first I promised my wife I would not make the attempt; then I determined that if one failed I would be the first to come. And I am here.

At 2.30 this morning I rose at the Terminus Hotel, at Calais, and at three o'clock departed with my friend M. Le Blanc in a motor-car to Baraques. On our way we noted that the weather was favourable to my endeavour. We therefore ordered the torpedo destroyer Escopette, generously placed at my disposal by our Government, to start.

At 3.30 a.m. we went to the garage and examined the aeroplane, which is my eleventh. I started the engine and found that it worked well. All was ready for the start.

At four o'clock I took my seat in the aeroplane and made a trial flight of one quarter of an hour around Calais and its environs. The circuit was about fifteen kilometres (9¼ miles). Having completed it I descended upon the spot on the cliff from which I intended to start.

Here I waited for the sun to come out, the conditions of *The Daily Mail* prize requiring that I should fly between sunrise and sunset.

At 4.30 we could see all round. Daylight had come. M. Le Blanc endeavoured to see the coast of England, but could not. A light breeze from the south-west was blowing. The air was clear.

Everything was prepared. I was dressed as I am at this moment, a "khaki" jacket lined with wool for warmth over my tweed clothes and beneath my engineer's suit of blue cotton overalls. My close-fitting cap was fastened over my head and ears. I had neither eaten nor drunk anything since I rose. My thoughts were only upon the flight, and my determination to accomplish it this morning.

4.35: Tout est prêt! Le Blanc gives the signal and in an instant I am in the air, my engine making 1,200 revolutions—almost its highest speed—in order that I may get quickly over the telegraph wires along the edge of the cliff. As soon as I am over the cliff I reduce my speed. There is now no need to force my engine.

"I BEGIN."

I begin my flight, steady and sure, towards the coast of England. I have no apprehensions, no sensations, pas du tout.

The Escopette has seen me. She is driving ahead at full speed. She makes perhaps 42 kilometres (about 26 miles) an hour. What matters? I am making at least 68 kilometres (42½ miles).

Rapidly I overtake her, travelling at a height of 80 metres (about 250 feet). The moment is supreme, yet I surprise myself by feeling no exultation. Below me is the sea, the surface disturbed by the wind, which is now freshening. The motion of the waves beneath me is not pleasant. I drive on.

LOST!

Ten minutes have gone. I have passed the destroyer, and I turn my head to see whether I am proceeding in the right direction. I am amazed. There is nothing to be seen, neither the torpedo-destroyer, nor France, nor England. I am alone. I can see nothing at all—rien du tout!

For ten minutes I am lost. It is a strange position, to be alone, unguided, without compass, in the air over the middle of the Channel.

I touch nothing. My hands and feet rest lightly on the levers. I let the aeroplane take its own course. I care not whither it goes.

For ten minutes I continue, neither rising nor falling, nor turning. And then, twenty minutes after I have left the French coast, I see the green cliffs of Dover, the castle, and away to the west the spot where I had intended to land.

What can I do? It is evident that the wind has taken me out of my course. I am almost at St. Margaret's Bay and going in the direction of the Goodwin Sands.

Now it is time to attend to the steering. I press the lever with my foot and turn easily towards the west, reversing the direction in which I was travelling. Now, indeed, I am in difficulties, for the wind here by the cliffs is much stronger, and my speed is reduced as I fight against it. Yet my beautiful aeroplane responds. Still steadily I fly westwards, hoping to cross the harbour and reach the Shakespeare Cliff. Again the wind blows. I see an opening in the cliff.

Although I am confident that I can continue for an hour and a half, that I might indeed return to Calais, I cannot resist the opportunity to make a landing upon this green spot.

Once more I turn my aeroplane, and,

describing a half-circle, I enter the opening and find myself again over dry land. Avoiding the red buildings on my right, I attempt a landing; but the wind catches me and whirls me round two or three times.

At once I stop my motor, and instantly my machine falls straight upon the land from a height of 20 metres (65 feet). In two or three seconds I am safe upon your shore.

Soldiers in khaki run up, and a policeman. Two of my compatriots are on the spot. They kiss my cheeks. The conclusion of my flight overwhelms me. I have nothing to say, but accept the congratulations of the representatives of *The Daily Mail* and accompany them to the Lord Warden Hotel.

Thus ended my flight across the Channel. The flight could be easily done again. Shall I do it? I think not. I have promised my wife that after a race for which I have entered I will fly no more.

Daily Mail, July 26, 1909

7

Poem: discussion
'To an Aviator'
A pupil/pupils should prepare this for reading aloud.

What is an aviator? Does he/she really travel near stars and meteors? What does the poet mean when he refers to the aviator's 'intimacy' and 'kinship' with these? What does 'lyric' mean? On whose behalf is the poet speaking (ref: the pronoun 'our')? Why should the aviator find earth 'common'? Which words suggest that flying is 'uncommon' and exciting?

In what ways is this poem similar to 'Let's go Ride' on page 2? etc.

Reading/Discussion: Bleriot extract

Some pupils should prepare the passage beforehand for reading to the class/group.

Background: Louis Bleriot (1872–1936) was a French motorcar engineer who became an aviator and later a manufacturer of aircraft. This article was probably dictated to a reporter from the *Daily Mail*, which had offered a reward for the first cross-Channel flight (Calais to Dover).

When did Bleriot set off? How long did his journey take? What do you think the Escopette was? What were the difficulties with (a) taking off? (b) landing? Was Bleriot expected in Dover? How do you know? etc.

Discussion: style

Bleriot was not a native English speaker, as shown in:
- simple sentence structures (see notes to pages 5–6);
- use of present tense;
- unusual use/phrasing of English;
- occasional French expressions.

Which aspects of the style suggest that the writer is not a native English speaker? (Help pupils to identify examples of all the indicators listed.)

a) *Find some groups of simple sentences – combine them into complex sentences. (See notes on clauses, etc. for page 6.)*

b) *In what tense would you expect the passage to be written? Why do you think Bleriot uses the present? What effect does it have on his story?*

c) *Which uses of English seem unusual to you, and how would you rephrase them to sound more natural?*

d) *From the context, what do you think the following mean:*
   Tout est prêt! (all is ready)   *Pas du tout* (none at all)   *Rien du tout* (nothing at all)

Discussion: Amy Johnson song

The biographical details of Amy Johnson on page 9 of Book 5 should be read before discussion of the song, the verses of which read:

There's a little lady who has
   captured every heart –
Amy Johnson, it's you!
We have watched and waited
   since the day you made
   your start –
Amy Johnson, it's true!
Since the news that you are
   safe has come along
Everyone in town is singing
   this song: *Chorus*

You deserve a lot of credit
   for your daring deeds –
Amy Johnson, that's true!
You are just the kind of
   person that the country
   needs –
Amy Johnson, that's true!
Yesterday you were but a
   nonentity,
Now your name will go down
   to posterity: *Chorus*

*If someone wrote a song
about Louis Bleriot, do you
think they would refer to
him as a 'little gentleman'?
In what other ways
(attitudes? language?)
does this song point up the
general attitude to women
(and their place) in 1930?
(Worksheet 4e consists of
a passage about Amy
Johnson's Australia flight
for sentence
punctuation.)*

Poems about flight

The following were among the many poems written about and by pilots during the Second World War:

Fighter Pilots

We're neither saint nor stoic,
Just craftsmen of the sky;
Our fighting's unheroic,
And quietly we die.
We have no heaven to buy with blood;
No heroes' world to give.
We do not fight to make men good –
Only, to let them live.

   (An anonymous Spitfire pilot)

For Johnny (written on the back of an envelope during the Blitz)

Do not despair
For Johnny-head-in-air;
He sleeps as sound
As Johnny underground.
Fetch out no shroud
For Johnny-in-the-cloud;
And keep your tears
For him in after years.
Better by far
For Johnny-the-bright-star,
To keep your head,
And see his children fed.

   (John Pudney)

Books

About the early days of flight, for Level 5 readers:
Flambards and *The Edge of the Cloud*, K M Peyton (Puffin)
Biggles (many titles), Capt W E Johns (Knight)
Going Solo, Roald Dahl (Puffin)

(page 9)

Amy Johnson

Obituary

MISS AMY JOHNSON

A GREAT AIRWOMAN

Miss Amy Johnson, C.B.E., whose death is now confirmed, will always be remembered as the first woman to fly alone from England to Australia. That flight took place in 1930 and her name at once became world-famous.

In the early days of the war she was employed in "ferrying" material to France for the R.A.F. Her cool courage, flying unarmed through the danger zone, was much admired by the R.A.F. pilots. Since that time she had flown a variety of aircraft many thousands of miles and she met her death while serving her country.

Amy Johnson was of Danish origin. Her grandfather, Anders Jörgensen, shipped to Hull when he was 16, settled there, changed his name to Johnson, and married a Yorkshire woman named Mary Holmes. One of their sons, the father of Amy, became a successful owner of Hull trawlers. Amy graduated B.A. at Sheffield University, and then went to London to learn to fly at the London Flying Club at Stag Lane, Edgware. After taking her "A" licence she passed the Air Ministry examination to qualify as a ground engineer. Before starting on her flight to Australia her only considerable experience of cross-country flying was one flight from London to Hull.

Having acquired a secondhand Moth with Gipsy engine, she started from Croydon on May 5, 1930, on an attempt to beat the light aeroplane record of 15½ days from England to Australia. Considering her lack of experience at that time as a navigator, it was a marvel that she found her way so well. She arrived safely at Darwin on May 24. Thence she flew to Brisbane, where, probably through her exhausted condition, she overshot the aerodrome and crashed her Moth rather badly. Australian National Airways Limited arranged for her to fly as a passenger in one of their machines to Sydney, and in the pilot of that machine she met her future husband, Mr. J. A. Mollison. She was accorded a great reception in Australia, and was received at Government House. King George V conferred on her the C.B.E. and the *Daily Mail* made her a present of £10,000. On her return to England she was met at Croydon by the Secretary of State for Air, the late Lord Thomson, in person.

In 1931 she made a fine flight to Tokyo across Siberia, and then back to England, and in 1932 she started off in another Puss Moth, Desert Cloud, to beat her husband's record to the Cape, which she did by nearly 10½ hours. The skill with which she crossed Africa proved that she had become a first-class pilot. In 1933 she and her husband acquired a D.H. Dragon aeroplane and set out to fly to New York. They successfully crossed the Atlantic, Newfoundland, Nova Scotia, Maine, and Massachusetts, but when they were approaching New York their petrol ran short and they therefore landed at Bridgeport, 60 miles short of New York, in the dark. The Dragon ran into a swamp and overturned. It was extensively damaged, and both of them were bruised and scratched. Her flight to the Cape and back in May, 1936, will rank as one of her greatest achievements. She beat the outward and the homeward records, the record for the double journey, and the capital to capital record. The Royal Aero Club conferred its gold medal upon her in October, 1936, in recognition of her Empire flights. Her book "Sky Roads of the World" was published in September, 1939.

Her marriage took place in 1932, but in 1936 she resumed her maiden name for the purposes of her career, and in 1938 the marriage was dissolved.

The Times, January 8, 1941

JOHNSON, Amy, C.B.E. 1930; B.A., A.R.Ae.S.I.; F.R.G.S.; F.S.E.; M.W.E.S.; aviator; e. d. of John William Johnson and Amy Johnson, Hull; m. 1932, J. A. Mollison (from whom she obtained a divorce, 1938). *Educ.*: Sheffield University (Degree in Economics). Commenced flying, Sept. 1928; took Pilot's A Licence at London Aeroplane Club; Engineer's Licence A (for rigging), C (for engines) also obtained; made an Associate of the Royal Aeronautical Society, April 1930, and a member of the Women's Engineering Society, May 1930; obtained Pilot's Commercial Licence in Australia, June 1930; first woman to fly alone from London to Australia, 1930, setting up a new record for a solo flight to India (Karachi in six days); flew to Japan and back, setting up records both ways, 1931; flew solo to Cape Town and back, making new records both ways, 1932; England to America non-stop via North Atlantic, with J. A. Mollison, in 39 hours, July 1933; President's gold medal from Society of Engineers, 1931; Egyptian gold medal for valour, 1930; International League of Aviators' Women's Trophy for 1930; Segrave Trophy for 1932; Holder (with J. A. Mollison) of present England-India record of 22 hours; regained London-Cape records in solo flight to Capetown via West Coast, and return via East Coast, 1936; Winner of Royal Aero Club's Gold Medal, 1936; President Women's Engineering Society, 1935-36-37; Member of Guild of Air Pilots and Navigators of the British Empire. *Publication*: Sky Roads of the World, 1939. *Recreations*: flying, riding, swimming. *Clubs*: Royal Aero, Forum (Pres. Technical Section). [*Died 5 Jan. 1941.*]

Who Was Who 1941–50

Thanks for the spin. Don't prang the bus.
Scribbling and rhyme? No dice, old scout!
But we were the chaps. Remember us.
Willco. Roger. Over. Out.

John Mole

9

Poem/Language (slang)

The Airman's Farewell
RAF **slang** (see Glossary): *What do you think the following words mean –* spin (ride); *prang* (crash); *bus* (vehicle); *no dice* (no chance); *willco* (end of call signal; I **will co**mply with instructions). *Do you use any slang words?* (e.g. words for 'good' and 'bad' etc.)

Reading for information/ Information sources

As well as encyclopaedias, local libraries have many other reference books and sources (e.g. newspapers on microfilm).

Who Was Who
From this extract what do you think the book Who Was Who *is for? What is the name of the current edition?* (Who's Who) *What sort of people would be listed? What sort of information does it give? etc.*

Obituary
What is an obituary? Which newspaper does this come from? What sort of attitude would an obituary take to its subject? Where does The Times *praise Amy Johnson? How is the information it gives different from that in* Who Was Who – *which contains more information? Which is more interesting to read?*

Writing: notes and prose
The *Who Was Who* extract is in **note form** (see Glossary) and the obituary is in formal connected **prose** (see Glossary).
What is the difference between notes and prose?

Writing
Class anthology
Pupils compile a 'Transport Who Was Who' about famous figures in the history of transport. Each pupil/pair chooses one figure; finds information from reference books, etc.; converts it into notes, arranged chronologically, modelled on the Amy Johnson entry.

Prose from notes
Pupils convert their own or someone else's notes into an obituary written in appropriate connected formal prose.

Class Who's Who
An alternative form of note-writing would be for pupils to compile their own entries for a class 'Who's Who'.

Wot go on at london airport? *(page 10)*

The extract is from *Back in the Jug Agane* by Geoffrey Willans and Ronald Searle, one of several Molesworth books now available as *The Compleet Molesworth* (Pavilion).

Reading/Written language

A group of pupils should split the passage up between them and prepare a presentation of it for the rest of the class. (Before this prepared presentation is given, it is worth asking all pupils to read part of the passage silently, and asking: *How does the incorrect spelling and punctuation affect your first attempts at reading the passage?*) Pupils should follow in their books as readers present the passage aloud.

Discussion: slang/ language

The boys of St Custard's have their own slang terms (see notes to page 9) for many things. Some of it is 1950s slang, some idiosyncratic. *What do you think the following mean?*

old h.b. (pencil)   blotch (blotting paper)
utterly wet (stupid)   our alma mater (their school)
new bug (new boy)   chiz
bungy (rubber)   jolly d.
yar boo sucks

*In what ways is Molesworth's prose **not** Standard English?*
(slang; spelling; punctuation; use of onomatopoeic non-words, e.g. ZOOOOOOOM!; use of figures for numbers; use of abbreviations; misuse of capital letters)

Reading/Comprehension/Interpretation

Questions for pupils to answer in writing (individually or in pairs) are given on **Worksheet 5a** (Section B).
Less experienced pupils will benefit from shared discussion of the text (see notes on next page) before attempting these questions.

During the 1950's, a team of boys from St Custard's School was sent to London Airport as part of a project on Transport, with instructions to find out "how it work, wot it do, ect." The story of the trip is told here by the inimitable Nigel Molesworth, self-styled "Curse of St Custard's".

ZOOOOOOOOOM!
    Two hours after leaving london the car which cary the st. custard's reporting team crawl past london airport, turn left, through the tunel and with a screech of brakes pull up at the door. 'Hullo planes, hullo passengers, hullo sky!' sa a gurly voice so you can guess that fotherington-tomas is here also peason, grabber, gillibrand and molesworth 2 it is no wonder the porters think we are bound for

belgrade and the guide who meet us make as if to run awa.
    'Wot go on here?' i rap, licking my old h.b. 'Tell us the whole story and make it snappy.'
    'You are "pasenger-processed".'
    This sound v. much like wot go on behind the bushes at st. custard's when a new bug hav been cheeky you kno we give him the works. But at the airport they just pass you through a chanel as they call it and, by the end, this is very much the same thing.
    'Imagine you are pasengers,' sa the guide. 'First you go up to this here desk (grammer) and hav tickets checked ect. Then yore baggage is put on a conveyor belt for the Customs, while you go up to the Concourse on a moving staircase to yore apropriate chanel. The grate thing about the system is that nothing can go wrong.'
    O-ho O-ho i think you are utterly wet if you think nothing can go wrong with st. custard's about you wate. As usual i am rite all the reporters zoom up the moving staircase then charge ta-ran-ta-rah down the other it is beter than the pleasure gardens and it is F R E E. It take the loudspeaker system to get them back.
    'WILL ALL BOYS ATACHED TO ST. CUSTARD'S *KINDLY* COLECT THEIR MARBLES AND PEASHOOTERS. TAKE LEAVE OF THEIR FRINDS AND PROCEED TO CHANNEL 6?'
    'Shan't,' sa molesworth 2.
    'WOT'S THAT? sa the loudspeaker, 'WILL ST. CUSTARD'S BOYS PROCEED TO CHANNEL 6 *IMMEDIATELY*.'

10

(page 11)

'Yar boo sucks.'

'LOOK 'ERE I DON'T WANT ANY MORE OF YORE LIP GET CRACKING OR ELSE.'

This, my dears, is language we can understand and it hav the desired effect. We asemble at the door where a beautiful A I R G U R L is standing she is absolutely fizzing more lovely even than prudence entwistle the under matron. My eyes pop and mouth open but all i can say is 'g . . . g . . . gug.'

'London airport,' sa the guide, 'process over 2 million passengers every year, in fakt, to be acurate last year it was 2,683,605.'*

'g . . . g . . . gug.'

'It can handle 30 planes an hour at peak period and over 119,000 each year. It is the busiest airport in the world in space. It hav 6 runways, the longest being number one which is 9,300 feet long.'

'g . . . g . . . gug.'

'Are you listening, boy?'

I come to with a start and take my eyes of the beautiful A I R G U R L. She hav a smile on her face can it be for me? Now gosh she is bending towards me can it be true? But wot do she sa? Her words are torture, e.g. 'You seme unhapy, little fellow. Do not cry for mummy she would not like that. Let me take you by the handy-pandy.'

And she do chiz chiz chiz chiz while all st. custards cheer. Well anybody who take *me* by the handy-pandy are taking a risk, they are never savoury hem-hem but i suppose

A I R G U R L S hav to be tuough. And so, hand in hand, the little toddler by her side, she lead the way into the C U S T O M S. i shall never live this down.

C U S T O M S ! brrh brrh it is like the cave in ali baba when the thieves come back quake quake wot will they do to you? and W O T is this? molesworth 2 hav come through on the moving belt with the bagage and they hav laid him on the counter. Well, if they make him declare wot is inside him i.e. 69 lickorice allsorts, 3 bubble gum, bits of bungy and 9 skool sossages they will get wot is coming to them. But i have not time to concentrate becos i am standing in front of a man who look like capt. hook in weedy peter pan and rap the counter with his hook.

'Hav you read this? Anything to declare? Come on, cough it up. We can tell when you are lying. No compasses, watches, bungy, blotch, cigs, bikes, magic lanterns, brownie No 0 or other dutiable goods? No cribs, woollen pants, white mice, caterpillers or doodle bugs?'

He glare at me and I meet his eye quake

'Come on, cough it up. We can tell when you are lying.'

11

Reading/Discussion/ Comprehension/ Interpretation

Molesworth refers to eight gallant souls in his party, but only five are named – who?

What sort of character is Fotherington-Tomas?

Why do you think their guide makes as if to run away?

What do the St Custard's boys do on the moving staircase?

What is the 'airgurl'?

What do you think an 'under matron' is? What is Molesworth's reaction to the airgurl? What is her reaction to him, and why do you think she reacts this way?

Where does she take them first? What are the customs men like? Where do they go next? What happens in Immigration?

What do you think has happened to the other six gallant men after Immigration?

Where does the airgurl finally take Molesworth and Fotherington-Tomas, and what happens to them there? etc.

Researching information

The 'London Airport' of the 1950s is now Heathrow, and there are several other airports in London. Up-to-date information (to contrast with that supplied by Molesworth's guide) can be found in BAA plc Airport Information booklets, from which an extract about Heathrow in 1991 is given on the next page. The booklets are obtainable from:

Public Affairs Department
D'albiac House
Heathrow Airport Ltd
Heathrow Airport
Hounslow
Middlesex TW6 1JH

Public Affairs Department
Gatwick Airport
PO Box 93
Gatwick
West Sussex RH6 ONH

Marketing and External Relations
Enterprise House
Stansted Airport Ltd
Stansted
Essex CM24 8QW

Standard English/ Punctuation/Spelling

Pupils, individually or in pairs, should attempt to render a few paragraphs of Molesworth's prose into correct Standard English. When corrections are complete, pupils should either:

- discuss their versions with teacher and class
- compare their versions with those of another pupil/pair, and amend as appropriate.

Worksheet 5d: Standard English

5d

This worksheet gives practice in recognising common examples of dialect grammars and converting them to Standard English equivalents. Some pupils may benefit from prior discussion of the Standard English form of the verb 'to be'.

quake i am about to confess when A I R G U R L sa: 'This little boy is v. sad for his mummy.' Thwarted he scribble rude things hem-hem in red chalk. 'Take him to Immigration.' S A V E D ! but at wot cost! Immigration is O.K. they just check yore crimes and look at yore passport and then you are through and free to wing away into the blue ect.

Here i check my men. Of eight gallant souls only 2 hav got through. e.g. me and fotherington-tomas. Weep hem-hem for the rest who have perished on the miserable journey which is the worst in the world.

Hist! but now wot is this? Still grasping my handy-pandy the A I R G U R L take me and fotherington-tomas to a door. She open it and take us through and wot grisly sight meet my tired eyes? It is a N U R S E R Y chiz chiz chiz chiz full of rocking horses and ickel pritty babies. On all sides are teddy bears and sea-saws 'O goody goody,' sa fotherington-tomas skipping weedily. 'Let us pla with the bears!' I turn to escape but the door hav closed. T R A P P E D ! Trapped with fotherington-tomas, a Nurse, 16 babies, 90 coloured balls, 56 teddy bears and a pedal car it is an uggly predicament.

There is only one course i shall hav to fite my way out. 'Listen,' i drawl, drawing a gat, 'the first baby that draw a bead on me gets plugged, see? I'm kinda hostile to babies and my finger mite slip on the trigger.'

W A M ! A mighty coloured ball which weigh 2 tons strike me on the nose and the party get ruough balls and teddy bears fly in all directions, a baby fly off the see-saw and strike his pritty locks on the ceiling and the N U R S E fante. Pausing only to shoot out the lights i make good my escape. Outside the guide is waiting.

'The London airport nursery service for children in transit is quite free. There children may be left in the care of a trained nurse and there are see-saws, shiny toys, teddy bears and baby's bottle can be quickly prepared.'

'G . . . g . . . gug.' I sa.

And so with this sobering thort we leave London Airport which is joly d. reely and and may be completely finished one day and return to the gloom and beetles of our alma mater chiz.

An extract from *Back In The Jug Agane* by Geoffrey Willans and Ronald Searle

". . . and return to the gloom . . ."

All the fakts are C O R E C T. They have been certified by the board of trade, ticked by Sigismund the Mad Maths Master and approved by the glassblowers union cheers.

12

Extract from Heathrow Airport Take-off Guide, Autumn 1991
Heathrow Airport Limited
Hounslow, Middlesex TW6 1JH
Telephone: (081) 759 4321 Telex: 934892 LHR LTD
Fax: (081) 745 4290   Open 24 hours

Heathrow is the world's premier international airport and the largest of London's four airports. In the year 1990/91 Heathrow handled 41.2 million passengers of which 34.1 million travelled on international routes and 7.1 million on domestic routes. The airport is used by over 80 airlines and is directly linked to over 200 destinations world-wide.

With its three runways and four passenger terminals, Heathrow Airport is situated 15 miles west of London. It has excellent motorway links and three underground stations connecting it with the capital.

NB There was no nursery at Heathrow in 1991.

Books
Hijacked, J M Marks (Puffin)
Thunder and Lightnings, Jan Mark (Puffin)

Refugees on the Train *(page 13)*

REFUGEES ON THE TRAIN

An extract from *The Silver Sword* by Ian Serraillier

THERE was still something left of the railway station at Posen, and the track had been mended. Of course there was no such thing as a time-table, but some trains – though much delayed – were getting through to Berlin, 250 miles to the west.

In one of these trains Ruth, Edek, Jan, and Bronia were travelling. It was crowded with refugees. They leaned from the windows, stood on the footboards, lay on the carriage roofs. Ruth's family was in one of the open trucks, which was cold but not quite so crowded.

'I don't like this truck,' said Bronia. 'It jolts too much.'

'Every jolt takes us nearer to Switzerland,' said Ruth. 'Think of it like that, and it's not so bad.'

'There's no room to stretch.'

'Rest your head against me and try and go to sleep. There, that's better.'

'It's a better truck than the other ones,' said Jan. 'It's got a stove in it. And we can scrape the coal dust off the floor. That's why I chose it. When it gets dark they'll light a fire and we shall keep warm.'

'The stove's right in the far corner. We shan't feel it from here,' said Bronia.

'Stop grumbling, Bronia,' said Ruth. 'We're lucky to be here at all. Hundreds of people were left behind at Posen – they may have to wait for weeks.'

'Edek was lucky to come at all,' said Jan. 'The doctor wanted to send him back to the Warthe camp, didn't he?'

'He said you wanted fattening up, as if you were a goose being fattened for Christmas,' laughed Bronia.

Ruth looked at her brother. Bunched up against the side of the truck, he was staring out at the fields as they swept by. It was over two and half years since she had last seen him. He was sixteen now, but did not look two and a half years older. So different from the Edek she remembered. His cheeks were pinched and hollow, his eyes as unnaturally bright as Jan's had once been, and he kept coughing. He looked as if he could go on lying there for ever, without stirring. Yet at the Warthe camp they had described him as wild.

She looked at Jan. Ruth could see that he was not entirely at ease with Edek yet. Did he resent his presence? There might be trouble here, for Edek must to some extent usurp the position that Jan had held, and Jan had a jealous nature.

She looked at Bronia. The child was asleep, her head in Ruth's lap, a smile on her face. Was she dreaming about the fairy-story that Ruth had been telling her, the one about the Princess of the Brazen Mountains? Perhaps in her dream

13

The extract is from *The Silver Sword* by Ian Serraillier (Puffin), which was first published in 1956. Serraillier's other book suitable for Level 5 readers, and featuring planes and espionage, is *There's No Escape* (Puffin).

Reading comprehension/ Writing in sentences

Questions about the extract for pupils to answer in writing are provided on **Worksheet 5a** (Section C).
These may be tackled either before or after shared reading and oral discussion of the passage, depending on how much support the particular group of pupils requires.

Reading aloud

A group of pupils should divide up the passage for prepared reading aloud, while the rest of the class follow in their books.

Oral discussion/Interpretation of the text

A map of Europe showing Posen, Berlin and Switzerland would be helpful.

Which three points in the first paragraph suggest that there has recently been a war in this area? What is a refugee? (Is there current coverage of refugees in the media?)

Where are the four children at the start of the extract? What is their immediate destination? What is their ultimate destination? Which sentence suggests that Ruth is the oldest of the children? During their first conversation, which child does not speak? Why do you think this is? What does this conversation tell you of the characters of Ruth/Bronia/Jan? What do we learn about from the conversation and subsequent paragraph? What do you think the Warthe camp was? What problem does Ruth foresee between Jan and Edek? (Ruth, Edek and Bronia are siblings, seeking their parents; Jan is an orphan found by Ruth amid the bombsites of Warsaw and 'adopted' during Edek's absence in Germany.) *Who and when were the Nazis? What facets of the refugees' stories suggest that there has been a war? How does Jan behave during Edek's story, and why do you think this is?*

What is a 'tall story'?

Spoken language/ Storytelling

Could each pupil 'earn a bed by the stove'?
Pupils think of a story they could tell in the family's situation – a fairy tale or folktale, a personal anecdote or tall story.
Discuss, e.g.:
What makes a good story/anecdote? Why are some stories boring? How long should a story be? etc.
Note the importance of familiarity with the story, fluency, timing and delivery of 'punchlines', etc.
Each pupil should jot down the main points of their story, and prepare and rehearse them before presentation to the class or group.

Bronia *was* the Princess, flying through the sky on her grey-blue wings. Then the Prince, who had searched for her seven long years, would be flying beside her, leading her to his mountain kingdom where they would live happily ever after. Fairy-stories always ended like that, and Ruth was happy to think that Bronia was still young enough to believe that it was the same in real life.

Ruth sighed. She leaned back, her head against the side of the truck, and dozed.

And the train, with its long stream of trucks and carriages all crammed to bursting-point with refugees, rattled and jolted on towards Berlin.

In the evening the train stopped and was shunted into a siding. Everyone got out to stretch his legs, but no one went far away in case it started again. As the night came on and it grew colder, they drifted back to their carriages and trucks. Coal dust was scraped from the floorboards and wood collected from outside, and the fire in Ruth's truck kindled. The refugees crowded round, stretching out their hands to the warmth.

It was the hour of the singer and the storyteller. While they all shared what little food they had, a young man sang and his wife accompanied him on the guitar. He sang of the storks that every spring fly back from Egypt to Poland's countryside, and of the villagers that welcome them by placing cart-wheels on the treetops and the chimney stacks for the storks to build their nests on. A printer from Cracow told the tale of Krakus who killed the dragon, and of Krakus's daughter who refused to marry a German prince. Others, laughing and making light of their experiences, told of miraculous escapes from the Nazis.

'I had a free ride on the roof of a Nazi lorry,' said one. 'It was eighty miles before I was seen. A sniper spotted me from the top of a railway bridge, but he couldn't shoot straight and I slid off into the bushes. The driver was so unnerved at the shooting that he drove slap into the bridge,

and that was the end of him.'

Another told of a long journey on the roof of a train.

'I can beat that for a yarn,' said Edek.

Everyone turned round to look at the boy slumped down at the back of the truck. It was the first time he had spoken.

'I'll tell you if you'll give me a peep at the fire,' he said. 'And my sisters, too. And Jan. We're freezing out here.'

Ungrudgingly they made a way for the family – the only children in the truck – to squeeze through to the stove. Ruth carried Bronia, who did not wake, and she snuggled down beside it. Jan sat on the other side, with his chin on his knees and his arms clasping them. Edek stood up, with his back to the side of the truck. When someone opened the stove to throw in a log, a shower of sparks leapt up, and for a few moments the flames lit up his pale features.

'I was caught smuggling cheese into Warsaw, and they sent me back to Germany to slave on the land,' he said. 'The farm was near Guben and the slaves came from all parts of Europe, women mostly and boys of my age. In winter we cut peat to manure the soil. We were at it all day from dawn to dark. In spring we did the sowing – cabbage crop, mostly. At harvest time we packed the plump white cabbage heads in crates and sent them into town. We lived on the outer leaves – they tasted bitter. I tried to run away, but they always fetched me back. Last winter, when the war turned against the Nazis and the muddles began, I succeeded. I hid under a train, under a cattle wagon, and lay on top of the axle with my arms and legs stretched out.'

'When the train started, you fell off,' said Jan.

'Afterwards I sometimes wished I had,' said Edek, 'that is, until I found Ruth and Bronia again. Somehow I managed to cling on and I got a free ride back to Poland.'

Jan laughed scornfully. 'Why don't you travel that way here? It would leave the rest of us more room.'

14

Discussion/Writing: refugees

Why do people become refugees? What would it be like to be a refugee? What problems would they have? How might they try to solve them?
What sorts of transport are available to refugees? What problems would there be?
Pupils imagine themselves into the person of a refugee in some historical/contemporary conflict (e.g. Israelites from Egypt, religious refugees throughout history, post Second World War, Boat People), and write about it in the first person.
Each should decide in advance of writing:
– from what they are escaping;
– their destination
– with whom they are travelling
– mode of transport
– problems
– possible solutions.
Preliminary discussion and rough drafting is essential for a piece of writing of this kind.
Writing could be in the form of:
• a short story
• a diary or letter
• a poem.

(page 15)

'I could never do that again,' said Edek.

'No,' said Jan, and he looked with contempt at Edek's thin arms and bony wrists. 'You're making it all up. There's no room to lie under a truck. Nothing to hold on to.'

Edek seized him by the ear and pulled him to his feet. 'Have you ever looked under a truck?' he said, and he described the underside in such convincing detail that nobody but Jan would have questioned his accuracy. The boys were coming to blows, when the printer pulled Jan to the floor and there were cries of, 'Let him get on with his story!'

'You would have been shaken off,' Jan shouted above the din, 'like a rotten plum!'

'That's what anyone would expect,' Edek shouted back. 'But if you'll shut up and listen, I'll tell you why I wasn't.' When the noise had died down, he went on. 'Lying on my stomach, I found the view rather monotonous. It made me dizzy too. I had to shut my eyes. And the bumping! Compared with that, the boards of this truck are like a feather bed. Then the train ran through a puddle. More than a puddle – it must have been a flood, for I was splashed and soaked right through. But that water saved me. After that I couldn't let go, even if I'd wanted to.'

'Why not?' said Jan, impressed.

'The water froze on me. It made an icicle of me. When at last the train drew into a station, I was encased in ice from head to foot. I could hear Polish voices on the platform. I knew we must have crossed the frontier. My voice was the only part of me that wasn't frozen, so I shouted. The station-master came and chopped me down with an axe. He wrapped me in blankets and carried me to the boiler-house to thaw out. Took me hours to thaw out.'

'You don't look properly thawed out yet,' said the printer, and he threw him a crust of bread.

Other voices joined in. 'Give him a blanket.' 'A tall story, but he's earned a bed by the stove.' 'Another story, somebody! One to make us forget.' 'Put some romance in it.'

The stories petered out after a while. When all was quiet, and the refugees, packed like sardines on the floor of the truck, lay sleeping under the cold stars, Ruth whispered to Edek, 'Was it really true?'

'Yes, it was true,' said Edek.

'Nothing like that must ever happen to you again,' said Ruth.

She reached for his hand – it was cold, although he was close to the stove – and she clasped it tight, as if she meant never to let go of it again.

15

Reading timetables
In happier times than those described in the story, successful railway travel depends upon the interpretation of timetables.

5e

Worksheet 5e
This includes a double page from a genuine railway timetable, which pupils must interpret in order to answer the questions at the end. Discussion with the teacher will be necessary before it is completed by individuals or pairs. Pupils may then devise further questions about the timetable to set for the rest of the group in an oral reading session.

Discussion: chunking for meaning
During reading of the passage, pupils will have paid attention to punctuation and layout in helping them to group words and ideas as the writer intended. This 'chunking' is done in three main ways:
- the basic unit of the **sentence** (delineated with a capital letter and a full stop);
- within sentences, chunking of groups of words is done by use of commas (see notes to page 5 and Worksheet 5b);
- sentences themselves are chunked by the way they are grouped into paragraphs (see notes to Book 4 page 34 and Worksheet 4j).

How does the author show how language is chunked for meaning by means of his punctuation and layout? What makes a sentence? When should we use commas? When should we give a new paragraph? etc.

5f

Worksheet 5f: Chunking for meaning
A passage containing a famous 'tall story', without punctuation or paragraphing, is provided on Worksheet 5f for editing by pupils, in pairs or individually. It could also be transferred onto a word-processor for editing.

Short story
Classic short story for Level 5 readers: 'Spit Nolan' in *The Goalkeeper's Revenge*, Bill Naughton (Puffin)

119

Night Mail

Background
This poem was originally written to accompany a 1936 promotional film for the General Post Office (directed by Edgar Anstey, now available on video). Wystan Hugh Auden (1907–1973) was a left-wing British poet, who emigrated to the USA before the Second World War and became an American citizen. He later returned to Europe and was briefly Poet Laureate.

Reading aloud/ Expression
The group of pupils preparing this poem for reading aloud will require support from the teacher.

Reading/ Comprehension/ Interpretation
Divide up those words of which pupils may be uncertain for individuals to check in the dictionary and report back, e.g.: postal order; gradient; apparatus; furnaces; receipted bills; applications for situations; circumstantial; financial; letters of condolence.

Where is the Night Mail going? Which border is it crossing? What do you think Beattock is? What sort of place is Glasgow? What do you imagine each of the various letters described would look like?
What do you imagine Edinburgh and Aberdeen would be like from the adjectives Auden gives them? etc.

NIGHT MAIL

I

This is the night mail crossing the Border,
Bringing the cheque and the postal order,

Letters for the rich, letters for the poor,
The shop at the corner, the girl next door.

Pulling up Beattock, a steady climb:
The gradient's against her, but she's on time.

Past cotton-grass and moorland boulder,
Shovelling white steam over her shoulder,

Snorting noisily as she passes
Silent miles of wind bent grasses.

Birds turn their heads as she approaches,
Stare from bushes at her blank-faced coaches.

Sheep-dogs cannot turn her course;
They slumber on with paws across.

In the farm she passes no one wakes,
But a jug in a bedroom gently shakes.

II

Dawn freshens, her climb is done.
Down towards Glasgow she descends,
Towards the steam tugs yelping down a glade
    of cranes,
Towards the fields of apparatus, the furnaces
Set on the dark plain like gigantic chessmen.
All Scotland waits for her:
In dark glens, beside pale-green lochs,
Men long for news.

16

Poetry/Rhythm and rhyme/Choral presentation
How does the rhythm of this poem reflect the movement of a train? Pupils might try tapping out the rhythm as they read the poem silently. Other poems creating the same effect can be found in Book 4, pages 18–19. *Which sections of the poem do you think don't sound like a train?* Split the class into choral reading groups (of up to 8 pupils) and divide the 'train-sections' between the groups, one or two lines at a time. Some lines are suitable for mass choral reading. Sections 2 and 4 may be more suitable for individual voices.
The class could rehearse a choral performance for presentation to an audience or for recording on tape.

(page 17)

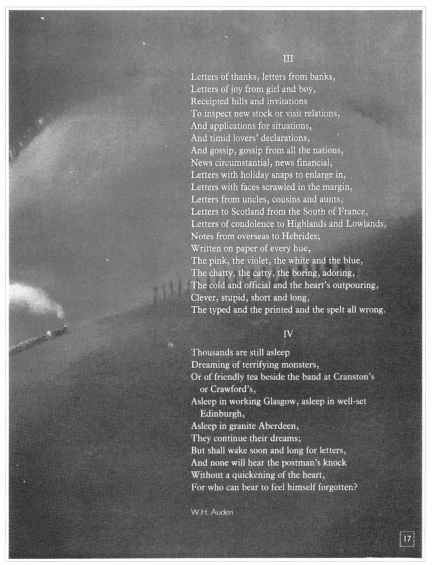

III

Letters of thanks, letters from banks,
Letters of joy from girl and boy,
Receipted bills and invitations
To inspect new stock or visit relations,
And applications for situations,
And timid lovers' declarations,
And gossip, gossip from all the nations,
News circumstantial, news financial,
Letters with holiday snaps to enlarge in,
Letters with faces scrawled in the margin,
Letters from uncles, cousins and aunts,
Letters to Scotland from the South of France,
Letters of condolence to Highlands and Lowlands,
Notes from overseas to Hebrides;
Written on paper of every hue,
The pink, the violet, the white and the blue,
The chatty, the catty, the boring, adoring,
The cold and official and the heart's outpouring,
Clever, stupid, short and long,
The typed and the printed and the spelt all wrong.

IV

Thousands are still asleep
Dreaming of terrifying monsters,
Or of friendly tea beside the band at Cranston's
  or Crawford's,
Asleep in working Glasgow, asleep in well-set
  Edinburgh,
Asleep in granite Aberdeen,
They continue their dreams;
But shall wake soon and long for letters,
And none will hear the postman's knock
Without a quickening of the heart,
For who can bear to feel himself forgotten?

W.H. Auden

17

Writing/Letters

Pupils could each choose one of the letters mentioned, research/ discuss the type of style/ format/language/contents and write their own versions for a class display (on paper of every hue).

Book

For Level 5 readers:
The Railway Children,
E Nesbit (Puffin)

Poems

Further poems about trains and railways:

A Train At Night

The frantic throb of the train
As we drop through the night,
The Night, a big black stain
Against my helpless sight,
Sets my heart also throbbing with pain
With the pain of its flight.

Like a lonely star dropping through space
To extinction rushing –
Towns, constellations, race
Past, and we're brushing
A brilliant station, the chase
Through ever onward night pushing.

(D H Lawrence, 1885–1930)

Also 'Skimbleshanks: The Railway Cat' in
Old Possum's Book of Practical Cats, T S
Eliot (Faber).
See also, Book 4 pages 18-19.

Adlestrop

Yes, I remember Adlestrop –
The name, because one afternoon
Of heat the express-train drew up there
Unwontedly. It was late June.

The steam hissed. Someone cleared his throat.
No one left and no one came
On the bare platform. What I saw
Was Adlestrop – only the name,

And willows, willow-herb, and grass,
And meadowsweet, and haycocks dry,
No whit less still and lonely fair
Than the high cloudlets in the sky.

And for that minute a blackbird sang
Close by, and round him, mistier,
Farther and farther, all the birds
Of Oxfordshire and Gloucestershire.

(Edward Thomas, 1878–1917)

Short Trips

Reading/Group work

Split the verses up between pupils in pairs, so that each pair can prepare a few for presentation to the class.

Discussion: language/poetry

Which of the verses do you think is the cleverest? the funniest? Which do you like/dislike most? In each case, why?
What do the following words mean: paradox; ennui; relativity?
Once pupils fully understand the poems, how does it affect their opinions/preferences?

Limericks

Two of the poems are limericks – which are they?

An old verse form, used e.g. by Shakespeare – acquired the name limerick after the town in Ireland, where soldiers used to sing humorous limerick songs. The making up of songs became a Victorian parlour game, and the form was then popularised by Edward Lear.

Rhyme schemes

What is the rhyme scheme of a limerick? (A, A, B, B, A) Using the same notation, work out the rhyme schemes of the other poems here. (The other two rhyming poems are both quatrains.)

'Knock knock' jokes

How many of these related to transport can pupils collect?

Poetry: learning by heart

After discussion, can any pupil close the book and recite any of the verses from memory? Given five minutes, how many of the verses can they commit to memory? *Which are the easiest/hardest verses to memorise? Why should this be?*

Some things will never change although
We tour out to the stars;
Arriving on the moon we'll find
Our luggage sent to Mars!

June Brady

The art of good driving's a paradox quite,
Though custom has proved it so long;
If you go to the left, you're sure to go right,
If you go to the right, you go wrong.

Anon

There was a young fellow called Bright
Who travelled much faster than light.
He set off one day
In a relative way
And returned on the previous night.

Anon

Space Joke?

'Knock knock' said the Astronaut.
'Who's there?' said the Alien.
'A Human Being' said the Astronaut.
'A Human being what?' said the Alien.

Julie Holder

There was a young man of the Tyne,
Put his head on the South-Eastern line;
But he died of *ennui*,
For the 5.53
Didn't run till a quarter past nine.

Anon

Writing: limericks and quatrains

Pupils could try their own mini-poems using these verse forms, preferably on transport themes. It is helpful to collect suitable rhyming words related to the topic before attempting to put a poem together.

Book

For Level 5 pupils on the subject of relativity:
The Time and Space of Uncle Albert, Russell Stannard (Faber)

Sad Story of a Motor Fan *(page 19)*

Sad Story of a Motor Fan

Young Ethelred was only three
Or somewhere thereabouts, when he
Began to show in divers ways
The early stages of the craze
For learning the particulars
Of motor-bikes and motor-cars.
He started with a little book
To enter numbers which he took
And, though his mother often said,
"Now, do be careful, Ethelred;
Oh, dear! oh, dear! what shall I do
If anything runs over you?"
(Which Ethelred could hardly know,
And sometimes crossly told her so),
It didn't check his zeal a bit,
But rather seemed to foster it;
Indeed it would astonish you
To hear of all the things he knew.
He guessed the make (and got it right)
Of every car that came in sight,
And knew as well its m.p.g.,
Its m.p.h. and £.s.d.,
What gears it had, what brakes, and what –
In short he knew an awful lot.

Now, when a boy thinks day and night
Of motor-cars with all his might
He gets affected in the head,
And so it was with Ethelred.
He called himself a "Packford Eight"
And wore a little number-plate
Attached behind with bits of string,
And cranked himself like anything,
And buzzed and rumbled ever so
Before he got himself to go.

He went about on all his fours,
And usually, to get indoors,
He pressed a button, then reversed,
And went in slowly, backmost first.
He took long drinks from mug and cup
To fill his radiator up
Before he started out for school
("It kept," he said, "his engine cool");
And when he got to school he tried
To park himself all day outside,
At which the Head became irate
And caned him on his number-plate.

So week by week he grew more like
A motor-car or motor-bike,
Until one day an oily smell
Hung round him, and he wasn't well.
"That's odd," he said; "I wonder what
Has caused the sudden pains I've got.
No motor gets an aching tum
Through taking in petroleum."
With that he cranked himself, but no,
He couldn't get himself to go,
But merely buzzed a bit inside,
Then gave a faint chug-chug and died.
Now, since his petrol-tank was full,
They labelled him "Inflammable",
And wisely saw to it that he
Was buried safely out at sea.
So, if at any time your fish
Should taste a trifle oilyish,
You'll know that fish has lately fed
On what remains of Ethelred.

H. A. Field

`19`

Reading poetry

A pupil/pair of pupils should prepare this poem for reading aloud while the rest of the group follow in their books.

The poem is later suitable for dramatisation – one pupil reading/reciting, while others take the parts of Ethelred, his mother and headmaster, miming and saying the relevant lines.

Discussion

For example: *What are/were m. p. g.; m. p. h.; l. s. d., and what would be their modern equivalents? At what point did Ethelred's behaviour become peculiar? What caused his death? Why was he buried at sea? etc. The poem is what is known as a 'cautionary tale' – what do you think this means? What is the rhyme scheme of this poem?*

Further cautionary verse
Selected Cautionary Verses, Hilaire Belloc (Puffin Classics)

Book
For Level 5 readers:
Chitty Chitty Bang Bang, Ian Fleming (Cape)

Petrol for Sale

The following pages are intended:
• as discussion material for:
  looking at language – investigating techniques of language use in advertising;
  looking at advertising – alerting pupils as consumers to the techniques used to influence them;
• then as a model for pupils' own attempts to devise a marketing and advertising campaign.

Discussion: marketing

Why do you think Esso chose a tiger for its symbol? How did the tiger's image change from the 1960s to the 1990s? Why? What slogan did the 1960s ad use? What about the 1990s ad? To what emotions/attitudes/beliefs were the two different adverts trying to appeal?
Other aspects of marketing to consider are:
brand name (Esso = SO = Standard Oil); logo; design/display at garages. What do pupils know about Esso's current image and display?
Which names have other petrol manufacturers chosen for their products? Can you think why in each case? What is the logo for each? The main elements of design/display? The thrust of current advertising campaigns? etc.

PETROL for SALE

Petrol companies, like most businesses with something to sell, are anxious to create the right image for their products. For about thirty years, the Esso tiger has helped to create Esso's image – although he has changed a lot over time, as these advertisements from the 1960s and 1990s demonstrate.

PUT A TIGER IN YOUR TANK
NEW ESSO EXTRA
...FOR QUICK STARTING

20

Group work/Spoken language: creating an image

In small groups, pupils invent their own brand of petrol and choose a marketing strategy (speed? convenience? greenness? family orientation? elitism?). Each designs a marketing campaign:
• deciding on an image;
• devising a name;
• designing logo/symbol;
• choosing a style/approach for an advertising campaign.
The groups can report back later to the class on what was decided and why.

Further information

Further information on advertising from:
The Office of Fair Trading, Room 500, Chancery House, Chancery Lane, London WC2A 1SP (071 242 2858)
Advertising Standards Authority, Brook House, 2–16 Torrington Place, London WC1E 7HN (071 580 5555)

Will life go more smoothly with unleaded petrol?

We live on a vulnerable planet. We must learn how to care for it.

During the next few weeks, many people in Britain will see the Esso Unleaded Airship taking to the air.

It is our way of drawing the motorist's attention to the environmental benefits of unleaded petrol.

Three years ago, Esso was the first oil company in Britain to provide unleaded petrol at service stations.

Today, it is increasingly available at Esso sites throughout the country.

We are planning ahead to develop the quality fuels of the future which will contribute still further towards improved environmental performance.

We intend to play our full part in improving the quality of the environment, whilst supplying the energy needs of future generations.

Esso Caring for tomorrow's quality of life.

21

Discussion: The language of advertising

If possible, collect examples of current petrol advertising campaigns (magazine ads; videos of TV ads) to analyse as below, along with the examples given. **Slogans and catchphrases** often rely on **alliteration** (see Glossary), **puns** (see Glossary to Book 4) or emotive 'buzz words' (e.g. caring).

Find these language techniques in the examples. Think of other examples in current advertising campaigns (not necessarily for petrol).

Emotive words often use **onomatopoeia** (see Glossary).

Think of some onomatopoeic words connected with motor transport.

The written information accompanying advertisements is known as 'copy'.

To what extent do you think people read copy? How can you attract their attention to it/persuade them to read it? What facets are important in its presentation? Is the copy in the example effective?

Music and advertising

Which current jingles do you know? What makes a good jingle? (Esso's jingle 'The Esso sign means happy motoring . . . Call at the Esso sign' was once set to the Toreador theme from 'Carmen'. Classical music in TV advertising includes: Greig's 'Morning' (Nescafé); Orff's 'Carmina Burana' (Old Spice); Bach's 'Air on a G String' from 'Suite no. 3' (Hamlet cigars). These and others are available on a tape TQ204 from Coombe Music International (1988).)

Popular songs are also used, some of which (like the Coca-Cola songs) are written for the advertisement and released in an amended form for the pop market.

Group work/Language

Designing an advertisement

Pupils collect 'good' words to associate with their product; look for rhyme, alliteration, onomatopoeia; devise ways of writing the brand names and key words to convey their meaning (e.g. use shape, colour, style); devise slogans or catchphrases to associate with their product; produce posters with illustrations and accompanying 'advertising copy'.

Pupils transform their slogans into jingles, by devising their own tunes, using tunes from classical or modern music.

Other products associated with transport which pupils might 'invent and market': airlines; ferry companies; railway companies; bicycles etc.

The Responsible Traveller's Charter *(page 22)*

Reading/Discussion

Who produced the leaflet shown here? What do you think this organisation is and how would it want to influence you? (It is a sort of 'green' AA.)
What arguments are given for using cars less? What do you think the people who wrote the Esso advertisements on pages 20–21 would say to these arguments? Which point of view do you agree with, and why? etc.

Research/Letter writing

Literature on the issue of transport and the environment is available from many agencies, e.g.:

The green lobby

Many leaflets available from:
The Environmental Transport Association
The Old Post House
Heath Road
Weybridge
Dorset KT13 8RS
(0932 828882)

Friends of the Earth
26–28 Underwood Street
London N1 7QJ
(071 253 4237)

Transport 2000
10 Melton Street
London NW1 2EJ
(071 388 8386)

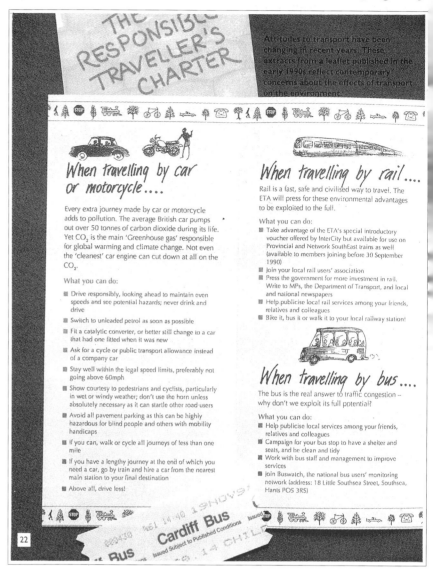

THE RESPONSIBLE TRAVELLER'S CHARTER

Attitudes to transport have been changing in recent years. These extracts from a leaflet published in the early 1990s reflect contemporary concerns about the effects of transport on the environment.

When travelling by car or motorcycle....

Every extra journey made by car or motorcycle adds to pollution. The average British car pumps out over 50 tonnes of carbon dioxide during its life. Yet CO_2 is the main 'Greenhouse gas' responsible for global warming and climate change. Not even the 'cleanest' car engine can cut down at all on the CO_2.

What you can do:

■ Drive responsibly, looking ahead to maintain even speeds and see potential hazards; never drink and drive
■ Switch to unleaded petrol as soon as possible
■ Fit a catalytic converter, or better still change to a car that had one fitted when it was new
■ Ask for a cycle or public transport allowance instead of a company car
■ Stay well within the legal speed limits, preferably not going above 60mph
■ Show courtesy to pedestrians and cyclists, particularly in wet or windy weather; don't use the horn unless absolutely necessary as it can startle other road-users
■ Avoid all pavement parking as this can be highly hazardous for blind people and others with mobility handicaps
■ If you can, walk or cycle all journeys of less than one mile
■ If you have a lengthy journey at the end of which you need a car, go by train and hire a car from the nearest main station to your final destination
■ Above all, drive less!

When travelling by rail....

Rail is a fast, safe and civilised way to travel. The ETA will press for these environmental advantages to be exploited to the full.

What you can do:

■ Take advantage of the ETA's special introductory voucher offered by InterCity but available for use on Provincial and Network SouthEast trains as well (available to members joining before 30 September 1990)
■ Join your local rail users' association
■ Press the government for more investment in rail. Write to MPs, the Department of Transport, and local and national newspapers
■ Help publicise local rail services among your friends, relatives and colleagues
■ Bike it, bus it or walk it to your local railway station!

When travelling by bus....

The bus is the real answer to traffic congestion – why don't we exploit its full potential?

What you can do:

■ Help publicise local services among your friends, relatives and colleagues
■ Campaign for your bus stop to have a shelter and seats, and be clean and tidy
■ Work with bus staff and management to improve services
■ Join Buswatch, the national bus users' monitoring network (address: 18 Little Southsea Street, Southsea, Hants PO5 3RS)

The motoring/petroleum lobby

Automobile Association	Group Public Affairs	Mail point 512
PO Box 50	Shell Group	Public Affairs
Basingstoke	Shell International Petroleum Co.	Esso UK plc
Hants RG21 2ED	Shell Centre	Esso House
(0256 20123)	London SE1 7NA	Victoria Street
		London SW1E 5JW

Pupils could write to these and other relevant agencies for current material on the subject of motoring and the environment.

(page 23)

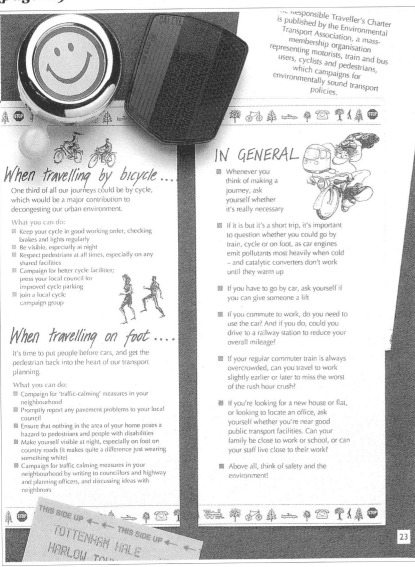

The Responsible Traveller's Charter is published by the Environmental Transport Association, a mass-membership organisation representing motorists, train and bus users, cyclists and pedestrians, which campaigns for environmentally sound transport policies.

When travelling by bicycle ....

One third of all our journeys could be by cycle, which would be a major contribution to decongesting our urban environment.

What you can do:
- Keep your cycle in good working order, checking brakes and lights regularly
- Be visible, especially at night
- Respect pedestrians at all times, especially on any shared facilities
- Campaign for better cycle facilities; press your local council for improved cycle parking
- Join a local cycle campaign group

When travelling on foot ....

It's time to put people before cars, and get the pedestrian back into the heart of our transport planning.

What you can do:
- Campaign for 'traffic-calming' measures in your neighbourhood
- Promptly report any pavement problems to your local council
- Ensure that nothing in the area of your home poses a hazard to pedestrians and people with disabilities
- Make yourself visible at night, especially on foot on country roads (it makes quite a difference just wearing something white)
- Campaign for traffic calming measures in your neighbourhood by writing to councillors and highway and planning officers, and discussing ideas with neighbours

IN GENERAL

- Whenever you think of making a journey, ask yourself whether it's really necessary

- If it is but it's a short trip, it's important to question whether you could go by train, cycle or on foot, as car engines emit pollutants most heavily when cold – and catalytic converters don't work until they warm up

- If you have to go by car, ask yourself if you can give someone a lift

- If you commute to work, do you need to use the car? And if you do, could you drive to a railway station to reduce your overall mileage?

- If your regular commuter train is always overcrowded, can you travel to work slightly earlier or later to miss the worst of the rush hour crush?

- If you're looking for a new house or flat, or looking to locate an office, ask yourself whether you're near good public transport facilities. Can your family be close to work or school, or can your staff live close to their work?

- Above all, think of safety and the environment!

23

Research/Debate

'This house believes that motor cars should be banned.' If, once pupils have become more informed on the subject, feelings about motoring and the environment run high, a formal debate might be organised. Explain vocabulary and procedure of a debate:
The **chairman** invites:
- a speech from the **proposer** in favour of **the motion**;
- a speech from the **speaker for the opposition** against the motion;
- a speech from the **seconder** of the motion;
- a speech from the **seconder** of the opposition;
- the chairman throws the debate **open to the floor**;
- the proposer **sums up** arguments for the motion;
- the opposing speaker **sums up** arguments against the motion;
- the chairman **puts the motion to the vote** and it is **carried** or **defeated.**

Fact and opinion
What is a fact? (see Glossary)
What is opinion? (see Glossary)
What is the difference between them? Might an opinion be a fact too? How can you tell the difference between fact and opinion? (e.g. Is there any proof? Might any reasonable person disagree with the premise?)

Worksheet 5g
This gives practice in identifying fact and opinion. Pupils might attempt it individually or in pairs.

5g

Discussion: for and against motoring
(This discussion will be more fruitful if pupils have obtained up-to-date material from the agencies listed opposite, or current advertising campaigns.)
Pupils should identify some points which they think are **facts** and some they believe are **opinions** in the advertisements and leaflets about road transport on pages 20–23 (and those they have collected).
Why do you believe that these points are fact/opinion? Do you agree with the opinions? Why/why not?
Is there any material which you consider **propaganda?** (see Glossary) etc.

Haikus on the road

Poetry/Language

All the verses are **haiku** (see Glossary). Pupils should count the **syllables** (see Glossary) in each line. *The poet has added the additional discipline of rhyme (which is not usually a feature of haiku).*
What is his rhyme scheme?
Can pupils find examples of the following (all defined in the Glossary)?

'Hiker's Haiku'
alliteration (slow steps; footpaths/fields)

'Biker's Haiku'
onomatopoeia (sizzling)
simile ('knees twiddling like thumbs', 'like an angry cat')
metaphor ('a silver carrot')

Punctuation

Attention to punctuation is very important in preparing short poems of this kind for reading aloud. The **comma** is used to chunk words together to convey the sense, as does the dash – a more abrupt separation of two ideas.
The **semi-colon** (;) is used for a more significant break (like a more powerful comma).
The **colon** (:) is the 'equals sign' of punctuation, suggesting some degree of balance between the information carried before and after it.

Reading aloud

Each pupil should prepare a reading of one haiku, to give maximum effect.

Haikus on the Road

Hiker's Haiku

i
This is the best way
To travel: on your two feet
Fuelled by bread and meat.

ii
On footpaths, through fields
Of daisies, cowslips, clear streams,
Alone with your dreams.

iii
Far from motorway's
Incessant roar, dust and stink –
Slow steps, time to think.

iv
Inhaling pure air
Seasoned with birdsong, green scent
No one could invent.

v
Quiet happiness,
Moving thoughtful, calm and slow;
The best way to go.

Biker's Haiku

i
The keen cyclist comes
Down country roads, helmeted,
Knees twiddling like thumbs.

ii
He crouches, his back
Arched above the sizzling wheels,
Like an angry cat.

iii
Unseen, they flow past –
Hedgerows, trees on a green breeze;
He is going too fast.

iv
Not even a glance
Can he spare, dreaming only
Of the *Tour de France;*

v
Tantalizing sight,
It shines, a silver carrot
He will never bite.

Vernon Scannell

24

Writing poems/haiku

Pupils choose a type or aspect of transport about which to compose a poem and brainstorm:
- onomatopoeic words on the subject;
- possibilities for alliteration;
- similes/metaphors.

These could be used as starting points for haiku (or other verse forms, if preferred).

Spelling: syllables

Writing haiku sensitises pupils to syllables. This may be capitalised upon when teaching spelling. Ask pupils to find examples of 1/2/3/4/5/6 syllable words, and break words into syllables with oblique lines, e.g. mul/ti/pli/ca/tion. Every syllable will contain a vowel (or y). Use syllabification to break down long spelling words.

Books

About bikes and motorbikes for Level 5+ readers:
Bike Run, Diane Wilmer (Lions)
The Freedom Machine, Joan Lingard (Puffin)
Handles, Jan Mark (Puffin)
Collision Course, Nigel Hinton (Puffin)

Transport Research Project *(page 25)*

The picture story provides a model of a Level 5 research project, showing the processes involved at each stage.

It is intended as the focus of discussion for pupils and teacher, preparing pupils to conduct their own small research projects on aspects of the Transport topic.

The picture story should never be used as a substitute for pupils' individual research work. However, where pupils are new to this kind of work, teachers may wish them to work through Steve's project or parts of it (e.g. looking up the subject of 'jet planes' along the guidelines Steve devises; taking notes from books according to his plan; writing up a page of project from Steve's notes). Such guided, structured work would help prepare pupils to work independently later.

Overview

Read through the entire picture story first with the class to familiarise them with the process as a whole. One pupil should read the narration, and others take the parts of Steve and Mr Uttley.

Then re-read the story, discussing each frame.

Discussion
Title: What is research?

Frames 1 and 2

It is difficult to make adequate book provision for all the pupils in a class to engage in research at once. For a class of around 35 pupils, at least 45 appropriate books are needed. This includes multiple copies where possible of particularly useful books. The local Schools Library Service, given notice, will usually supply a 'project box' which can be added to books from the school's own library, the local children's library, other resource centres, teachers and pupils in the school. Cataloguing and record-keeping are then essential, and a useful experience in itself, drawing attention to titles/authors, etc. We recommend that the books used by Steve in his project are supplied as part of the project collection: details on page 132.

Frames 3 and 4

Pupils often want to start making a project book immediately, before they have had time to read around the subject or reflect about it. This tends to lead to copying verbatim from books, and should be avoided. A period of browsing is essential to allow pupils to select a subject area for study and build up a basic framework of knowledge about it. *What other subject areas might someone study in a transport project?*

Frames 1 and 2

Pupils should be encouraged to consult simple books, to look at pictures and read captions and short passages on their chosen subject. This helps them develop the vocabulary and concepts required to understand more difficult material.

Considerable reading is usually required before pupils are familiar enough with the subject to work out the main areas they will have to cover in their research.

The use of an index is covered in Book 3, page 21 and Worksheet 3h; and further indexing skills in Book 4, page 8 and Worksheet 4d.

Frames 3 and 4

The framing of suitable questions about a project is difficult, and even at this stage many pupils will require assistance in developing their questions. However, once questions are decided they provide a coherent framework for research-reading and note-taking, and can therefore become **section headings** for the pupil's own work.

Why does Steve have to think up questions? What questions might you ask about e.g. steam locomotion/motorcars/the bicycle/sailing clippers?

Adequate space is needed for notes under each headings. Steve's three pages are due to constraints of space within the picture story: a page per heading is more appropriate.

Do you think Steve has left enough space for his notes?

TAKING NOTES

We had a poster to remind us about the rules for note-taking.

RULES FOR NOTE-TAKING

1. Just key words – not sentences.

2. Neatness not important.

3. Where poss. use short ways of writing things –
   initials, e.g. U.K. U.S.A.
   short forms, e.g. km/h, sub.
   symbols, e.g. &, –, %, ditto marks

4. Leave plenty of space – to add notes later.

5. Use arrows, etc. to show connections.

6. Use diagrams/pics. – sometimes easier than writing explanations. Labels v. important.

I went back to the books on jets, starting with the easiest ones. I noted down points which answered my questions. The facts ended up in a different order from the way they were written in the books but Mr Uttley said that was a good thing.

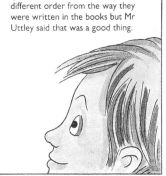

This is how my note papers looked after I'd finished making notes from the first book.

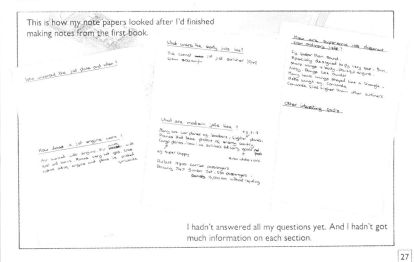

I hadn't answered all my questions yet. And I hadn't got much information on each section.

27

Frame 1: note-taking

These rules should be discussed at length, e.g.:

What are key words? Why don't you need to write sentences?
What is 'poss' short for? What other short forms of words might you use?
What are ditto marks?
What sort of diagrams might you draw? When might a quick picture be better than words? Why are labels on pictures so important?
This poster is in note form – what aspects of note-taking does it demonstrate?

A similar wall-poster should be provided for pupils' ready reference.

Frame 2

Note-taking under headings forces pupils to reorganise the information they find in books, a process which many find inhibiting (hence verbatim copying).

Frame 3: early notes

This is an illustration of Steve's first attempts at following the note-taking rules.

How well has Steve taken his notes? What note-taking strategies has he used?

Frame 1: consulting many sources

Stress that research involves consulting a variety of resources:

a) The information provided in a book is not always correct. The accuracy of statements may be affected by, e.g.:
  - the age of the book (check copyright details);
  - the interests, experience and opinions of the author;
  - the level of difficulty at which information is tackled.
  Consulting a number of sources helps check facts.

b) Pupils' understanding of a topic will develop through encountering similar information expressed from a variety of viewpoints.

c) Different books include more or less information on different aspects of the topic.

See Glossary for definition of 'Bibliography'.

Do any books in the project collection have bibliographies? How might a bibliography be useful to a reader? etc.

Frame 2: finished notes

Steve's notes now reflect the extent of his reading:

How long do you think it took Steve to collect these notes? Are there many words you don't understand? What should you do if you find yourself writing a word you don't understand in your own notes?

How can you tell that he wasn't being very careful about handwriting and spelling? Does it matter? How has he used arrows in the notes?

Books

Main books used by Steve in his research project:

Eyewitness: Flying Machines (Dorling Kindersley)
Jets (Usborne)
Look it up: Flying (Macmillan)
Let's Look at Aircraft (Wayland)
Things That Fly (Usborne)

(page 29)

In the end, I even went to the local library in town, to check out the encyclopedias.

JUNIOR REFERENCE LIBRARY

While I was there, I had a look at a hard book, written for adults. I was really surprised that I could understand most of what it said about jets. I wouldn't have understood it before starting my project!

ADULT NON-FICTION

WRITING UP

The last thing was to write up my project. This was when I got jealous of the people in my class who'd been allowed to make notes on the computer. They could easily expand the notes into sentences.

I had to write it all out in neat handwriting!

29

Frame 1: consulting a library
Library skills are covered in Book 4, pages 7–9. An opportunity to visit the local library might be arranged at a suitable point in the pupils' research, to benefit from the use of encyclopaedias and, possibly, the adult library.

Frame 2: difficult books
Once vocabulary and concepts about the topic are firmly established through work on easier books, and research-reading skills have also been well practised, pupils' reading level in non-fiction material is often surprisingly high.

Frames 3 and 4: writing up a project
All pupils should at some time have the opportunity to make notes on a word-processor and expand these into sentences. This process involves a number of further linguistic and Information Technology skills.

The handwriting of final projects is time-consuming and requires great concentration. It is often best tackled over a period of time, in short bursts.

Final frames

Mr Uttley's advice to Steve is important. Pupils may now be so well informed on their particular subject that they are not explicit enough in their writing up, assuming a similar degree of knowledge on the part of their readers.

The potential audience (the rest of the class if project books are to be put into the library), should be stressed, and help given in achieving the right degree of explicitness in the first paragraphs.

Is Steve's first paragraph clear enough? Which parts of his notes does it cover? Does he explain the meaning of any difficult words? etc.

If the browsing and note-taking processes have been successful, the pupils' final project should be in his/her own words and organised according to his/her own intentions.

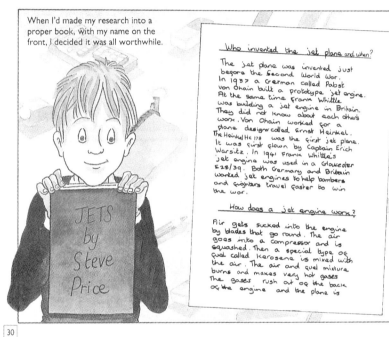

TRANSPORT BOOK 5 TRANSPORT BOOK 5 TRANSPORT BOOK 5 TRANSPORT

Sea Views *(page 31)*

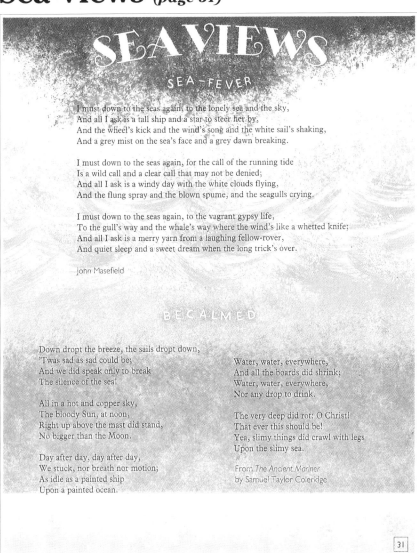

SEA VIEWS

SEA-FEVER

I must down to the seas again, to the lonely sea and the sky,
And all I ask is a tall ship and a star to steer her by,
And the wheel's kick and the wind's song and the white sail's shaking,
And a grey mist on the sea's face and a grey dawn breaking.

I must down to the seas again, for the call of the running tide
Is a wild call and a clear call that may not be denied;
And all I ask is a windy day with the white clouds flying,
And the flung spray and the blown spume, and the seagulls crying.

I must down to the seas again, to the vagrant gypsy life,
To the gull's way and the whale's way where the wind's like a whetted knife;
And all I ask is a merry yarn from a laughing fellow-rover,
And quiet sleep and a sweet dream when the long trick's over.

John Masefield

BECALMED

Down dropt the breeze, the sails dropt down,
'Twas sad as sad could be;
And we did speak only to break
The silence of the sea!

All in a hot and copper sky,
The bloody Sun, at noon,
Right up above the mast did stand,
No bigger than the Moon.

Day after day, day after day,
We stuck, nor breath nor motion;
As idle as a painted ship
Upon a painted ocean.

Water, water, everywhere,
And all the boards did shrink;
Water, water, everywhere,
Nor any drop to drink.

The very deep did rot: O Christ!
That ever this should be!
Yea, slimy things did crawl with legs
Upon the slimy sea.

From *The Ancient Mariner*
by Samuel Taylor Coleridge

31

Fiction
Nautical fiction for Level
5+ readers:
Dolphin Island, Arthur C
Clarke (Puffin)
The Dolphin Crossing, Jill
Paton Walsh (Puffin)
*Twenty Thousand Leagues
Under the Sea*, Jules Verne
(Puffin)
Swallows and Amazons,
etc. Arthur Ransome
(Puffin)
Treasure Island, Robert
Louis Stevenson (Puffin)
*Voyage of the Dawn
Treader*, C S Lewis (Puffin)

Further poem
O to sail in a ship,
To leave this steady unendurable
 land,
To leave the tiresome sameness
 of the streets, the sidewalks
 and the houses,
To leave you, O you solid
 motionless land, and entering a
 ship,
To sail and sail and sail!

(Walt Whitman 1819–92)

Reading poems
Each poem should be prepared by a pupil/pupils for reading aloud while the rest of the group or class follow in their books.

Discussion
'Sea-fever'
John Masefield (1878–1967) ran away to sea early in life, went to America where he had many humble jobs, then returned to Britain to be a journalist and poet. He remained obsessed with the sea and many of his poems are about it. He was Poet Laureate (1930–67).
Find examples of alliteration in this poem. How does the poet use repetition to help achieve his effect? What is the rhyme scheme? How does he give the impression of 'waves' of words? (the build-up of lists using repetitive sounds – and … and … and …) etc.

'Becalmed' from *The Ancient Mariner*
Samuel Taylor Coleridge (1772–1834), friend of the poets Wordsworth and Southey, wrote many mystical poems, often under the influence of opium, to which he was addicted.
The Ancient Mariner is telling his story to a guest at a wedding: on a voyage to the South Pole he shot and killed an albatross, which caused a curse to fall on the ship. While becalmed all the crew except the Mariner died of thirst, and though he at last breaks the curse he is condemned ever after to wander, telling his story as a warning to others.
How is this poem so different from the first? (differences in weather, freshness, movement, colour, etc.) *What is the simile in stanza 3? What is the rhyme scheme? Find some examples of alliteration and repetition. Which poem do you like best, and why? Which do you think is the better description of the sea, and why?*

Jason and the Argonauts

(page 32)

The play is suitable for group reading and performance. There are 12 parts, but some are very short.

In smaller groups, some parts could be doubled, e.g.:

  Pelia/Hylas
  Old woman/Medea
  Argos/Aeetes

Note:

The play is an introduction to characters from classical mythology, including some of the major heroes of Ancient Greece. Further stories about these heroes can be found with the notes to pages 33–35. Younger pupils may find the play easier to follow if they know something about the characters in advance. The play is also an introduction to classical theatre. The play is constructed on similar lines to classical Greek drama, e.g. using a chorus and offstage action. Some background information on the Greek theatre can be found with notes to page 38.

Reading/Comprehension/Interpretation

These questions may be used:
• as the basis of oral discussion
• and/or some written on the board for pupils to answer in writing.

Scene One

1 *What do these words and phrases mean? prophet; family feud; use your wits; words of counsel*
2 *Of which two people was King Pelias frightened, and why?*
3 *How did Jason lose his shoe?*
4 *How did King Pelias trick Jason?*
5 *What sort of a person do you think King Pelias was, and why?*
6 *What sort of a person do you think Jason was, and why?*

Scene Two

7 *What do these words and phrases mean? trophy; I hope the craft is equal to the journey; squire; volunteers*
8 *Why did Jason call his ship the 'Argo'?*
9 *What sort of personalities were these heroes? Give at least three adjectives or phrases for each of them:*
  Hercules   Theseus   Atalanta

Scenes Three and Four

10 *What do these words and phrases mean? brazen-footed; motley crew; betrothed*
11 *What sort of a personality was Medea? Write at least three adjectives or phrases to describe her.*
12 *What was Medea's attitude to Jason?*
13 *What task did Aeetes set for Jason?*
14 *How did Aeetes try to trick Jason?*
15 *How did Orpheus help Jason steal the fleece?*
16 *How did Medea slow down her father's ships so that the Argonauts could escape?*

Books

Stories from Greek and Roman mythology:
Tales of the Greek Heroes, Roger Lancelyn Green (Puffin)
The Tale of Troy, Roger Lancelyn Green (Puffin)
Myths of Greece and Rome, H A Guerber (Harrap)
Favourite Greek Myths, L S Hyde (Harrap)
Kingfisher Book of Myths and Legends, Anthony Horowitz (Kingfisher)

(page 33)

(He sits down. Enter old woman.)

Woman   Good day, young sir.

Jason   Good day, mother. Where are you bound?

Woman   My home in yonder mountains. But I fear I shall not be able to cross the stream today. The rains have made it deep and I'm unsteady on my feet.

Jason   Never fear, mother, I'll help you out. Just let me rest for a minute or two, and I'll gladly carry you over.

Woman   You are a kind young man. I wish you well. Where does your journey take you, sir?

Jason   It's a long story, but I'm on my way to make peace with my uncle, King Pelias. Our family quarrelled when I was a baby, and I have been brought up far away in the mountains. But I see no point in these family feuds and I have come to be a peace-maker and set his heart at rest.

Woman   Then you are the Lord Jason? It is a pleasure to meet you, my lord, and especially to hear of your peaceful intent. The people of Iolcus will be glad to know the feud is over. So will King Pelias, for his heart is heavy. You may see him before you reach the city – every day he walks these hills, watching for strangers.

Jason   Indeed? Then let us hasten to meet him. I will carry you across.

(Jason lifts the old woman and struggles across the mud, losing his sandal as he does so.)

Jason   There. The ground is firmer here.

Woman   Oh thank you, my Lord Jason. But you have lost your shoe.

Jason   It doesn't matter. If, as you say, I will meet my uncle soon, I'm sure he will replace it for me.

Woman   I hope so, my lord. You are indeed the kindest of men. I wish you good fortune. *(Exit)*

Jason   *(Smiling to himself.)* Oh dear, I hope I won't have to walk very far half-shod!

(Enter Pelias and servants. Pelias sees Jason, and eyes him nervously.)

Pelias   Who are you, fellow? Where are you bound?

Jason   My name is Jason, sir, and I'm bound for Iolcus to seek King Pelias.

Pelias   Are you indeed? Then you need look no further. I am King Pelias.

33

Orpheus

A gifted musician, married to a beautiful young dryad called Eurydice, who died after being bitten on the foot by a snake. Like all the dead, Eurydice travelled to the banks of the River Styx where she paid her fare and was ferried across into the Underworld.

Meanwhile Orpheus, heartbroken at the loss of his wife, decided to journey to the Underworld and try to get her back. He was helped by his music: he played on the lyre to persuade the ferryman to take him across the Styx; then to soothe Cerberus, the three-headed guard dog; then to the King of the Underworld to persuade him to give Eurydice back. The King at last agreed that Eurydice could follow Orpheus home, but she must stay behind him, and if he looked back before they left the Underworld, he would lose her again.

Orpheus set off with Eurydice following. He had almost reached the gates of the Underworld when he became obsessed with the thought that she might have lost him. He glanced round to check that she was still there. She was, but the moment he set eyes on her she was pulled back into Pluto's land.

Heroes and heroines: further background
Atalanta

Her father, a king, abandoned Atalanta on a mountainside when she was a baby, because he wanted a son, not a daughter. She was found and raised by a she-bear, and grew up to be a great huntress and warrior. She joined with other heroes (including Jason and Theseus) in the hunt for a dangerous boar which was threatening the people of Calydonia, and was the first to wound it. She joined in some Greek games, and beat the men at everything (including wrestling).

At the games her father recognised her, apologised for what he had done, and welcomed her back to the family. He wanted her to marry, but she refused to marry any man who could not beat her in a running race. All her suitors had to race her: if they won they would marry her; if they lost they would die. Many young men died, until one called Hippomenes got some help from the goddess Aphrodite (goddess of love). She gave him three golden apples (probably the ones stolen from the Hesperides – see Heracles' notes on next page), which he threw down during the race. Atalanta kept bending to pick them up, which slowed her down so that Hippomenes won the race.

Atalanta and Hippomenes were married and had a son. Eventually, they displeased Zeus, the King of the Gods, and he changed them into lions.

Heracles
(Roman name: Hercules)

The strongest man in Greece. He strangled a serpent while still in his cradle, and as a boy killed his music teacher by hitting him with his lyre when the teacher tried to punish him. For this he was sent to mind cattle on the hillside, where he killed his first lion with his bare hands, at the age of 18. As a man he could beat whole armies and vanquish beasts and monsters. He was hounded all his life by the goddess Hera, who arranged for him to be set twelve terrible tasks by King Eurystheus:

1 To kill the Nemean lion, whose skin could not be pierced. (Hercules choked it to death.)
2 To kill the many-headed Hydra, which grew two new heads whenever you cut one off. (Hercules got his charioteer to burn the stumps as he cut the heads off.)
3 To catch the fleet-footed Erymanthian boar. (Hercules chased it into deep snow to slow it down.)

Jason   You are? Then I am your long-lost nephew. Let me greet you, uncle!

(Jason limps towards Pelias, who looks horrified.)

Jason   Fear not, uncle, I come in peace!

Pelias   *(Noticing the missing sandal and backing away.)* Ah!

Jason   What is it, uncle? I mean you no harm.

Pelias   Do you not? What happened to your shoe?

Jason   I lost it in the mud here. It is no matter.

Pelias   *(Aside)* No matter to you perhaps. But it seems to me that both my nightmares come to claim me at once. I must do what I can to destroy him. Careful, Pelias, use your wits – and don't let him guess how frightened you are. *(Smiling to Jason.)* So you are my missing nephew? How good of you to come and find me. *(Embraces Jason.)* You must come back with me to the palace.

Jason   Oh uncle, I hope that I can bring peace to our family, and reunite you with my father. My only wish now is to serve you.

Pelias   Indeed, nephew, perhaps you can. I am in need of help and counsel at this time. I am troubled constantly by a prophecy of doom.

Jason   Uncle, that is terrible. What can I do?

Pelias   Perhaps you can advise me, nephew. I have been told that I will recognise the bringer of my downfall. But I cannot decide how best to deal with him. Tell me, what would be your way of dealing with a man who is destined to destroy me?

Jason   I should send him away, uncle. Send him on some journey from which he would never return. Then you'd be safe. I know, I'd send him to fetch the Golden Fleece from the far land of Colchis! That is an impossible task.

Pelias   Excellent advice, nephew. And I shall take it at once. YOU are the man the prophecy warned about, and fortunately you have sealed your own fate. You must travel to the distant land of Colchis and bring me the Golden Fleece. Your words of counsel have saved me and ruined you!

(Exit Pelias, laughing, with his servants.)

Jason   What have I done? What task have I set myself? *(Exit Jason.)*

34

4 To catch the even fleeter-footed Arcadian hind. (Hercules chased it across the world for a year until it was exhausted.)
5 To chase away the Stymphalian birds which were terrorising people with their poisoned feathers. (Hercules frightened them away with a huge bronze rattle.)
6 To clean the Augean stables, which held 3000 oxen and hadn't been cleaned for 30 years. (Hercules did it in a day by diverting two rivers through them.)
7 To capture the Cretan bull from King Minos. (Hercuies picked it up and carried it to Eurystheus.)
8 To capture the flesh-eating horses belonging to King Diomedes. (Hercules fed their master to them, and then tamed them.)
9 To steal the girdle of Queen Hippolyta, queen of the warlike Amazons. (Hercules fought off all the Amazons and killed Hippolyta.)
10 To capture the oxen belonging to Geryon, a three-headed monster. (Hercules killed Geryon and carried back the oxen.)
11 To capture the three-headed dog Cerberus, which guarded the way to the Underworld. (Hercules got all its heads in a headlock.)
12 To steal the golden apples of the Hesperides, the beautiful maidens who lived a the ends of the earth. (Hercules killed the dragon who guarded the apples and brought them back.)

Scene Two: Some months later.
A street in Iolcus, outside a house where Jason is staying.

Chorus So Jason came in peace but found a task
That would for all his life keep him from peace:
To sail to far-off Colchis, there to find,
That trophy of the gods – the Golden Fleece!
But he was young and strong and did not fear:
He found a ship-builder, the best in Greece,
And sent a summons out across the land,
For heroes who could help him win the Fleece!

(Enter Argus and Jason)

Argus I hope you are pleased with the ship I have built for you, Lord Jason.

Jason Pleased! It is magnificent, Argus. I knew that if anyone could build a ship fit to carry me to Colchis and home again, you were the one. Your skill as a ship-builder is spoken of all over Greece.

Argus It was a hard task, my lord. I only hope the craft is equal to the journey.

Jason It will be, Argus. I'm sure it will. And I have chosen a name for it, one which will remind me always of the skill which went into the making of the craft. What to do you think of . . . the *Argo*?

Argus Oh, my lord. I am honoured.

Jason Now you must meet the crew who are to sail the *Argo*. I sent out a message through the whole of Greece, telling of my task. The response was better than I could ever have dreamed. Come, let me introduce you to some of them.

(They enter the house, and find Hylas, Heracles, Theseus, Atalanta, and Orpheus.)

Jason Hail, everyone. This is Argus, the ship-builder, who has prepared our craft.

35

Further background on the story of the Argonauts

Golden Fleece
The fleece came from a ram which was sent by the gods to save two children who were being mistreated by their stepmother. The ram was later sacrificed to the gods, and the fleece hung in a temple until taken by Aeetes.

Voyage of the *Argo*
The Argonauts' adventures on their voyage to Colchis included:
– the kidnapping of Hylas by some water nymphs who were bewitched by his startling good looks;
– the driving away of the terrible Harpies (monstrous winged creatures);
– the passage through the cliffs of Symplegates, which moved on their bases, crushing almost everything that passed between them.

Capturing the Fleece
The task Aeetes gave to Jason (page 39) would have been impossible without Medea's help. She was the niece of the witch Circe, and knew of an ointment (made from yellow flowers grown in human blood) which would make Jason invulnerable to fire and iron so that he could yoke the fire-breathing bulls. She also told him how to confuse the army of warriors which sprung up where he threw the dragon's teeth – he had to throw stones among them, so that the warriors thought their companions were attacking them and started to fight amongst themselves.

Theseus
Theseus was the son of King Aegeus of Athens. Athens had to send a tribute of seven youths and seven maidens every year to King Minos on the island of Crete, to feed the bull-like monster which Minos kept there. It was known as the Minotaur and Minos kept it in an underground maze called the Labyrinth.

When Theseus was old enough, he volunteered to go as one of the young men, in order to kill the Minotaur. He arranged with his father that, if he failed, the ship which took him would come back carrying a black sail to give King Aegeus the bad news; if he succeeded the sail would be white.

King Minos' daughter, Ariadne, fell in love with Theseus, helped him sneak into the Labyrinth, and gave him a ball of twine to unwind so that he would be able to find his way out. Theseus found the Minotaur unawares, and killed it with his bare hands. He returned triumphantly to Athens (leaving poor Ariadne behind him), but forgot to raise a white sail. His father saw the black one approaching and, heartbroken, threw himself into the sea (which was afterwards known as the Aegean).

Medea and Jason
The Argonauts passed through many more dangers on their way home, and this time luck seemed always to be against them. Jason married Medea, who kept up her wifely involvement by killing King Pelias (she chopped him into little bits and boiled him). They had two children, but Jason eventually could stand her witchcraft no longer and left her for a princess called Glauce. Medea used her craft to kill Glauce and, for revenge on Jason, her own children. She went off to exercise her black arts elsewhere and Jason was left, a tragic, broken figure, wandering Greece. At last he found the wreck of the *Argo* on a beach and climbed into it for shelter. A beam fell from the ship and killed him.

139

Punctuation: direct speech

5h

Worksheet 5h

Section A provides discussion material on the difference between narrative writing and a playscript. Section A should be discussed at length before pupils proceed to Sections B and C.

The following vocabulary will be helpful (see Glossary for definitions):
dialogue-carrier
speech marks

Discussion

For example: *In the narrative passage, which words have been added to the words from the playscript?* (Pupils could underline these.)

When has the narrative writer started a new paragraph? Where has he placed speech marks? Is the original punctuation of speeches from the play inside or outside the speech marks? What happens to a full stop at the end of a speech if a dialogue-carrier follows it?

(It becomes a comma, e.g.:

Old woman: Good day, young sir.

becomes

'Good day, young sir,' said the old woman.)

When a dialogue-carrier is inserted halfway through a speech, what punctuation is required?

(1 Where the dialogue-carrier comes at the end of a sentence, the punctuation is standard, e.g.:

Jason: Good day, mother. Where are you bound?

becomes

'Good day, mother,' said Jason. 'Where are you bound?'

2 Where the dialogue-carrier is inserted in mid-sentence, commas are used before and after it, and there is no capitalisation of the first letter when the direct speech recommences, e.g.:

Jason: It's a long story, but I'm on my way …

becomes

'It's a long story,' sighed Jason, 'but I'm on my way …')

When pupils are clear about the rules governing punctuation of direct speech, they may complete Worksheet 5h individually or in pairs.

Herac   (*Jumping up.*) You mean it's ready! We've got a ship! Wonderful – let's get on with the quest!

Hylas   Calm down, my lord. We have to wait for the wind and the tides.

Herac   Wind and tides! What do they matter to Heracles? I've done more than tame the wind and the tides in my time!

Argus   (*Amazed*) Heracles! Don't say this is the great Heracles told of in the stories?

Herac   I am indeed! Glad to meet you, Argus. From what I've heard, you're as good at ship-building as I am at strangling serpents and doing impossible tasks! When are we setting off, Jason – I'm itching to go!

Jason   (*Smiling*) Soon, Heracles, soon.

Hylas   Good day, Argus. I am Heracles' squire, Hylas. I tend to my master's needs, keep his armour bright, and try to stop him rushing into trouble too quickly!

Herac   Ha! That's what you think, is it? You young scallywag – you only tend to my needs when you're not sighing after some young woman or other!

Hylas   (*Laughing*) My lord!

Jason   Let me introduce you to Theseus, Argus.

Argus   (*Taken aback.*) Theseus – the King of Athens? The man who killed the dreaded Minotaur, and freed his people from a terrible curse?

Theseus   I'm glad to know you've heard of me, my good man. It was nothing, of course – a mere trifle. But to tell the truth, life's been rather boring since I got back to Athens. Just ruling my people all day long. Frightfully dull stuff, you know. I've been looking for a bit of excitement ever since. I hope this excursion will be a nice little distraction for me.

Argus   Distraction, sire! They say there is a terrible dragon guarding the Fleece.

Theseus   Dragon, eh? Good show!

Herac   Dragon? Dragon? Let me at him!

Hylas   Calm down, my lord!

Atalan   Honestly, you men. If you don't show off in one way, you show off in another. It's just as well you'll have me along to keep you in order.

Argus   A woman! You mean, you're part of the crew?

36

Atalan (*Bristling*) Yes indeed. What's wrong with that?

Jason This is Princess Atalanta, Argus. The swift-footed huntress who is honoured by gods and men alike.

Argus (*Impressed*) Oh, I see – Your Highness, I crave pardon for my impertinence.

Atalan Very well, I'll overlook it this once. But remember in future that there are heroines as well as heroes, and I'm more than a match for any man. I can race and wrestle with any man in Greece, and I can think a darn sight more clearly!

Theseus We are proud that you have joined us, madam.

Argus Lord Jason, I cannot believe all this. Your crew will be made up of the most distinguished heroes – and heroine – in all the world.

Jason Yes, is it not marvellous? And there are many more – every hero in Greece seems to want to join our quest. And not just heroes. We have volunteers of all kinds – here is Orpheus, Greece's most famous musician and singer, who is coming along to entertain and soothe us on the voyage.

Orpheus Good day, Argus. It is always good to meet another artist.

Argus Good day, Orpheus. I am honoured to meet you. I have heard tales of the wonders of your singing.

Orpheus (*Sadly*) Hmm. Well, it's been so wonderful that it's brought me nothing but sorrow! I'm coming on this quest to try and forget the terrible things that have happened in my life.

Jason Our voyage will heal you, Orpheus. Now, my crew . . . No – "crew" is a poor sort of word to describe the company here – I have a better word for us. We sail in the *Argo*, so let us call ourselves . . . the Argonauts! (*Everyone makes noises of approval.*) It is time we set off.

Orpheus Then may the wind speed the Argonauts on our quest.

Atalan Let's bring back the Golden Fleece!

Herac You heard what the lady said! Bring back the Golden Fleece!

All Bring back the Golden Fleece! (*All except Jason exit, cheering.*)

Jason I am indeed blessed with the greatest of good fortune! (*Exit*)

37

Punctuation

it's and its

Once pupils are secure in their understanding of the apostrophe to show ownership, ensure they recognise the difference between it's and its.

1 Apostrophes to show ownership are only necessary with nouns. Possessive pronouns such as **his**, **yours** and **ours** do not require them.
2 **its** is a possessive pronoun, e.g. the dog ate its food.
3 The apostrophe is used in **it's** to show the shortened form of it is, e.g. It's a cold day today.

The use of the apostrophe

Once pupils understand all the uses of the apostrophe, they can survey the ways in which it is used throughout the play, converting examples to the ' . . . of . . . ' form for ownership or the complete version of shortened forms.

Language/ Punctuation: the apostrophe to show ownership

(see Glossary)
The use of the apostrophe in shortened forms (e.g. we've) has been covered in Book 4 and Worksheet 4c.

Worksheet 5i `5i`

This provides an introduction to the use of the apostrophe to show ownership. Pupils new to the topic would benefit from discussion of the worksheet before completing it. It is also important to discuss pupils' errors in Section 4 to ensure that they know when apostrophes are **not** required as well as when they are.
Ask pupils to look out for examples of misused apostrophes in signs and notices (e.g. spotted in a shop window: 'Lot's more dresse's upstair's')

Worksheet 5j `5j`

This worksheet should not be introduced until pupils are secure in their understanding of the work on Worksheet 5i. Discuss Section 3 with pupils to ensure they understand how the position of an apostrophe can show whether the owner is singular or plural.

Indirect speech

Pupils who are secure in their understanding of direct speech, may be introduced to the concept of **indirect speech** or **reported speech** (see Glossary).

The old woman wished Jason good day and he responded, asking her where she was bound. She replied that she was going to her home in the nearby mountains, but that she was afraid she would not be able to cross the stream that day. The rains had made it deep and she was unsteady on her feet.

Jason told the old woman not to fear. He would help her out. Once he had rested for a moment or two he would gladly carry her over the stream. The old woman was very grateful. She called Jason a kind young man and wished him well. Then she asked where his journey was taking him.

Jason sighed and replied that it was a long story. He was on his way to make peace with his uncle, King Pelias …

After discussion of the differences between a direct speech version and an indirect speech version (e.g. the changes involved to pronouns), pupils could attempt **orally** to convert some parts of the play into indirect speech.

Scene Three: A room in King Aeetes' palace

Chorus Northwards they sailed, the bravest souls in Greece,
Cheered on their way by Orpheus' sweetest songs,
And many adventures had they on their way:
A fair nymph lured young Hylas from the ship,
And Heracles, while searching, lost his way,
Was left behind on Mysia's gloomy shores;
Heroes were killed in battles, fought with gods,
Tussled with harpies, strove on land and sea;
Until at last they reached the land they sought –
Colchis, where King Aeetes keeps his court.
Jason had heard of this most wicked king –
Heard of his wizardry, his blackest arts,
Heard of his daughter, beautiful Medea,
Witch like her father, versed in evil's ways.
Cautiously he and all his Argonauts,
Approached the palace and their journey's end.

(Enter Aeetes, Medea, Jason and the Argonauts, except Heracles and Hylas.)

Aeetes Welcome, Jason, and your most distinguished company. We had heard of your approach across the wild Black Sea, and wondered that mortals could make such a journey.

Jason But how could you know, King Aeetes? No messenger could get here before us.

Aeetes You think not? As it happens, you are wrong. Someone did reach here who knew about your quest. He set off with your Argonauts all those months ago but was separated from you.

Jason Heracles!

Aeetes Indeed. He reached here but a few hours ago, exhausted after his long haul overland. Only the strongest man in Greece could have achieved it, of course. Anyway, he was able to give us notice of your arrival. He is resting now, but you will be reunited tomorrow.

Jason You haven't harmed him?

Aeetes *(Slyly)* Of course not. Why should I? You have nothing to fear from me.

Atalan *(Secretly to Jason.)* No one could harm Heracles, Jason. Don't trust this man.

Jason I think you're right, Atalanta.

38

Greek Theatre

Greek dramas were performed in horseshoe-shaped open-air theatres, with a space in the middle called the **orchestra**, where the chorus (one person or a group speaking in unison) performed. At the back of the orchestra was a raised stage called the **scena** where the actors appeared. The actors wore built-up shoes to make them appear taller and masks to represent their characters. Little action occurred on the stage – any activity was described as happening offstage (ob scena, from which we get our word 'obscene').

There were two main types of drama: comedy and tragedy. Tragedies were the story of sad and terrible events which came about because of human frailty (and, often, the vengeance of the gods). A technique frequently used by Greek dramatists was 'dramatic irony', where the audience knows something of which the protagonists are unaware, and the audience is therefore privy to the coming tragic consequences.

Drama/Presentation

Pupils could produce the play, as Greek or modern drama, with appropriate music and costumes, for a school audience.
Pupils who become sufficiently interested in the story to read about the Argonauts' adventures on the voyages to and from Colchis might add extra scenes portraying these sections in more detail. The play could also be performed as a puppet play or as a 'radio play' recorded on to tape with suitable sound effects and musical accompaniment.

(page 39)

Orpheus   And Hylas? What about him? Heracles left us to seek for him.

Aeetes   No sign of him, I'm afraid. It appears he was lured away by some beautiful water nymph, and drawn deep into her wells below the ground. I don't think you'll see him again.

Atalan   Oh, honestly – men!

Orpheus   Alas, poor Hylas.

Aeetes   So welcome again, Jason and the famous Argonauts. We know all about your quest. Now let me introduce you to my daughter, Medea, who has been looking forward to your arrival.

Medea   (*Smiling slyly.*) Good day, my lords and (*looking Atalanta up and down*) . . . lady.

Jason   Good day, princess.

Medea   So you are Jason, whom I've heard so much about. You are certainly handsome enough. That lout Heracles tells me you are noble and honourable too.

Jason   My friend Heracles is no lout, madam.

Medea   And loyal, eh? I like that in a man.

Aeetes   Silence, Medea, Do not let my daughter annoy you, Lord Jason. She meets so few men of noble birth here in Colchis.

Jason   I see, King Aeetes. Well, if you know all about our quest, we need waste no more time. I am here to take the Golden Fleece. Will you allow me to do so, or must my Argonauts and I fight you for it?

Aeetes   Tush, tush, Jason. You have much to learn about me. Fighting will get you nowhere against my wizardry.

Atalan   That's true, Jason. Beware of him.

Aeetes   But it amuses me to offer you a challenge. I will *give* you the Golden Fleece . . . on one condition. In the field out there I have two brazen-footed bulls which breathe fire from their nostrils. If you – and you alone, no help from your motley crew here – can yoke my bulls, plough a field with them, and sow it with dragon's teeth, the Fleece is yours! That's my only offer. I'll leave you to to think it over. (*Exit Aeertes, laughing.*)

Theseus   Bulls, eh? Wish I could take the challenge.

Atalan   Oh, be quiet, Theseus. Even you can be burned by fire. Even Hercules. I don't see how Jason can possibly manage the task, especially as there's probably more trickery involved. Aeetes is one of the evillest wizards ever known – his challenge won't be straightforward.

39

Poems

Two poems about women on board ship. Like Medea, both proved to be unlucky.

The Wreck of the Hesperus

It was the schooner Hesperus,
That sailed the wintry sea;
And the skipper had taken his little
                              daughter,
To bear him company.

Blue were her eyes as the fairy-flax,
Her cheeks like the dawn of day,
And her bosom white as the
                    hawthorn buds,
That ope in the month of May.

The skipper he stood beside the
                              helm,
His pipe was in his mouth,
And he watched how the veering
                    flaw did blow
The smoke now West, now South.

Then up spake an old Sailor,
Had sailed to the Spanish Main,
"I pray thee, put into yonder port,
For I fear a hurricane.

"Last night, the moon had a golden
                              ring,
And to-night no moon we see!"
The skipper, he blew a whiff from
                    his pipe,
And a scornful laugh laughed he.

Colder and louder blew the wind,
A gale from the Northeast,
The snow fell hissing in the brine,
And the billows frothed like yeast.

Down came the storm, and smote
                    amain
The vessel in its strength;
She shuddered and paused, like a
                    frighted steed,
Then leaped her cable's length.

"Come hither! come hither! my
                    little daughter,
And do not tremble so;
For I can weather the roughest gale
That ever wind did blow."

He wrapped her warm in his
                    seaman's coat
Against the stinging blast;
He cut a rope from a broken spar,
And bound her to the mast.

"O father! I hear the church bells
                    ring,
Oh say, what may it be?"
"'Tis a fog bell on a rock bound
                    coast!" –
And he steered for the open sea.

"O father! I hear the sound of guns,
Oh say, what may it be?"
"Some ship in distress, that cannot
                    live
In such an angry sea!"

"O father! I see a gleaming light,
Oh say, what may it be?"
But the father answered never a
                    word,
A frozen corpse was he.

Lashed to the helm, all stiff and
                    stark,
With his face turned to the skies,
The lantern gleamed through the
                    gleaming snow
On his fixed and glassy eyes.

Then the maiden clasped her hands
                    and prayed
That saved she might be;
And she thought of Christ, who
                    stilled the wave,
On the Lake of Galilee.

And fast through the midmight dark
                    and drear,
Through the whistling sleet and
                    snow,
Like a sheeted ghost, the vessel
                    swept
Tow'rds the reef of Norman's Woe.

And ever the fitful gusts betweeen
A sound came from the land;
It was the sound of the trampling
                              surf
On the rocks and the hard
                    sea-sand.

The breakers were right beneath
                    her bows,
She drifted a dreary wreck,
And a whooping billow swept the
                    crew
Like icicles from her deck.

She struck where the white and
                    fleecy waves
Look soft as carded wool,
But the cruel rocks, they gored her
                    side
Like the horns of an angry bull.

Her rattling shrouds, all sheathed in
                    ice,
With the masts went by the board;
Like a vessel of glass, she stove and
                    sank,
Ho! ho! the breakers roared!

At daybreak, on the bleak sea-
                    beach,
A fisherman stood aghast,
To see the form of a maiden fair,
Lashed close to a drifting mast.

The salt sea was frozen on her
                    breast,
The salt tears in her eyes;
And he saw her hair, like the brown
                    seaweed,
On the billows fall and rise.

Such was the wreck of the
                    Hesperus,
In the midnight and the snow!
Christ save us all from a death like
                    this,
On the reef of Norman's Woe!

Henry Wadsworth Longfellow

Jason   No, but I must take it. Listen, Argonauts – will you leave me to think
         about this for a while?

Atalan   Of course, come men. (*Atalanta leads the Argonauts away. Medea
         remains.*)

Medea   Well, Jason. Alone at last!

Jason   Please leave me, madam.

Medea   No. I can't do that. You see, I am your only hope. I can give you
         ointment to keep you safe from the bulls' fiery breath. But there is
         more. Your female friend there was right when she warned you of
         trickery – when you sow the field with dragon's teeth, a harvest of
         armed men will spring from the ground, all ready to slaughter you.

Jason   (*Hopelessly*) I might have guessed. And my friends cannot help.

Medea   But I can. I know how to defeat them. And I will tell you how, Jason,
         but first I too have one condition that I must make.

Jason   It seems I have no choice but to take your help. What is your
         condition?

Medea   When you leave with the Fleece, you must take me too. As your wife.

Jason   What? Your father will never allow it!

Medea   We'll deal with him when the time comes. Well, do you want my
         help or not? (*Medea leads a devastated Jason away.*)

Scene Four: The deck of the Argo

Chorus   Lord Jason had no choice, his fate was sealed;
         He took Medea's help, and by her art
         Vanquished Aeetes' army.
                    Then with Orpheus
         He crept to where the dragon of the gods
         Guarded the Golden Fleece.
                    Orpheus played,
         The dragon slept, and Jason took his prize.
         And now the Argonauts by night made haste
         To escape from Colchis and the wizard-king.
         The sails were set, the anchor raised aboard,
         The Argo set her course. And on her decks,
         The witch Medea laughed to gain her prize . . .

         (*Enter all the Argonauts, Jason and Medea.*)

40

Sir Patrick Spens

I. *The Sailing*

The king sits in Dunfermline town,
Drinking the blude-red wine;
"O whar will I get a skeely skipper
To sail this new ship o' mine?"

Up and spak an eldern knight,
Sat at the king's right knee:
"Sir Patrick Spens is the best sailor
That ever sail'd the sea."

Our king has written a braid letter,
And seal'd it wi' his hand,
And sent it to Sir Patrick Spens,
Was walking on the strand.

"To Noroway, to Noroway,
To Noroway o'er the faem;
The king's daughter o' Noroway,
'Tis thou maun bring her hame."

The first word that Sir Patrick read
A loud laugh laughed he;
The neist word that Sir Patrick
                    read,
The tear blinded his e'e.

"O wha is this has done this deed
And tauld the king o' me,
To send us out, at this time o' year,
To sail upon the sea?

"Be it wind, be it weet, be it hail, be
                    it sleet,
Our ship must sail the faem;
The king's daughter o' Noroway,
'Tis we maun fetch her hame."

They hoysed their sails on
                    Monenday morn
Wi' a' the speed they may;
They ha'e landed in Noroway
Upon a Wodensday.

(page 41)

Medea	We beat him, Jason. You won your prize and I won mine. Now I shall be your wife.
Jason	Yes, Medea, I made a promise and I shall not break it. But it will not be easy to escape from Colchis. See, your father's ships are already in sight. He is angry with me for taking the Fleece, and for taking you.
Medea	Of course he is angry, but we have a secret weapon. I'll show you. Absyrtus, come here! (*Enter Absyrtus. frightened.*)
Jason	Who is this?
Medea	My little brother, my father's youngest son.
Jason	(*Suprised*) Welcome, young sir. I didn't know we were bringing more of Medea's family home to Greece with us.
Medea	We aren't. This is my secret weapon. Come here, brother. I can see my father's ship in sight now, and my father on the prow. This will stop him. (*Medea draws a knife, stabs Absyrtus, and throws his body into the sea. The Argonauts exclaim and gasp but are too stunned to stop her.*)
Medea	There, Aeetes won't come after us until they've pulled out the body of his precious son. Make haste, Argonauts, and use the advantage I have gained for you. See what a clever wife you have, Jason.
Jason	(*in despair*) On, ye gods above. What have I done? Why did I listen to you?
Medea	(*Laughing*) You must always listen to me. I got you the Fleece!
Theseus	By Athene!
Herac	The woman's mad!
Atalan	What wickedness are we taking back to Greece?
	(*Medea's laughter is drowned by a roll of thunder; darkness falls.*)
Chorus	Jason had won the Fleece, but what the cost? His fair betrothed had shown herself the worst Most wicked witch that ever walked the earth, And now she'd haunt him every day he lived. Aeetes seeing thus his young son slaughtered, Called on the Argonauts his blackest curse, The darkest of all curses in his art. And so they sailed, heroes and heroine – Their triumph turned to ashes by the witch – Away they sailed, into a sea of blood, Into a sea of darkness, trials and death! . . . .

41

---

ii. *The Return*

"Mak ready, mak ready, my merry
                   men a'!
Our gude ship sails the morn." –
"Now ever alack, my master dear,
I fear a deadly storm!

"I saw the new moon late yestreen
Wi' the auld moon in her arm;
And if we gang to see, master,
I fear we'll come to harm!"

They hadna' sailed a league, a
                league,
A league but barely three,
When the lift grew dark, and the
                wind blew loud,
And gurly grew the sea.

The anchors brak, and the topmast
                lap
It was sic a deadly storm;
And the waves cam owre the
                broken ship
Till a' her sides were torn.

"O whar will I get a gude sailor
To tak my helm in hand
Till I get up to the tall topmast
To see if I can spy land?" –

"Oh here am I, a sailor gude,
To tak the helm in hand,
Till you go up to the tall topmast,
But I fear you'll ne'er spy land."

He hadna gane a step, a step,
A step but barely ane,
When a bolt flew out of our goodly
                ship,

And the saut sea it came in.

"Gae fetch a web o' the silken
                claith,
Another o' the twine,
And wap them into our ship's side,
And let na' the sea come in."

They fetched a web o' the silken
                claith,
Another o' the twine,
And they wrapped them round that
                gude ship's side,
But still the sea cam in.

O laith, laith were our gude Scots
                lords
To wet their cork-heel'd shoon;
But lang or a' the play was play'd
They wet their hats aboon.

And mony was the feather bed
That flatter'd on the faem;
And mony was the gude laird's son
That never mair cam hame.

O lang, lang may the ladies sit,
Wi' their fans into their hand,
Before they see Sir Patrick Spens
Come sailing to the strand!

And lang, lang may the maidens sit
Wi' their gowd kames in their hair,
A' waiting for their ain dear loves!
For them they'll see nae mair.

Half-owre, half-owre to Aberdour,
'Tis fifty fathoms deep;
And there lies gude Sir Patrick
                Spens
Wi' the Scots lords at his feet!

                Anon

Skeely, skilful; *braid*, plain; *faem*, foam; *maun*, must; *neist*, next; *hoysed*, hoisted; *lift*, sky; *gurly*, stormy; *lap*, sprang; *saut*, salt; *claith*, cloth; *wap*, wrap; *laith*, unwilling;

Language on the Move

(page 42)

Non-fiction reading on the subject of language.

Language/Discussion/Research

Discuss and expand upon the information in the explanatory passage as appropriate, e.g.:
How long ago were the Roman, Anglo-Saxon, Viking invasions? Do you know of any words they brought? (e.g. names of months and days, local place names) *Can you think of words which have been brought to English by British explorers and travellers?* (e.g. **algebra**, **zero**, **caravan** from the Middle East; **potato**, **tomato**, **tobacco** from the Americas; **giraffe**, **zebra**, **okra** from Africa; **pyjama**, **verandah**, **curry** from India; **kangaroo**, **boomerang**, **budgerigar** from Australia)
Discussion of word derivations is interesting in itself, can motivate pupils to take a greater interest in language, and may be helpful in the learning of spelling.
Most dictionaries provide indications of word origins, and specific reference books are also available, e.g. *Concise Oxford Dictionary of English Etymology* (OUP, 1986).
Pupils may be asked to investigate the origins of other names and words which interest them.

LANGUAGE ON

The English language has a long and complicated history. The words we use come from many other languages, such as Latin (the language of the Romans), Norse (the language of the Vikings, Anglo-Saxon (a mixture of languages spoken in Northern Europe about fifteen hundred years ago) and Old French. These languages were brought to our country by invaders long ago, and they gradually combined together to make the English language we speak. As English-speaking people travelled the world, new words were added to the language all the time.

The words we use to talk about transport show what a mixture our language is. The word "transport" itself, for instance, comes from two Latin words (*trans* – across; *porto* – I carry). Various types of transport seem to have their origins with different invaders. "Boat" is from an Anglo-Saxon word (*bat*), while "cart" may have come over with the Vikings (Old Norse: *kartr*). "Car" is a shortened form of "carriage", which is from an Old French word (the verb *carier*, meaning "carry in a vehicle").

New words are being added to English all the time to define and describe new ideas, inventions and occupations. Sometimes words make a complicated journey through the ages to reach a modern home. The word "caravan", for instance, set off long ago in the Middle East (Persian: *karwan* – a group of desert travellers). It travelled to France (*caravane*), where it was used to mean a group of travellers, or the carts on which they carried their belongings, By Victorian times it had arrived in Britain to describe a third-class railway carriage. Somewhere along the way, it also turned into the name for a mobile home.

(page 43)

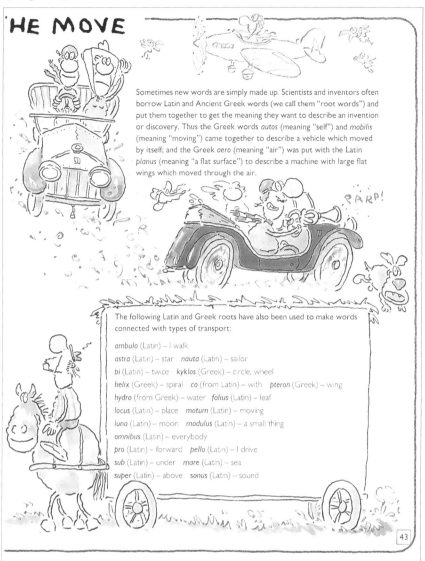

HE MOVE

Sometimes new words are simply made up. Scientists and inventors often borrow Latin and Ancient Greek words (we call them "root words") and put them together to get the meaning they want to describe an invention or discovery. Thus the Greek words *autos* (meaning "self") and *mobilis* (meaning "moving") came together to describe a vehicle which moved by itself; and the Greek *aero* (meaning "air") was put with the Latin *planus* (meaning "a flat surface") to describe a machine with large flat wings which moved through the air.

The following Latin and Greek roots have also been used to make words connected with types of transport:

ambulo (Latin) – I walk

astra (Latin) – star   *nauta* (Latin) – sailor

bi (Latin) – twice   *kyklos* (Greek) – circle, wheel

helix (Greek) – spiral   *co* (from Latin) – with   *pteron* (Greek) – wing

hydro (from Greek) – water   *folius* (Latin) – leaf

locus (Latin) – place   *motum* (Latin) – moving

luna (Latin) – moon   *modulus* (Latin) – a small thing

omnibus (Latin) – everybody

pro (Latin) – forward   *pello* (Latin) – I drive

sub (Latin) – under   *mare* (Latin) – sea

super (Latin) – above   *sonus* (Latin) – sound

PARP!

43

Discussion/Language/Spelling

The Latin and Greek words listed provide roots for the following 'transport words':
**ambulance,
perambulator (pram)
astronaut, nautical
bicycle, biplane, tricycle
helicopter, co-pilot
hydrofoil
locomotive, motor
lunar module
bus
propeller
submarine, mariner
supersonic**
Note also the non-transport words which share these roots, e.g.:
**amble, astronomy,
bisect, circle,
pterodactyl, cooperate,
hydrant, dehydrated,
location, promotion,
marina, superman,
sound.**

Discussion/Language: names

Individual items of transport are given proper names by which they can be identified.
Why do you think the owners/builders gave these names to their ships: Santa Maria, Discovery, Titanic? What other ships' names do you know, and why do you think they were chosen?
Why did the manufacturers choose these names for makes of plane: Spitfire, Tornado, Comet, Concorde? What others can you think of?
Brand names are chosen to influence people's attitudes to a car – why should manufacturers have chosen the names Jaguar, Scimitar, Fiesta, Mini and Escort? What other names do you know and where do you come from? etc.

A Steamboat on the Mississippi

Background

Mark Twain was the pen name of the American writer Samuel Clemens (1835–1910) who became a pilot on a Mississippi steamboat in 1857. He took his pen name from the leadsman's call indicating the water level (twain = two). When he later became the most popular American writer of his day, he often wrote about the river. His most famous book, *Huckleberry Finn,* is an epic about a boy's adventures on the Mississippi.

Reading aloud/ Expression

The pupil(s) preparing this passage for reading aloud will require support from the teacher.
Pupils should know the background to the passage in advance of discussion.

Reading/ Comprehension/ Interpretation

Divide up those words of which pupils may be uncertain for individuals to check in the dictionary and report back, e.g.: ambition, transient, gaudy, packet, clerks, wharf, fragrant, prodigious, gilded device, husbanded grandeur, forecastle, picturesque, gauge, freight, facilitate.
Re-read the passage, asking the relevant pupils to explain the meanings of their words as they come to them.
The words 'skids', 'point', 'gingerbread' and 'texas' are in **inverted commas** *– why? (see Glossary) What do you think they might mean here? Does Mark Twain really mean the drunkard was fragrant? Are there any more examples of irony? How had the steamboat made the black smoke it was giving off as it arrived, and why? How many other things about the steamboat were false? How does Twain build up to the arrival of the boat? Compare the length of the build up to the length of the description of its departure. etc.*
This poem is another example of a romantic attitude to transport – compare with 'Let's Go Ride' on page 2 of Book 5.

STEAM BOATS on the MISSISSIPPI

When I was a boy, there was but one permanent ambition among my comrades in our village, on the west bank of the Mississippi River. That was, to be a steamboatman. We had transient ambitions of other sorts, but they were only transient. When a circus came and went, it left us all burning to become clowns; the first negro minstrel show that came to our section left us all suffering to try that kind of life; now and then we had a hope that if we lived and were good, God would permit us to be pirates. These ambitions faded out, each in its turn; but the ambition to be a steamboatman always remained.

Once a day a cheap, gaudy packet arrived upward from St. Louis, and another downward from Keokuk. Before these events, the day was glorious with expectancy; after them, the day was a dead and empty thing. Not only the boys, but the whole village, felt this. After all these years I can picture that old time to myself now, just as it was then: the white town drowsing in the sunshine of a summer's morning; the streets empty, or pretty nearly so; one or two clerks sitting in front of the Water Street stores, with their splint-bottomed chairs tilted back against the wall, chins on breasts, hats slouched over their faces, asleep; a sow and a litter of pigs loafing along the sidewalk, doing a good business in watermelon rinds and seeds; a pile of "skids" on the slope of the stone-paved wharf, and the fragrant town drunkard asleep in the shadow of them; two or three wood flats at the head of the wharf, but nobody to listen to the peaceful lapping of the wavelets against them; the great Mississippi, the majestic, the magnificent Mississippi, rolling its mile-wide tide along, shining in the sun; the dense forest away on the other side; the "point" above the town, and the "point" below, bounding the river-glimpse and turning it into a sort of sea, and withal a very still and brilliant and lonely one. Presently a film of dark smoke appears above one of those remote "points"; instantly a negro drayman, famous for his quick eye and prodigious voice, lifts up the cry, "S-t-e-a-m-boat a-comin'!" and the scene changes! The town drunkard stirs, the clerks wake up, a furious clatter of drays follows, every house and store pours out a human contribution, and all in a twinkling the dead town is alive and moving. Drays, carts, men, boys, all go hurrying from many quarters to a common centre, the wharf. Assembled there, the people fasten their eyes upon the coming boat as upon a wonder they are seeing for the first time. And the boat *is* rather a handsome sight, too.

44

Books

For Level 5+ readers:
Tom Sawyer, Mark Twain (Puffin)
Huckleberry Finn, Mark Twain (Puffin)

(page 45)

She is long and sharp and trim and pretty; she has two tall, fancy-topped chimneys, with a gilded device of some kind swung between them; a fanciful pilot-house, all glass and "gingerbread", perched on top of the "texas" deck behind them; the paddle-boxes are gorgeous with a picture or with gilded rays above the boat's name; the boiler deck, the hurricane deck, and the texas deck are fenced and ornamented with clean white railings; there is a flag gallantly flying from the jack-staff; the furnace doors are open and the fires glaring bravely; the upper decks are black with passengers; the captain stands by the big bell, calm, imposing, the envy of all; great volumes of the blackest smoke are rolling and tumbling out of the chimneys – a husbanded grandeur created with a bit of pitch pine just before arriving at a town; the crew are grouped on the forecastle; the broad stage is run far out over the port bow, and an envied deck-hand stands picturesquely on the end of it with a coil of rope in his hand; the pent steam is screaming through the gauge-cocks; the captain lifts his hand, a bell rings, the wheels stop; then they turn back, churning the water to foam, and the steamer is at rest. Then such a scramble as there is to get aboard, and to get ashore, and to take in freight and to discharge freight, all at once and the same time; and such a yelling and cursing as the mates facilitate it all with! Ten minutes later the steamer is under way again, with no flag on the jack-staff and no black smoke issuing from the chimneys. After ten more minutes the town is dead again, and the town drunkard asleep by the skids once more.

Mark Twain

45

Extract from another piece on transport by Mark Twain, from *What is Man?* (1906):

Learning to ride a bicycle

Mine was not a full-grown bicycle, but only a colt – a fifty inch, with the pedals shortened up to forty-eight – and skittish, like any other colt. The Expert explained the thing's points briefly, then he got on its back and rode around a little, to show me how easy it was to do. He said that dismounting was perhaps the hardest thing to learn, and so we would leave that to the last. But, he was in error there. He found, to his surprise and joy, that all he needed to do was to get me on the machine and stand out of the way: I could get off myself. Although I was wholly inexperienced, I dismounted in the best time on record. He was on that side shoving up the machine; we all came down with a crash, he at the bottom, I next, and the machine on top...

Then he limped out to a position, and we resumed once more. This time the Expert took up the position of shortstop, and got a man to shove up behind. We got up a handsome speed and presently traversed a brick, and I went out over the top of the tiller and landed, head down, on the instructor's back, and saw the machine fluttering in the air between me and the sun. It was well it came down on us, for that broke the fall, and it was not injured.

Five days later I got out and was carried down to the hospital and found the Expert doing pretty fairly. In a few more days I was quite sound... During eight days I took a daily lesson of an hour and a half. At the end of this twelve working-hours' apprenticeship I was graduated – in the rough. I was pronounced competent to pedal my own bicycle without outside help... Before taking final leave of me, my instructor inquired concerning my physical strength, and I was able to inform him that I hadn't any... Then he left me, and I started out alone to seek adventures. You don't really have to seek them – that is nothing but a phrase – they come to you... It took time to learn to miss a dog, but I achieved even that... Get a bicycle. You will not regret it if you live.

Space Travel

(page 46)

Reading

Apart from 'The Launch', which is not suitable for reading aloud, pupils can prepare the poems for reading to the class as they follow in their books.

Discussion/Writing

'The Launch'

This reads:

In ten seconds' time, new words will be needed: sputnik, skylab, astronaut, spaceflight, spacecraft. Inventions no one believed in will be worth a million. Cranks will be rehabilitated as geniuses. In ten seconds' time science will do what once needed magic and Science fiction will come true. *Can anyone work it out? Why is it written this way?* (Apart from the visual effect, the technique slows down the reading, making the words seem 'newer': you can't guess it, just as you can't guess the future) *When must the poem have been written?* (first Sputnik, 4th October 1957) etc. Pupils could attempt shape poems of their own, using different forms of transport. They should draw a silhouette of the subject, brainstorm for ideas and words related to it, then find the most effective way of fitting them into or around the shape.

Space Travel

Space Pilot

The land sinks back
The rockets shoot their bolt,
Earth's pull weakens and dies.
I breach space and become a celestial body,
Moving with planets and suns
Through darkness, silence and cold,
But having no place in this void
My weight lost, my breath in an envelope,
My eyes replaced by intricate instruments.
There is no place for the heart
Here, needing the light and the seasons,
But the soul perhaps?
Released from all that I could not carry with me
I shall stare unhindered into the face of God.

John Blackie

The space race! The space race!
What has it all been for?
Stockpiling satellites
To wage a nuclear war?

The space race! The space race!
Wouldn't it have been more worth
Spending all that money
To improve life on Earth?

John Foster

Discussion: 'Space Pilot'

What is a celestial body? How are the pilot's 'weight lost'? 'breath in an envelope'? 'eyes replaced by instruments'? Why is there no place for the heart in space? What is the soul? Why is the pilot free now to look at God? etc.

Discussion/Debate: The Space Race

Fact or opinion? (see page 23 and Worksheet 5g)
Do you agree? Why/why not? This is another topic which can provide the basis of a

---

Books

On space travel themes for Level 5+ readers:
Islands in the Sky, Arthur C Clarke (Puffin)
Space Hostages, Nicholas Fisk (Puffin)
Wheelie in the Stars, Nicholas Fisk (Puffin)
The Time and Space of Uncle Albert, Russell Stannard (Faber)

(page 47)

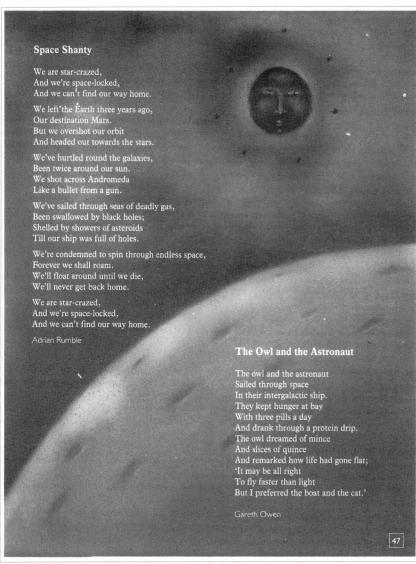

Space Shanty

We are star-crazed,
And we're space-locked,
And we can't find our way home.

We left the Earth three years ago,
Our destination Mars.
But we overshot our orbit
And headed out towards the stars.

We've hurtled round the galaxies,
Been twice around our sun.
We shot across Andromeda
Like a bullet from a gun.

We've sailed through seas of deadly gas,
Been swallowed by black holes;
Shelled by showers of asteroids
Till our ship was full of holes.

We're condemned to spin through endless space,
Forever we shall roam.
We'll float around until we die,
We'll never get back home.

We are star-crazed,
And we're space-locked,
And we can't find our way home.

Adrian Rumble

The Owl and the Astronaut

The owl and the astronaut
Sailed through space
In their intergalactic ship.
They kept hunger at bay
With three pills a day
And drank through a protein drip.
The owl dreamed of mince
And slices of quince
And remarked how life had gone flat;
'It may be all right
To fly faster than light
But I preferred the boat and the cat.'

Gareth Owen

47

Discussion/Research/Writing
'Space Shanty'
What is a shanty and who usually sings it? How could the various things which have happened to these astronauts be compared to what happened to sailors long ago? (Look back to page 31, and compare 'Sea Fever' to 'Space Pilot' and 'Becalmed' to 'Space Shanty'.) *What do you imagine will happen to these travellers in the end?*
Pupils could research sea shanties and revise them as space shanties.

Poetry/Discussion
'The Owl and the Astronaut'
This poem is a tribute to 'The Owl and the Pussycat' by Edward Lear, another example of a poem about the romance of transport:

The Owl and the Pussycat went to sea
In a beautiful pea-green boat.
They took some honey, and plenty of money,
Wrapped up in a five pound note.
The Owl looked up to the stars above,
And he sang to a small guitar;
'Oh lovely Pussy, oh Pussy my love,
What a beautiful Pussy you are, you are,
What a beautiful Pussy you are.'

Pussy said to the Owl, 'You elegant fowl,
How wonderfully sweet you sing.
Pray let us be married, too long we have tarried,
But what shall we do for a ring?'
They sailed away for a year and a day
To the land where the Bong tree grows
And there in a wood a Piggiwig stood
With a ring through the end of his nose, his nose
With a ring through the end of his nose.

'Dear Pig, are you willing to sell for one shilling,
Your ring?' Said the Piggy, 'I will!'
So they took it away and were married that day
By the Turkey who lived on the hill.
They dined on mince, and slices of quince,
Which they ate with a Runcible Spoon;
Then hand in hand along the sand
They danced by the light of the moon, the moon,
They danced by the light of the moon.

accent (n.)
The way a person pronounces words – this is affected by tone of voice and speech rhythms. Accents vary from one part of the country to another, and the same words can sound different if spoken in a different accent. Particular accents sometimes go with particular dialects of English.

alliteration (n.)
Repetition of the same sounds, often at the beginnings of words,
e.g. "where the wind's like a whetted knife."

antonym (n.)
A word which means the opposite of another word, e.g. an antonym for *fast = slow*.

apostrophe (n.)
A punctuation mark like a flying comma. It shows
1. where letters have been missed out of a word or words,
   e.g. *it'll = it will; can't = cannot*
2. possession, e.g. *the plane's engines* (sing.),
   the planes' engines (pl.)

BBC English (n.phr.)
Standard English (so called because BBC announcers speak it).

bibliography (n.)
A list of books about a particular topic, sometimes found at the back of a non-fiction or reference book. It gives the title and author of each book and sometimes the publisher and date of publication.

clause (n.)
A group of words, including a verb, which go together to make sense. It can be a main clause or a subordinate clause.

databank (n.)
Information about a particular subject classified and stored for reference on a computer.

dialect (n.)
A way of speaking the language which is particular to one part of the country or ethnic group. There are dialect words (such as *drag* for *sledge*) and dialect grammars (such as *We was there* for *We were there*). Dialects often have an accent to go with them. [See also Standard English]

dialogue-carrier
In direct speech the words which are inserted to show who is speaking, and which are shown outside the speech marks, e.g. in the example below, the dialogue-carrier is underlined:
"Well Jason," said Medea, "Alone at last!"

direct speech (n.)
The actual words someone speaks, as shown in a piece of writing. [See also speech marks]

haiku (n.)
A form of three-line poem from Japan. There are five syllables in the first line, seven in the second, and five in the third. There are several examples on p. 24.

indirect speech
A reported version of the words someone has spoken. Indirect speech does not use exactly the same words as direct speech and does not need speech marks around it.
e.g. direct speech:
   "My friends cannot help," said Jason.
   indirect speech:
   Jason said that his friends could not help.

inverted commas (n.phr.)
Another name for the punctuation marks we have called speech marks ("   "). They are also sometimes used:
a) to show titles (e.g. "Night Mail")
b) to show words are being quoted (e.g. The St. Custard's boys had to find out "how it works, wot it do, ect.")
c) to show you are talking about a word, rather than using it in the usual way (e.g. "creto" is a poor sort of word to describe the Argonauts)
d) to show that words are being used in an unexpected way, (e.g. CO_2 is the main "Greenhouse gas" responsible for global warming.)

italic print (n.)
A type of print which leans towards the right. It is used to draw attention to particular words. The most common reasons for the use of italic print are:
1. for the titles of books, films, etc. (instead of using inverted commas, see above)
2. to show that a word should be *stressed* when read aloud, e.g. "Will all boys attached to St. Custards *kindly* take their marbles away."

joining word (n.phr.)
A word which joins words or groups of words together, e.g. *and, but, when, so, as, while, because, although.*

main clause (n.phr.)
A clause which makes sense on its own.
A single main clause is the same as a simple sentence.

myth (n.)
A story about ancient gods or heroes.
mythology (n.)
A collection of myths.
mythological (adj.)
To do with mythology.

noun phrase (n.phr.)
A phrase of two or more words which act together as the name of something (i.e. like a noun).

opinion (n.)
Something that a person believes, which may or may not be true.

part of speech (n.phr.)
The job a word is doing in a phrase or sentence.
e.g. noun (naming word),
   verb (word of doing or being),
   adjective (a word which describes a noun),
   adverb (a word which describes a verb),
   pronoun (a word which stands in place of a noun).

phrase (n.)
A group of words which go together to make sense, but do not make a complete sentence or clause.

propaganda (n.)
Information which is spread about to try and change people's ideas and attitudes. Propaganda often presents opinions as though they were facts.

prose (n.)
Writing which is not in verse.

punctuation marks (n.phr.)
In general, these are to help the reader make sense of a piece of writing. They show how words are grouped together in phrases and sentences to make sense. Some also show what tone of voice is needed to read the words (? !). The apostrophe is an exception.

quotation marks (n.phr.)
Another name for inverted commas.

received pronunciation or R.P. (n.phr.)
The accent used in English public schools, which is usually associated with BBC English.

reported speech (n.phr.)
See indirect speech.

sentence (n.)
A group of words that go together to make complete sense, consisting of one or more clauses.

simile (n.)
A striking comparison, usually in writing; e.g.
"As idle as a painted ship
Upon a painted ocean."

slang (n.)
A way of speaking, usually associated with a particular age-group, which is not accepted as correct Standard English, and should not be used in formal writing.

speech marks (n.phr.)
Punctuation marks that look like this "   ". They are placed around passages of direct speech (and any punctuation associated with it) to show the exact words which someone has spoken.
e.g. "And loyal, eh?" said Medea "I like that in a man."

Standard English (n.)
The dialect of English which is used in written language. It is also the dialect spoken by many people (such as newsreaders) who wish to be understood by all groups of English speakers.

style (n.)
The way something is done, written or spoken. Different sorts of writing tasks require different styles,
e.g. a formal letter would be written in a different style from a letter to a friend.

subordinate clause (n.phr.)
A clause (usually beginning with a joining word) which is linked to a main clause as part of a sentence. If separated from the main clause, it would not make complete sense on its own.

syllable (n.)
A beat in a word, e.g. syll/a/ble has three syllables. he/li/cop/ter has four.

synonym (n.)
A word similar in meaning to another word, e.g. a synonym for *car = automobile*.

thesaurus (n.)
A book which lists words systematically by their meaning, so that you can find synonyms and antonyms. (From the Greek for "treasure-store".)

vocabulary (n.)
The words a person uses (e.g. "She had a wide vocabulary") or the words associated with a particular subject (e.g. scientific vocabulary).

The teacher is referred to the Glossary when a new term is mentioned in the Teacher's Notes. It is intended as:
a) a source of shared definitions of the meta-language used to discuss the resource material;
b) a reference for pupils as they gradually build up their repertoire of meta-language.
Generally, terms which have been introduced in previous books are not included.
Definitions require plenty of discussion with the teacher. Pupils should then experience the concept concerned within the context of their own reading and writing.
By the time pupils have finished the book they should be familiar with the terms included in the Glossary. A method of checking their understanding is to copy the words and their definitions on to separate pieces of card and ask pupils to match them up correctly.
See also notes re punctuation with Glossary to Book 3.

(back cover)

Transport non-fiction books for Key Stage 2

Here is a list of non-fiction/reference books which will support your topic in the classroom. The emphasis is on books which will appeal to the children and which they will be able to use themselves.

ARDLEY, N, *My science book of movement*, Dorling Kindersley 1992 (0863187951)

BARRETT, N, *Flying machines*, Franklin Watts 1991 (0749607270)

BARRETT, N, *Transport machines*, Franklin Watts 1991 (0749607076)

BENDER, L, *Channel Tunnel*, Franklin Watts 1990 (0749607238)

CATHERALL, E, *Wheels*, Wayland 1992 (0853409188)

DALLOWAY, J, *Making a motorway*, Wayland 1992 (0750204761)

DAVIES, E, *Transport on land, road and rail*, Franklin Watts 1992 (0749606177)

DAY, J, *The Hindenburg tragedy*, Wayland 1988 (1852104309)

FIDDY, P & FOX-DAVIES, D, *Traffic computer*, A & C Black 1986 (0713627255)

GAFF, J, *Buildings, bridges and tunnels*, Kingfisher 1991 (0862725593)

LAFFERTY, P & JEFFERIS, D, *Pedal power*, Franklin Watts 1990 (0749601671)

GRAHAM, I, *Helicopters*, Franklin Watts 1989 (0863139388)

HERNANDEX, X & BALLONGA, J, *A seaport through history*, Wayland 1991 (0750201347)

HEWISH, M, *The young scientist book of jets*, Usborne 1982 (0860200507)

HUMBLE, R, *Ships, sailors and the sea*, Franklin Watts 1991 (0749605480)

JOHNSTONE, H, *Land and sea transport*, Franklin Watts 1989 (0863139582)

KERROD, R, *Motorcycles*, Franklin Watts 1989 (0863139353)

KERROD, R, *Transport*, Wayland 1991 (0750200693)

LINES, C, *Exploring transport*, Wayland 1988 (1852100036)

LORD, T, *Amazing cars*, Dorling Kindersley 1992 (0863187307)

MACDONALD, F, *A 19th century railway station*, Simon & Schuster 1990 (0750002158)

PETTY, K & CASH, T, *Bridges*, A & C Black 1990 (0713633158)

PETTY, K & CASH, T, *Canals*, A & C Black 1990 (071363314X)

PETTY, K, *New bike*, A & C Black 1991 (0713534820)

PETTY, K & CASH, T, *Roads*, A & C Black 1990 (0713633123)

PETTY, K & CASH, T, *Tunnels*, A & C Black 1990 (0713633131)

RICHARD, G, *Spacecraft*, Wayland 1986 (0850786231)

SMALLEY, M, *Transport in Europe*, Wayland 1991 (0750201509)

SUTTON, R, *Car*, Dorling Kindersley 1990 (086318412X)

TAYLOR, B, *Force and movement*, Franklin Watts 1990 (0749601450)

TRIER, M, *Supercar*, Franklin Watts 1988 (086313775X)

The visual dictionary of cars, Dorling Kindersley 1992 (0863188354)

The visual dictionary of ships and sailing, Dorling Kindersley 1991 (0863187021)

WALPOLE, B, *Speed*, A & C Black 1992 (0713635460)

WOOD, S, *Trains and railways*, Dorling Kindersley 1992 (086318815X)

Programmes of Study for Key Stage 2, England and Wales

Speaking and listening

Pupils should be given the opportunity to learn how to:
- express and justify feelings, opinions and viewpoints with increasing sophistication;
- discuss increasingly complex issues;
- recount events and narrate stories;
- assess and interpret arguments and opinions with increasing precision and discrimination;
- present their ideas, experiences and understanding in a widening range of contexts across the curriculum and with an increasing awareness of audience and purpose;
- give increasingly precise questions;
- ask increasingly precise or detailed questions;
- respond to increasingly complex instructions and questions;
- present factual information in a clear and logically structured manner in a widening range of situations – discriminate between fact and opinion and between relevance and irrelevance, and recognise bias;
- listen and respond to an increasing range of fiction, non-fiction, poetry and plays, including those which have been seen;
- recite and read aloud in a variety of contexts, with increasing fluency and awareness of audience;
- work with or devise an increasing range of drama scripts, taking on a variety of dramatic roles;
- use, and understand the use of, role-play in teaching and learning, *e.g. to explore an aspect of history, a scientific concept or a piece of literature*;
- communicate with other group members in a wide range of situations, *e.g. an assignment in science or mathematics where a specific outcome is required*;
- discuss issues in small and large groups, taking account of the views of others, and negotiating a consensus;
- report and summarise in a range of contexts;
- reflect on their own effectiveness in the use of the spoken word;
- engage in prediction, speculation and hypothesis in the course of group activity.

The range of opportunities provided should:
- not be restricted to English lessons but be available across the curriculum;
- allow pupils to work in groups of various size, both single sex and mixed where possible, with and without direct teacher supervision;
- encourage pupils to contribute individually in class discussions;
- enable pupils to talk with wider audiences, *e.g. in representing the views of a group or taking part in group or class presentations*;
- include the use, where appropriate, of audio and/or video recorders, radio, television, telephone and computer;
- allow pupils to undertake activities on behalf of others, *e.g. by making use of the telephone, or in representative roles.*

The range of activities should include:
- the preparation of presentations, *e.g. to the class, the school assembly or to parents*;
- planning and problem-solving activities across the curriculum;
- assignments where specific outcomes are required;
- talking about stories, poems, playscripts and other texts;
- taking part in shared writing activities;
- role-play, simulations and group drama.

Teaching about language through speaking and listening, which should have started by the time pupils are working towards Level 5, should focus on:

- regional and social variations in accents and dialects of the English language and attitudes to such variations;
- the range of purposes which spoken language serves;
- the forms and functions of spoken Standard English.

Pupils should have increasing opportunities to develop proficiency in spoken Standard English, in appropriate contexts.

Pupils should be encouraged to respect their own language(s) or dialect(s) and those of others.

Reading

Pupils should read an increasingly wide range and variety of texts in order to become more experienced readers. they should be encouraged to develop their personal taste in reading with guidance from the teacher and to become more independent and reflective.

The reading materials provided should include a range of fiction, non-fiction and poetry, as well as periodicals suitable for children of this age. These should include works written in English from other cultures. School and class libraries must provide as wide a range as possible. The material available must pose a significant challenge to pupils; for example, poetry should not be confined to verse written for children; folktales and fables might include translations from original sources. Pupils should discuss with others and with the teacher what has been read.

Pupils should:

- hear stories, poems and non-fiction read aloud;
- have opportunities to participate in all reading activities, *e.g. preparing and reading a selection of poems, reciting some from memory, or taking part in storytelling sessions or dramatic activities;*
- select books for their own reading and for use in their work;
- keep records of their own reading and comment, in writing or in discussion, on the books which they have read;
- read aloud to the class or teacher and talk about the books they have been reading;
- be encouraged to respond to the plot, character or ideas in stories or poems, and to refer to relevant passages or episodes to support their opinions;
- be encouraged to think about the accuracy of their own reading and to check for errors that distort meaning;
- be shown how to read different kinds of materials in different ways, *e.g. 'search' reading to find a scientific or geographical fact;*
- learn how to find information in books and databases, sometimes drawing on more than one source, and how to pursue an independent line of enquiry.

Writing, Spelling and Handwriting

Pupils should continue to have varied and frequent opportunities to write. They should know for whom they are writing, *e.g. themselves (to help in their thinking, understanding or planning of an activity), their classmates, their teacher, younger children in the school, their parents or other trusted adults.* In writing for others they will learn that writing for a public audience requires more care to be taken with the finished product than writing for oneself as an aid to memory.

Listening

Listening has implications for speech development, thinking, and learning generally. Though talking and listening often occur in proximity to each other (in, for example, discussion) they are separable for educational purposes and are regularly in practice – for example, listening to a talk, to a teacher, to radio, to a series of instructions.

In the early years, listening is the main means by which knowledge is acquired but teachers at all stages must be attentive to pupils' abilities and capacities, nurturing them in constructive, interesting ways, and noting and attending to specific problems which may impede the learning process. For pupils who may have difficulty in learning the skills of reading and writing, it is the oral components that will, perhaps, provide the main basis for thinking about experiences, expressing feelings and engaging with society.

Listening effectively is an active process. It has much to do with the knowledge and experience of the listener, with motivation and involvement, and with the individual situation in which listening takes place. People listen best when the information is of importance to them, when they have to take some action on it or have the opportunity to reply or participate. Listeners, therefore, have to learn to select relevant information from what they are hearing or seeing.

It cannot be assumed that children will have acquired the necessary skills – of concentrating, and of thinking about and recalling what they hear and see – by the age of 5: some may already possess good general alertness; others will not have acquired the basic habits; a few may reveal signs of physical difficulties in hearing which will require treatment.

In the early stages the pupils will:
- be encouraged to sit comfortably and quietly, face the source of the message and not interrupt; they will also begin to learn how to conduct themselves in discussion;
- regularly listen to good stories and particularly to tales and poems which incorporate the 'three Rs' of listening for young pupils – Repetitions, Rhythms and Rhymes; many of these will be of Scottish origin; some will be live performances by teacher or pupils; others will be audio or video recordings;
- engage in a programme linked to the early teaching of reading and writing, which will involve developing auditory discrimination and matching sounds with pictures, printed letters and words.

At all stages, in ways appropriate to their age and attainments, pupils will:
- work regularly in pairs or groups;
- undertake practical activities which give them an interesting purpose for their listening;
- listen to messages or narratives in order to predict at various stages likely outcomes and to locate with increasing accuracy genre, purposes and audience;
- play listening games and other activities designed to develop skills in attention and recall and the identification of sounds;
- use tape or video recorders to allow them to hear, watch and reflect upon what they themselves and their classmates have said;
- listen to speakers and to messages that employ Scottish language features;
- encounter a range of dialects and accents to enhance their linguistic competence and social confidence making use of radio, television, film, audio and video tapes, and song;

- discuss terms associated with knowledge about language where these help to clarify meaning;
- be given opportunities to associate listening with other forms of communication such as body language, music, set and costume designs;
- demonstrate a response to their listening in a variety of media – writing, pictures, graphics, speech, and performance.

Contexts for Listening as pupils get older will become more complex. There will be a corresponding need for listeners to be more aware of purposes and of the uses to which the listening is to be put. They will also be able to listen selectively at some times; pay close attention at other, more important times; adapt their mode of listening to their intention in listening; recognise the genre of the communication and be able to recall it. Assessment of listening should be varied. It would be wrong for a pupil's listening development to be stunted by asking for too much evidence of it in a component like writing which is still proving difficult.

Talking

Talking helps us sort out what we think and is the main means of social communication and interaction. It is through talking with peers, teachers and other adults that much of pupils' learning will occur. From the earliest stages, pupils should talk together about the issues within their common experience. Contexts for talking should be varied, with opportunities to discuss, to question, and to respond to books, other texts, and pupils' own talk and writing.

The whole curriculum offers a widening set of contexts for talk and it is through talk that the pupil makes sense of the range of ideas in that curriculum. Through personal experiences in and out of school, children should be encouraged to develop a growing awareness of the language appropriate to different audiences, purposes and situations. Most children will have acquired skills in talking before they come to school, but teachers at the early stages will ensure that pupils are given opportunities to:
- learn the disciplines of effective talking – sitting comfortably, taking turns, keeping still and quiet, listening to the other speaker;
- talk in the reading and writing programme;
- use talk in structured play to arrive at outcomes.

At all stages, in ways appropriate to their age and attainments, pupils will:
- talk to peers, other pupils, teachers and adults in the context of their classwork;
- engage in practical activities which will require them to talk together to produce an outcome;
- make use of audio or video recorders to hear and to discuss their own and their classmates' performance;
- play games and engage in simulations and role–play, to develop their confidence and competence, and to facilitate talking;
- talk in Standard English, and their own dialect, as appropriate;
- give individual presentations to stimulate interest and command the attention of an audience;
- be given opportunities for talking in drama and performance;
- develop language awareness through talk and discussion.

Reading

Learning to read accurately and with discrimination becomes increasingly important as pupils move through their education. Reading and writing are reciprocal skills; attainment in one is usually paralleled by a similar attainment in the other; teaching one is closely related to teaching the other.

Pupils should be encouraged to read for enjoyment and, with support from the teacher, to maintain a personal reading programme. They should be helped to develop their own tastes in fiction and non-fiction and at the same time to gain confidence in speaking and writing about them. To foster this, it is essential that the class library is well stocked with colourful and interesting reading material.

The importance of meaning should be stressed at all stages. The activity of reading should take place, wherever possible, in an appropriate context, and it should be concerned with the gaining of meaning from a suitable text. Reading should always have a purpose which is clear to both the teacher and the pupil.

At the earliest stages learning to read is dependent upon the spoken language that pupils bring to school. It will also be influenced by the knowledge they have gained in the pre-school years about the conventions of print itself. Some pupils in P1 will be familiar with story-books, poems, nursery rhymes, and print in their environment; some may have already started to recognise single words and even letters. However, for many pupils the experience of hearing stories read aloud and talking about pictures will be encountered for the first time as part of the school's early reading programme. At this stage pupils will:
- be involved in pre-reading activities to develop skills of matching, discrimination, left-to-right eye movement, and sequencing;
- learn to enjoy books by listening to stories and talking about them;
- create and read short texts with teacher support;
- learn the basic skills of reading through a systematic and progressive programme.

As pupils' reading becomes less supported by illustrations, they must learn to recognise the commoner patterns in fiction and non-fiction. As texts become more complex and various in form, the teacher needs to deploy a widening range of techniques such as: sequencing, prediction, cloze procedure, evaluating the text, making deductions, marking text, comparing and contrasting different texts.

At later stages, reading activities should demand that pupils shown an overall grasp of a text, and understanding of specific details and how they contribute to the whole, make inferences, supply appropriate supporting evidence and identify intended audience, purpose and features of style. In longer reading activities, for example novels, teaching the strategies which will help them to make sense of aspects such as plot, characters and themes is essential. In all of these activities, pupils will be helped by developing, through discussion, knowledge about language.

In teaching reading through all stages, in ways appropriate to pupils' ages and attainment, the teacher can focus on texts:

before reading
- by priming pupils for the task, for example, by alerting them to unfamiliar content or ideas;
- by directing them into the task;

during and after reading
- by providing questions which ask for literal, inferential and evaluative responses;
- by asking them to demonstrate understanding by doing or speaking;
- by asking readers to use the text as a model for their own writing.

Writing
Writing helps pupils to clarify their thoughts and experiences, and to give them personal meaning. Through writing, pupils can define, order and understand ideas. Because writing is essential for communication within society, it is important that pupils learn precision in its conventions.

Handwriting skills will be formally taught, especially in the early years. Later, pupils will pay attention to handwriting in the normal course of composing their own writing.

For the most part, writing will be developed in association with the other three components. Acquiring writing skills begins in the earliest years, and at all stages the teacher should be involved in listening, discussing and assisting with the selection of ideas, overseeing content, organisation and form. The teacher will also demonstrate and require different writing strategies. For example, in producing writing the following strategy of drafting and re-drafting should be used:

- presenting ideas;
- discussing them with teacher and/or peers;
- selecting what is appropriate;
- developing them in expanded text (writing, drawings, storyboarding, word processing or simple flowcharts, as appropriate);
- discussing this with teacher and/or peers;
- producing a re-draft (which may be the final copy).

At the early stages, the teacher should respond to the content and structure of what is being written, leaving spelling and simple punctuation to the final draft. But with regular practice the pupil should be taught to give increasing priority to surface features of the text such as spelling, punctuation and presentation.

As pupils begin to read more widely so their writing will develop and become more varied. From writing about events drawn from their day-to-day lives they will write about matters which go beyond their real-life experiences. They will demonstrate that they can write for a larger number of audiences and purposes, and from points of view other than their own. They will attempt more complex narratives and will be asked to extend their ability to write non-narrative test, for example, reports, letters, and news items.

Teachers will, therefore, spend time devising programmes which will provide contexts in which pupils will be asked to write in a variety of forms. Pupils will also write for a number of readerships, in language registers and with degrees of formality that will depend on the writer's familiarity – which may be real or imaginary – with the target readership. In such programmes and contexts, teaching approaches, tasks and experiences will motivate and support pupils, especially those with special needs, as they gain a set of essential but complex skills.

The combination of purpose, form and readership will influence pupils' choice of appropriate language and they should be faced with tasks which clearly demand the use of a variety of styles. Mostly this will involve forms of Standard English, but from time to time the child's own dialect will also be used for appropriate purposes, and attention given to enriching it.